P9-DEZ-257

HOW NOT TO WRITE A PLAY

BY

Walter Kerr

BOSTON
THE WRITER, INC.
PUBLISHERS

PUBLISHED BY ARRANGEMENT WITH
SIMON AND SCHUSTER, INC.
REPRINTED 1972

LIBRARY OF CONGRESS CATALOG CARD NUMBER: 55-7756
MANUFACTURED IN THE UNITED STATES OF AMERICA

for my wife

ACKNOWLEDGMENTS

THE AUTHOR is grateful for permission to quote brief excerpts from the following:

All My Sons, by Arthur Miller, copyright 1947 by Arthur Miller

Anna Christie, by Eugene O'Neill, reprinted by courtesy of Random House, Inc.

Aspects of the Novel, by E. M. Forster, reprinted by courtesy of Harcourt, Brace & Company

A Streetcar Named Desire, by Tennessee Williams, copyright 1947 by Tennessee Williams, reprinted by permission of the publisher, New Directions

Beyond the Horizon, by Eugene O'Neill, reprinted by courtesy of Random House, Inc.

Burning Bright, by John Steinbeck, reprinted by courtesy of The Viking Press, Inc.

Camino Real, by Tennessee Williams, copyright 1953 by Tennessee Williams, reprinted by permission of the publisher, New Directions

Collected Poems, by Kenneth Fearing, reprinted by permission of the author

Collected Poems, by T. S. Eliot, reprinted by courtesy of Harcourt, Brace & Company

Come Back, Little Sheba, by William Inge, reprinted by courtesy of Random House, Inc.

Death of a Salesman, by Arthur Miller, reprinted by courtesy of The Viking Press, Inc.

Dramatic Opinions and Essays, by George Bernard Shaw, reprinted by permission of The Public Trustee and The Society of Authors

Home of the Brave, by Arthur Laurents, reprinted by courtesy of Random House, Inc.

Judgment Day, by Elmer Rice, copyright, 1934, by Elmer Rice. Copyright (Acting Edition), 1938, by Elmer Rice. All rights reserved. Reprinted by permission of the author and Samuel French, Inc.

Lazarus Laughed, by Eugene O'Neill, reprinted by courtesy of Random House, Inc.

Letter from George Tabori to *The Saturday Review*, reprinted by courtesy of *The Saturday Review*

Men in White, by Sidney Kingsley, reprinted by courtesy of the author

Morning's at Seven, by Paul Osborn, copyright, 1939, by Paul Osborn under the title *Summer Solstice*. Copyright, 1940, by Paul Osborn. All rights reserved. Reprinted by permission of the author and Samuel French, Inc.

Of Mice and Men, by John Steinbeck, reprinted by courtesy of The Viking Press, Inc.
Paul Kauvar, by Steele MacKaye, reprinted by permission of Percy MacKaye, son of Steele MacKaye
Playwright at Work, by John van Druten, reprinted by courtesy of Harper & Brothers
Poets at Work, by W. H. Auden, reprinted by courtesy of Harcourt, Brace & Company
Shakespeare of London, by Marchette Chute, copyright, 1950, by E. P. Dutton & Co., Inc.
Summer and Smoke, by Tennessee Williams, copyright 1948 by Tennessee Williams, reprinted by permission of the publisher, New Directions
Swann's Way, by Marcel Proust, reprinted by courtesy of Random House, Inc.
The Ascent of F6, by W. H. Auden and Christopher Isherwood, copyright 1936 by Wystan Hugh Auden and Christopher Isherwood. Reprinted by permission of Random House, Inc., and Faber and Faber, Ltd.
The Emperor's Clothes, by George Tabori, copyright, 1952, by George Tabori. Copyright (Acting Edition), 1953, by George Tabori. All rights reserved. Reprinted by permission of the author and Samuel French, Inc.
The Eve of St. Mark, by Maxwell Anderson, reprinted by courtesy of Anderson House
The Glass Menagerie, by Tennessee Williams, reprinted by courtesy of Random House, Inc.
The Lady's Not for Burning, by Christopher Fry, copyright 1949, 1950 by Christopher Fry. Reprinted by permission of Oxford University Press, Inc., and Oxford University Press of London.
The Oxford Companion to English Literature, edited by Sir Paul Harvey, reprinted by courtesy of The Clarendon Press, Oxford
The Theatre of the Nineties, by George Bernard Shaw, reprinted by permission of The Public Trustee and The Society of Authors
The Time of the Cuckoo, by Arthur Laurents, reprinted by courtesy of Random House, Inc.
The Voice of the Turtle, by John van Druten, copyright 1943, 1944 by John van Druten
Tomorrow the World, by James Gow and Arnaud D'Usseau, reprinted by courtesy of Charles Scribner's Sons
Under Milk Wood, by Dylan Thomas, copyright 1954 by New Directions, reprinted by permission of the publisher, New Directions
Watch on the Rhine, by Lillian Hellman, reprinted by courtesy of Random House, Inc.
Winterset, by Maxwell Anderson, copyright, 1935, by Anderson House and Maxwell Anderson

CONTENTS

PART FOUR
Arthritis in the Joints

INTRODUCTION

America is, at the moment, in possession of a highly unpopular theater. For twenty-five years the taste for legitimate drama has steadily waned. Each successive year finds fewer theaters in operation, fewer plays produced, fewer successes among those that are produced.

In 1929 there were seventy-five playhouses in operation in New York City. Now there are thirty-one.

In 1929 managers were able to get 224 productions on the boards. Nowadays they are lucky to hit seventy.

Only eight or nine years ago a producer figured that the chances of failure were four to one. Now he must expect that they will be about seven to one.

The average professional actor's salary is now $790 a year.

The most alarming thing about the contemporary American theater is the absolute regularity of its march toward extinction. The figures just quoted would not be half so frightening if they represented a sudden, sharp break with a normal prosperity. Nineteen twenty-nine, for instance, was a disastrous financial year in every way, and if the number of playhouses and productions had been sliced in half immediately after the stock-market crash and then remained stable at the lesser figure, there would be cause for dismay—but not for despair. Stability at any level would be encouraging, and the theater might seem simply to be biding its time in quiet confidence of an eventual upturn.

It didn't happen that way. Instead of staggering with the general economy, and then slowly sharing in its recovery, the theater has undergone a continued, season-by-season process of attrition. There has been no single fatal blow, only a casual and apparently irreversible dwindling away.

Nothing—not the gradual recovery of the dollar during the 1930s, not the war boom of the 1940s, not the fantastically easy money of the early 1950s—has halted the shrinkage. The general economy may go wherever it likes; the theater goes right on down.

There is nothing to indicate that the decline will not continue. Since the theater seems to profit not at all from the customer's fattened pocketbook, since it is clearly following a course of its own against the grain of the universal economy, there is no reason to suppose that we will not go on closing theaters and curtailing production at the same annual rate that has prevailed for twenty-five years. Should this happen—what is there to say that it won't?—we may expect to find the New York stage confined to two theaters and seven annual productions within another twenty years. Any time thereafter the theater as we know it may cease to function entirely.

You don't believe this. Neither do I. But where does our courage come from? From the mere pious repetition of the thought that "the theater cannot die"?

The road is just about dead. Most of us have some personal memory of it when it was alive. My own earliest recollection—I was about nine, and beginning to be dazzled by the theatrical advertisements—is of spreading open the Sunday pages of the Chicago Tribune on the living-room floor and studiously memorizing the names of the playhouses: the Apollo, the Garrick, the Four Cohans, the Illinois, the Studebaker, the Selwyn, the Harris, the Grand, the Great Northern, the Erlanger. There may have been twenty theaters in regular operation. Today Chicago is lucky when it has four open.

During my high-school days, in a community of 70,000 I was able to see every successful play of the twenties in stock. Stock no longer operates in that community.

Graduating from college, I went to work in a city boasting

four playhouses. During an eight-year period I watched one of them turn into a parking lot, one into a warehouse, two into motion-picture theaters.

Few major American cities now require more than a single legitimate theater; not many of these offer more than a fragmentary season. Most smaller communities have abandoned all thought of keeping a building available for those three or four discouraged companies that might straggle through during the winter months. Managers cannot hope to send out reasonably good plays, featuring fairly well-known people, and turn a profit. Even hits have been known to lose their New York earnings in vain flings at the road.

The iceberg inches its way into New York. New York is, after all, only another community of increasingly disaffected playgoers—larger, but in the long run no less vulnerable, than Chicago, St. Louis, or Cleveland.

That's the condition of the contemporary theater as a working professional might look at it. How does the audience look at it?

There is no longer any such thing as habitual theatergoing. The audience neither plans to attend the theater two or three times a month nor does it drop in casually at a Broadway show. An occasional production receives such an overwhelming accolade in the New York press, thus becoming a suitable subject for cocktail conversation, that social pressure drives a large number of people into seeing it; the play that does not generate this sort of social pressure might better never have been born. Drama is not thought tolerable as a steady diet; it is something that must be endured now and then in the interests of intellectual upkeep.

There are exactly enough habitual theatergoers left in New York City to fill a single theater for a single evening. Opening nights are crowded. Second nights—unless the newspapers have put the pressure on—are empty. I spent a year as a second-night regular, reviewing plays for a magazine; it was the lonesomest year of my life. I quickly grew used to the fact that there is no audience for a play which has not been made socially unavoidable. I never quite adjusted myself to a more startling fact: that not even theater people are interested in theater. At these desolate second nights I saw no producers studying the work to find out what was wrong with it. I saw no playwrights analyzing the failure of a fellow craftsman. I saw no directors. I saw no actors. I saw twenty-five or thirty magazine reviewers, present under duress, and that was it. On one occasion a saddened management scurried down the aisles to ask the reviewers to bundle together in the center of the house so that the actors might be encouraged to go on.

Nobody—but nobody—is willing to subject himself to any contemporary theatrical experience he can get out of. A rival medium has but to rear its head to draw off yet another portion of that public which had once been regarded as the theater's. The invention of the motion picture saw hordes of happily released playgoers fly in enchantment to something that pleased them more. Radio found people curling up comfortably at home, yearning not at all for the excitement of a theatrical night out. Television is a splendid excuse for making the breach permanent. No one has yet devised an entertainment form poor enough, dull enough, or monotonous enough to send anyone back to the apparently poorer, duller, and more monotonous theater.

For one reason or another, the contemporary American cannot be persuaded that the legitimate drama is a tolerable form of entertainment. All sorts of persuasions are repeatedly tried. The newspaper reviewers, for instance, flirt with perjury in the nightly effort to make the theater seem gay. One recent Broadway season was, by common consent, the worst in the memory of man. The plays which went to make up this season were described in the daily press as "stunning," "magnificent," "exuberant," "distinguished," "exhilarating," "enormously enjoyable," "enchanting," "extraordinary," and "filled with wit, talent, and splendor." The playgoer remained skeptical.

Hurt and unable to imagine that it is in any way lacking in what advertisers call "personal daintiness," the theater likes to picture itself as the victim of economic forces, and so works very hard to lure the reluctant customer through lowered prices. A New York organization known as City Center offers popular stars at very low prices, and is normally unable to play twelve days to capacity or to scrape through a season without a substantial loss. A survey by the show-business weekly, Variety, indicates that it is the cheapest seats in the balcony which have gone begging in recent years.

In short, the fun-loving American finds the theater infinitely resistible—and at any price. He vaguely acknowledges its superiority over the media he actually patronizes. He apologizes profusely for his inability to keep up with it. He makes a point of knowing who Tennessee Williams is by carefully studying the theatrical columns of Time; anything he misses will be supplied by his wife, who will have been briefed on the shows she hasn't seen by a woman's-club lecturer who is paid to see them. Caught up in a theatrical conversation, he will expand handsomely on a performance he will never forget, probably a performance of Lightnin'.

A rat catcher came to my house yesterday, to catch rats. Discovering that I was a newspaper reviewer, he snapped his fingers in an "of course" gesture and went on to say how long he had read me and, in particular, how completely he had agreed with my review of Oklahoma!. I have been on a newspaper for four years. Oklahoma! opened twelve years earlier. It was, of course, the last show he had seen and conversation had perforce to radiate from that point. Nor are the rat catchers of the world the only social group to have seceded from the theater. In the course of lecturing to groups deeply committed to cultural activity of all sorts, I am everlastingly invited to dwell on the merits of The Barretts of Wimpole

Street, and in another five years I confidently expect to be asked what I think of Harvey. Even the intellectual avant-garde continues to busy itself with the dashing experimentation of e.e. cummings' him (1921). A President of the United States, confronted with a dramatic group which had strayed into the White House, beamed merrily and made the strangers at home with a glowing account of the finest "play" he had ever seen—Mrs. Miniver.

The average American, from President to rat catcher, knows that the theater exists, though he is not quite sure why. Buzzing about on the fringes of his consciousness is a peculiar activity supported by specialists, worthy of encouragement if the encouragement can be given in absentia, apparently valuable in some dim educative, intellectual, or historical way, like Williamsburg, Virginia, or Shaker furniture, or the novels of Thackeray. The notion that, when he is looking for a good time, he might deliberately choose playgoing over poker, golf, movies, detective stories, or bourbon on the rocks does not seriously enter his head.

He has been to the theater—once or twice. He has been going with a girl and isn't quite certain how else they are going to pass the earlier hours of the evening. He has been invited to a dinner party which must, dinner being over, be carried out of the house—somewhere, anywhere—so that the maid can go home. He has come in from out of town, is lonesome and of high moral character, and has finally spent the evening at a show he can talk about when he goes back out of town.

The problem that faces the contemporary American theater is this: once the customer has been there, it doesn't occur to him to go back. The visit will have had a certain ritualistic value; but it will not have brightened the man's life, caught his fancy, stirred his soul, or fired a brand-new passion. If the visitor never sees another legitimate play so long as he lives, he will feel no sense of loss.

I don't think this is an economic problem, a competitive

problem, or a sociological problem. I think it is a playwriting problem. I don't think the fault is in our stars; I think it is on our stage.

It is very difficult, though, to convince either a professional or a playgoer that this is so. The professional prefers to assume that the drama is first-rate but that the audience is feeble-minded. The audience, half suspecting that it is feeble-minded, obligingly agrees that the drama is first-rate and stays away from it.

All of us, whenever we make note that the American theater is unpopular, indulge in a crafty mental reservation. We are willing to acknowledge that the theater is unpopular in the sense that people don't go to it. We are not willing to admit that it is unpopular in the sense that people don't like it.

Yet we shall never solve the problem of shrinkage unless we first solve the problem of affection. I'd like to put this book to the task of asking what there is about the contemporary theater that leaves audiences indifferent to it, what happens on our stages that flatly bores the good folk out front.

There is no point in pretending that this is not going to be an argumentative book, or that overemphasis isn't going to crop up pretty frequently in the chapters that follow. The face of our theater is so familiar to us that we shall never see its features without blowing them up a bit, one by one. And it does seem to me that we had better do some arguing—quick.

PART ONE

The Way Things Are

1. Young Blood

MOST YOUNG PLAYWRIGHTS nowadays want to learn "how to" write a play. This seems to me to be a mistake.

"How to" write a play is apparently the easiest thing in the world to learn. As nearly as I can figure—from the number of manuscripts that are copyrighted every year, from the somewhat smaller but still quite large number of manuscripts that are actually circulated by theatrical agencies, and from the very much smaller but nevertheless quite imposing number of "first plays" that are offered on Broadway each year—virtually every American who has learned to put carbon paper in a typewriter right side up has also learned "how to" put a play together.

We have made it remarkably easy. We have placed at everyman's disposal a number of reasonably trustworthy playwriting manuals, textbooks that tell a man, a woman, or an indefatigable grandmother (half the grandmothers I know are writing sex plays; the other half are writing allegories about world peace) how to get characters on and off stage without having one of them say "tennis, anyone?", how to slip a piece of vital exposition into an apparently innocuous telephone conversation, how to get the second-act curtain down without having used up all of the material for Act Three, and how to spell out the commoner stage dialects (North Carolina, upper and lower Bronx, and Eugene O'Neill Irish).

We have almost made it possible for the well-rounded youngster to pick up this sort of information without interrupting his college education. A good many universities offer courses in playwriting and a good many of these courses are good ones. Here the serious-minded student will apply himself to the structural subtleties of Ibsen's *An Enemy of the People,* ferreting out the play's underlying thesis, examining the position of each character in relation to the thesis, and reveling in the masterly showmanship with which Ibsen fused an unfolding purpose and a stinging theatrical excitement.

He will examine the symbolism of O'Neill (the horizon, the jungle, the illusion-ridden saloon run by Harry Hope), the muted tension of Chekhov ("The fact is, Constantin has shot himself . . ."), the delicate balance between robust humor and grinding tragedy that O'Casey sustains throughout *Juno and the Paycock.* Nor will he confine himself to the modern masters. He will give due attention to the effective mechanics of *Three Men on a Horse,* learning how to place the key word in a calculated gag in just the right rhythmic position to make the line explode. (You mustn't swallow your kicker by writing "Temptation is the one thing I can't resist"; you must swing around and write, with Oscar Wilde, "I can resist anything except temptation.")

Moss Hart was recently heard to announce that playwriting courses were a waste of time, that valid theatrical know-how can be acquired only in the theater. This isn't quite true. Any tyro can be taught, let's say, that he must make his audience ask questions. He quickly sees the inadvisability of marching a couple of characters on stage, having one explain to the other that he is in possession of a letter he doesn't want his wife to discover, and having him subsequently stash the letter away in a convenient bookcase. Better to bring the man on alone, let him glance apprehensively at the letter, tuck it nervously into its hiding place, and then play a short scene in which he makes no reference whatever to the matter. By the time he does get around to explaining himself, the audience will have spent a few moments wondering what he is up to. It will be demanding the exposition, rather than sullenly resisting it. The ABC's can be communicated somewhere short of Broadway.

In fact, when the modern novice is through doing his homework, he will know quite a bit about the indispensable mechanics of his trade. He may talk a rather grandiose game of "organic structure," but he will at least realize that he has got to wrap up the evening in a big scene somewhere and that—if the scene isn't going to seem wildly irrelevant—he has got to begin preparing for it from the rise of his first curtain. He may make finicky distinctions between direct and indirect characterization, but he does know the difference between having a man announce his temperament in the manner of Iago and having the audience deduce his temperament from certain revealing things he does. He will know how to blend scenes smoothly, how to conceal information suspensefully, how to introduce coincidences casually, how to imply larger values in a limited domestic situation ("It's not just you, Mother. It's not just me. It's all of us—all of us together."). He will, in fact, be quite a glib young man.

Structural gaucherie is relatively rare on our stage. In two recent seasons on Broadway, twenty-six "first" plays were produced—the fledgling efforts of our most promising youngsters. If twenty-three of them failed, it was not for want of technical dexterity. There wasn't a transparently clumsy piece of playbuilding among them.

There was the carefully articulated labor play. Scene: the Dockyards. Act One: the heroine decries any sort of violence, makes her lover swear he will never resort to force. Act Two: the lover, attacked, meets force with force, and is scornfully denounced by the girl, who will henceforth have none of him. Act Three: the girl's pacific attitude results in the death of her father and the severe mauling of her lover, whereupon she clasps her lover's bloody head to her breast, recognizes that evil must be fought, and faces up to the sorry challenge of the modern world. Curtain line: "If this goes on, night after night, what will we all be?" The play moved forward with an always professional fluidity.

There was the psychopath play. Scene: Central Park. Act One: a detective explains to his fiancée that she oughtn't to come into the park alone; there have been stranglings recently; near by a mild-mannered young man sits on a bench with his doting mother. Act Two: the fiancée keeps coming into the park, begins to feel sorry for the lonesome young man, is in a nice position to be strangled as the curtain comes down. Act Three: the fiancée is rescued in the nick of time, whereupon she is not so much grateful as incensed. She now speaks, in ringing accents, the thesis of the play: neurotics aren't criminals; they're sick. Don't put them in jail; put them in hospitals. There were no real flaws in the author's management of his scenes.

There were two environmental studies. One found the younger generation, in a south-side Chicago tenement, looking in horror on the disintegration of the older generation, and vowing violently to escape the same fate. Sample environmental detail: the young hero, who is of a rather poetic turn of mind, announces that he is going to puke, and attempts to do so into a large basin. (He does not succeed.) The other detailed the efforts of an ineffectual jeweler, living above his all but bankrupt shop, to bind his frustrated wife, his wayward daughter, and his drunken son into some sort of family unit. In Act Three, everybody left home. Neither play betrayed ineptitude at the surface; each was well enough made to win production.

Then there were the three or four rewrites of *An Enemy of the People*. In one a druggist discovered that he was manufacturing a harmful medication, that his businesslike board wanted him to go right on manufacturing it, and that, if he were going to be a man of integrity in a corrupt society, he would have to stand alone. In another a television executive discovered that he had harbored a friend suspected of Communist sympathies, that his employers wanted him to disavow his friendship, and that, if he were going to be a man of integrity in a panicky society, he would have to stand alone. In yet another a political ghost writer discovered that his employer was guilty of slandering an opponent, that he was expected to write a speech confirming the slander, and that, if he were going to be a man of integrity in a venal society, he would have to stand with his arm around his girl, defiant. This last was a comedy, and perhaps doesn't count. One of these rewrites was a model of mechanical deftness; the others revealed a comfortable acquaintance with the standard practices of the stage.

All of this is the work of our most promising newcomers, eager young men and women who are talented enough to have earned the interest of theatrical agents, the devotion of theatrical producers, and the money of theatrical backers. It is not crude work. On the contrary, it is noticeably slick work, rich in "know-how." It is, however, dead at the heart.

Why is so much competence so lifeless when we look at it?

I think there are several reasons for our out-of-hand rejection of work that is almost always proficient and often energetic. One of them is that the particular models that are being analyzed, assimilated, and imitated by the young are themselves unbearably tired and ripe for the junk heap. The best new brains are feeding on dead tissue.

2. *The Tired Model*

NO DRAMATIC FORM, good or bad, has enduring vitality. The great Greek theater, with its godlike heroes, its spare structure, and its lyric chorus, wore out its inspiration in less than eighty years. The Elizabethan theater, with its riotously complex structure and its bustling poetic realism, spent its energies in less than fifty-five. The best-known period of French drama, embracing all of the professional work of Corneille, Molière, and Racine, lasted forty-two.

These are the major dramatic impulses, the most fecund and the most dynamic we have had. Minor impulses have occasionally dragged themselves on for a little longer, possibly out of sheer inertia: it took nearly seventy years to kill off sentimental comedy in eighteenth-century England. Plautus and Terence, however, can account for no more than forty years between them, and England's Restoration Comedy was through in twenty-five.

The point here is that the time comes when every dramatic style, and hence every useful model, disintegrates and disappears. Though the theater itself has gone on for quite a long time, no one manifestation of it—no one set of conventions, no one notion of what constitutes suitable subject matter for the stage—has ever outlived the oldest man in the audience.

Dramatic activity operates in lively short-term cycles. Each brief cycle takes its peculiar shape, and its impetus as well, from whatever is most urgent in the society around it. A society that is enthusiastically bent on swallowing the whole known world, and is fairly romantic about its ability to do so, is apt to produce something pretty much like the Elizabethan theater—or perhaps the German theater of Goethe and Schiller. A society that prides itself on its capacity for leading a thoroughly rational emotional life is quite likely to find itself admiring the compact, Q.E.D. couplets of Racine—or, in another art form and in another age, the poetry of Pope. A society that is intensely hardheaded by day ("there is no friendship in business") and piously generous by night ("give me simplicity of mind, friendship, good nature, and honor") is bound to turn up the genteel hypocrisies of the eighteenth-century comedy of Steele. A society that is dedicated to the scientific method is certain to write even its plays in prose. And so on.

As each age mirrors its own temper, there will be a period of discovery, a period of polished reflection, and a period of waning light. Greece begins to find its own most accurate image in the groping but powerful work of Aeschylus; England begins to hear its own roaring voice in the thunders of Marlowe. One or another young playwright detects what is in the wind. Fumbling a bit, he gradually—or perhaps, with a lucky strike, suddenly—hits upon the sort of dramatic machinery that will best give back to his society the radiations it is sending out.

Naturally the society responds to its own image, to this figurative—sometimes quite literal—demonstration of its own drives. The form becomes popular and is imitated. Shakespeare, and a dozen lesser men, steal Marlowe's thunder. Sophocles listens to Aeschylus and improves on the orchestration. Imitation, with some pruning here and some seeding there, brings the cycle to maturity. For a time it thrives gloriously.

Times change, visions alter, ambitions die. (An ambition can die of either failure or success.) The social impulse shifts its course, sheds one skin and tries another. The theater, like all institutional structures, lags a little behind and now enters either a ritualistic period of placid echoes or a somewhat more excitable but markedly decadent period of bitter disillusion. Fletcher follows Shakespeare with graceful but empty gestures; Webster, trying harder, follows him with feverish thrashings that suggest nothing so much as death throes. After Molière, the French comic theater relaxes into lazy repetition; after Sophocles, Euripides all but burns the Attic house down in the violence of his attempt to restore a dying dynamic. This last period of either gentle or frenzied rehash continues until people stop going to the theater (which they frequently have done), or until the next social impulse is detected and successfully mirrored.

When the next impulse does acquire a theatrical shape, it

is apt to be wholly unrecognizable to an old-timer. After Euripides, the next Greek mirror to take on a shine is the homely, hearthbound mirror of Menander. After Webster, the next English cycle to wear an air of authority is the dandified artifice of the amoral, witty, and bewigged Restoration.

The life span of any one of these discovery-maturity-decline cycles would average out, in a generous estimate, at about sixty years. Our own cycle is now seventy-five years old.

It dates from the appearance, in 1877, of Ibsen's *Pillars of Society*. Before this time Ibsen had been putting himself through the conventional gestures of an earlier and exhausted form, the romantic historical play in verse. He had floundered through a few interesting experiments, one of which (*Peer Gynt*) had been an attempt to fuse the verse romance with the oncoming vein of social criticism.

With *Pillars of Society* the new form jelled. The age had discovered a set of theatrical conventions, an arrangement of dramatic attitudes, that it was willing to accept as its own image. Ibsen quickly developed and exploited the style. *An Enemy of the People*, still the leading contender among contemporary models, was written in 1882. The American theater began to investigate the possibilities of this curious new dramaturgy almost immediately; Modjeska was playing *A Doll's House* here in 1883. True, the Ibsen format did not wholly dominate American creative and critical thinking until some time after the turn of the century. But no matter how late we date it as a specifically American phenomenon, we have still got a form that is pushing sixty.

There has been no substantial alteration of the shape of our drama since *Pillars of Society*. There have been certain brief and unassimilated cross-influences, such as the influence of Strindberg on O'Neill. There have been continuing modifications via Chekhov. But in every important respect the revelation of 1877 remains the routine, largely unquestioned playmaking of today.

Pillars of Society is a prose play. It is written in four acts (we have trimmed this to three). It takes place in a single setting. The setting is domestic: an upper-middle-class living room. The furnishings are carefully realistic: sofa right, table left, pictures on the walls, "a small table on which two pots of flowers are standing." The speech is idiomatic, the gestures lifelike, the stage business familiar: "On a table lie great piles of linen garments and other articles of clothing, some half finished and some merely cut out."

The characters are plausibly fashioned so as to seem to be going about their own business while they are, in fact, conscientiously articulating various social points of view:

> "Oh, it was you knocking?"
>
> "Mr. Bernick sent for me."
>
> "He did; but he cannot see you. He has deputed me to tell you—"
>
> "Deputed you? All the same, I would much rather——"
>
> "—deputed me to tell you what he wanted to say to you. You must give up these Saturday lectures of yours to the men."
>
> "Indeed? I supposed I might use my own time——"
>
> "You must not use your own time in making the men useless in working hours. Last Saturday you were talking to them of the harm that would be done to the workmen by our new machines and the new working methods at the yard. What makes you do that?"
>
> "I do it for the good of the community."
>
> "That's curious, because Mr. Bernick says it is disorganizing the community."
>
> "My community is not Mr. Bernick's."

These are the first words of the new dispensation. With minor changes in idiom, they are still the most familiar words on our stage today.

The action of the play has to do with a businessman who

is sending faulty ships to sea. As the evening approaches its climax, there is some possibility that his own son may be on one of those ships.

(Arthur Miller's success of 1947, *All My Sons*, has to do with a businessman who has been sending out faulty airplane parts. As the evening approaches its climax, there is some possibility that his own son has gone down in an airplane equipped with one of those parts.)

Pillars of Society is two things: a literal milieu study, and a liberal moral document. The fusion of these two points of technique—a photographic surface, a socially significant content—became the pattern for the drama of the first half of the twentieth century. The pattern perfectly reflected the principal passions of the age in which it appeared.

There was, on the one hand, the passion for the scientific method as such, the conviction that all truth could be arrived at by the precise measurement of things actually observed; hence photographic backgrounds and stenographic speech.

On the other hand stood the two newest and most exciting intellectual structures to be born of this method, the social and political sciences; hence the sociological and political content of the narrative.

Time was when the audience—or at least a certain segment of the audience—stood up and cheered these innovations in style and content.

The first time an actor shuffled slowly across the stage, sat at a table, stirred his chocolate and sipped it quietly while he read a newspaper, the house went wild. The vision—an accurate duplication of familiar life—was exhilarating. For the moment, a man sipping his chocolate was more exciting than a man battling brigands. A shuffle was more astonishing than a stride.

In the course of more than half a century, however, we have fairly thoroughly explored the possibilities of chocolate-sipping. Our actors have learned to shuffle; all of them can do it. Over the years a good many tables have been set, meals consumed, newspapers read, shades drawn, lights switched on and off, cocktails mixed, doorbells answered, bookshelves dusted, flowerpots watered, telegrams received, pianos strummed, coats removed, brief cases opened, cigarettes lighted, parcels delivered, and sofa cushions fluffed. It may be that every inconsequential thing that can be done in a living room *has* been done in a living room—and done eight times a week for forty weeks for fifty years.

The first time a playwright used his characters to illustrate the immediate issues of the day a thrill ran through the theater. Here was no idle fiction, but a pertinent and responsible coming-to-grips with things that really mattered. From a sleepy dalliance with conventional romance the drama had plunged wholeheartedly into the thick of the modern battle. The stage became a forum in which the most progressive arguments could be acted out, a storm center in which honest and angry men could call a corrupt society to task, a laboratory in which environments could be examined and measured. The playgoer was surprised and stimulated to find himself debating war, workmen's wages, women's rights, slums, syphilis, and political malfeasance. He was no longer required to check his most urgent concerns with his hat and coat at the door; he could bring them into the auditorium with him, hold them up for study under a new and very bright light. The theater was participating, and—to the most thoughtful minds of the time—it seemed the more vital for it.

As of 1955 the theater continues—at its most significant level—to participate. It gives attention, as the newspaper headlines dictate, to the refugee problem, to the police state, to the Congressional witch hunt, to racism, fascism, and communism. On a somewhat quieter, less engaged, level, it pursues the dispassionate study of milieu.

It does not, however, stir the blood or startle the intelligence in quite the same way that it did. Though the topic for the day has frequently changed, the playmaking pattern—and even the point of view which informs it—has become safely predictable.

Act One: the infected social area is explored; the hero comes in contact with it.

Act Two: the hero hesitates to deal with the infection, because of his job, his wife, his social indifference, or his innate cowardice.

Act Three: the hero is forced to deal with the infection, which he does successfully (converting his opponent and marching toward a more hopeful future with a child on each arm), or unsuccessfully (suffering death or social dishonor, but at an enormous gain in personal integrity).

Win or lose, he makes a speech:

> "And we—we have a long earnest day of work ahead of us; I most of all. But let it come; only keep close round me, you true, loyal women. I have learnt *this*, too, in these last few days; it is you women that are the pillars of society."
>
> "You have learnt a poor sort of wisdom, then, brother-in-law. No, my friend. The spirit of truth and the spirit of freedom—they are the pillars of society."

The playwright doesn't live who hasn't rewritten this speech.

Maxwell Anderson, in *The Eve of St. Mark*:

> All right, boys. You go out and make things over your way. . . . We old folks, we'll stay here—and milk the cows and run the baler. . . . Make a new world, boys! God knows we need it!

Sidney Kingsley, in *Men in White*:

> There isn't a man in medicine who hasn't said what you've said and meant it for a minute—all of us, George. And you're

right. We are groping. We are guessing. But, at least our guesses today are closer than they were twenty years ago. And twenty years from now, they'll be still closer. . . . That's what we're here for. Mm . . . there's so much to be done. And so little time in which to do it. . . .

Elmer Rice, in *Judgment Day:*

Why . . . Why should I be careful? Could caution save me now, even if I were cowardly enough to think only of my own safety? No! A man who may never be heard again must not be careful. He must be bold—he must speak while he can. Shall I waste my precious time discussing evidence? There is no evidence—only a fantastic collection of lies. . . . We have all understood it perfectly. Not one of us here has been taken in for an instant . . . the people have not been taken in, either. The trick has been performed but it has deceived no one. The tide is rising higher, the voices of the people grow louder. . . .

Lillian Hellman, in *Watch on the Rhine:*

Well. He stole bread. The world is out of shape, we said, when there are hungry men. And until it gets in shape, men will always steal and lie and—kill. But for whatever reason it is done, and whoever does it—you understand me—it is all bad. I want you to remember that. Whoever does it, it is bad. But you will live to see the day when it will not have to be. All over the world, in every place and every town, there are men who are going to make sure it will not have to be. . . .

James Gow and Arnaud d'Usseau, in *Tomorrow the World:*

. . . Every time anybody tells you anything, you've got to ask why! In our country we're not afraid of questions. We *want* people to ask questions. Lee says you can be turned into a human being. Pat seems to think so, too. Perhaps they're right. But get this straight, Emil. What happens is really up to you. You can be a decent member of society if you want to. . . .

Arthur Laurents, in *Home of the Brave:*

> I was crazy . . . yelling I was different. I *am* different! Hell, you're different! Everybody's different—but so what? It's O.K. because underneath, we're—hell, we're all guys! We're all—O Christ! I can't say it, but am I making any sense?

The most earnest exhortation, repeated often enough, becomes as pat as a television commercial. After a while, because I know everything the man is going to say and even the tone of voice in which he is going to say it, I will very likely dial him out. This does not necessarily indicate a lack of sympathy, or a disagreement about social aims, on my part. On the contrary, it is possible that I have reached a state of almost total agreement with the contemporary playwright, that we have achieved a meeting of minds so absolute as to induce a kind of conversational paralysis. I can anticipate every argument, every illustration, every conclusion he is prepared to offer (I am confident that he is not going to come out in favor of lynching), and, if I am ever going to be honest about it, I must admit that the good fellow bores me. He is on the side of the angels; so am I. He is going to develop his argument along certain lines; I know them. He is going to complete his charge to the jury in a burst of warm rhetoric; I can recite it in my sleep. I am all for him, you understand. But we are such old hands at this game, the playwright and I, that, hearing he has brought off yet another new "challenge," I can send a check to my favorite charity and stay home in perfect complacence.

I have seen this man's play, perhaps a thousand times. And, however much I may admire its integrity, its candor, and its passionate purposefulness, I do not really want to see it again.

The meaning is familiar; the method is transparent. A play that I can anticipate in every mechanical and editorial detail is a play which no longer shocks, surprises, or delights me.

A few years ago my wife was having her hair done by a gentleman barber who had exhibited some interest in the theater. A new Lillian Hellman play, *Montserrat,* was due to open the following Monday, and my wife asked if he were going. He didn't say he wasn't. He simply lifted his eyes heavenward, raised one shoulder, and murmured in weary pain, "Insurrections in Bolivia?"

A short descriptive phrase in the advance publicity had made it perfectly clear to him that his presence was not required.

The Ibsen-inspired theater has entered its ritualistic, or hardened-arteries, phase. This is in part due to the noticeable fraying of a once fashionable form, the rusting of much-used machinery. It is also due to a shift in the social view, to a subtle alteration in man's image of himself, his problems, and the possible means by which those problems may be solved.

The forward-looking man of 1880, of 1910, of 1925, and even of 1940 believed, let us say, that munitions makers were the cause of war. Forward-looking playwrights wrote a good many forward-looking plays on the subject; Robert E. Sherwood earned a Pulitzer Prize for one as late as 1936. These plays said in effect: take the profit out of munitions and you will be through with warfare forever. This was a simple problem in the science of economics; if you took the laws of a science seriously enough, and applied them literally enough, you could solve the problem handily.

It is doubtful that many men continue to believe in the proposition, or to place full confidence in the method which gave us the proposition.

In 1884 Ibsen opened a glorious new world to womankind by sending Nora Helmer beyond her own front door. In 1951 Samson Raphaelson wrote a play called *Hilda Crane* in which

Nora, under the name of Hilda, came back looking for some of the things she had left behind her. The structure of the play remained expert Ibsen; the body of belief on which it rested had changed beyond recognition.

It is too early to know what fresh inquiries and fresh beliefs will dominate, and come to characterize, the next movement of twentieth-century thought. What is clear, however, is that some subterranean movement is under way. In an atomic age it is no longer possible to conceive of science as taking care of everything; somebody is going to have to take care of science. There is no sure way of putting it, but I suppose we might say that the social focus is turning away from the perfectible machine and turning toward the imperfectible man. The next accent is likely to be less mechanistic, more humanistic, less concerned with evolving a sociological slide rule and more concerned with seeking some understanding of the complex, cantankerous personal soul. Should this be the case, we are likely to abandon, in the theater as in life, our reliance on the photographic negative, the tape-recorder, and the environmental statistic; we are also likely to cease posing and solving our dramatic contests in the manner of sociological, economic, or political equations.

At the moment American playmaking continues to make the passionless gestures of a vision that has not so much been discredited as superseded. We do not really regret our age-long belief in "perfection through the social sciences"; the sciences have given us too much for that, and they will certainly give us more. But we have begun, I think, to assign these sciences a somewhat different and more limited value; we have begun to look for a larger format that will embrace them without allowing them to define absolutely the whole range of human—and, sooner or later, artistic—activity. This underground burrowing is, fairly patently, under way. The theater stands perfectly still.

What was wholly valid for a vision of sixty years ago is

tediously out of touch today. It should come as no surprise that youthful, earnest, and accomplished work studiously modeled on so aged a form should display an internal ennui.

Weariness finally defeats the best of forms, and our theater was bound, sooner or later, to lose champions. But weariness is not the only cause of the theater's current decline. Our particular form came equipped with a built-in decline; its champions were always few. The very model we are tired of was designed to be unpopular in the first place.

3. *The Day the Shopgirl Got Her Notice*

We have, with the best will in the world, consciously and deliberately created for ourselves an unpopular theater. We knew what we were doing every step of the way, and we did it because we wanted to do it.

I am going to have a hard time turning George Bernard Shaw into a villain, but I shall have to begin somewhere and Shaw was helpfully articulate.

Along about 1896 Shaw glanced at the London theater around him. It was, commercially speaking, a flourishing institution. Large theaters were regularly filled with shopgirls, clerks, jacks-of-all-trades. There was a habit of theatergoing, and it was a commonplace habit. There were no extraordinary cost problems, critical problems, or competitive problems. The drama on which so much affection was lavished was commonplace, too: melodrama not much past the blood-and-thunder stage, fancy-dress intrigues in fashionable drawing rooms, gay, pointless, and ephemeral comedies. Perhaps very little can be said for the intellectual content of that theater. One thing can be said for it: it was popular.

Shaw did not like it. In all of this buzzing, thronging, superficially dazzling activity, he complained, there was not a single play he could take William Morris to see.

"We have no theater for men like Morris: indeed, we have no theater for quite ordinary cultivated people. I am a person of fairly catholic interests: it is my privilege to enjoy the acquaintance of a few representative people in various vortices of culture. I know some of the most active-minded and intelligent of the workers in social and political reform . . . they don't go to the theater. . . . Nobody goes to the theater except the people who also go to Madame Tussaud's. . . . It has no share in the leadership of thought: it does not even reflect its current. . . . And yet you ask me why Morris did not go to the theater . . . you could not induce him to spend his evenings at a modern theater."

Shaw wanted a theater he *could* bring William Morris into, regularly. With all of the wit, invective, and critical ingenuity at his command, he set about creating one.

Ibsen had just come over the British horizon, and the imitation of Ibsen seemed to Shaw imperative. In essay after essay, and in an influential little book called *The Quintessence of Ibsenism*, the fire-eating Irishman rammed the fire-eating Norwegian down the nation's throat. Ibsen was not only superior to Madame Tussaud's waxworks; he was superior to Shakespeare's waxworks. Shaw wanted a revolution, fought for a revolution, and, looking back a little later, he told us how successful his revolution had been:

"Until then [the nineties] Shakespear had been conventionally ranked as a giant among psychologists and philosophers. Ibsen dwarfed him so absurdly in those aspects that it became impossible for a moment to take him [Shakespear] seriously as an intellectual force."

Ibsen's was the superior intellect; hence Ibsen's was the superior art.

The early twentieth-century theater listened carefully to these broadsides and, having considered the matter, lined up with Shaw. The shape of the theater must be changed. It would be difficult, this business of shattering one kind of taste and imposing another, but it would be done. After a considerable struggle it has been done. We are at last in possession of a theater for William Morris. This is an entertainment to which the self-respecting intellectual can devote himself without demeaning himself, a form of activity in which the serious aesthete and the responsible thinker can engage without loss of caste. That the new state of affairs represents a gain, in certain respects, over the old is perfectly clear: the modern drama is more literate and more responsible than the drama of 1896.

It has, and always did have, one drawback: William Morris does not constitute much of an audience.

There was never any secret about this. The men and women who shaped the modern theater knew it. The new drama was meant to appeal to a cultivated, alert, "advanced," and therefore necessarily limited segment of the social whole. The shopgirl was no longer to be catered to. If the new aesthetic vision were to become a reality, the garish and sentimental popular theater would have to be killed off. The jack-of-all-trades who liked his action livid and his prose fairly purple would, in the new order of things, have to put up or shut up. The noisy lowbrow with his bag of peanuts would have to go along with his betters or, if he chose, get out.

Actors, managers, and playwrights saw in the new revelation a chance—even a challenge—to improve themselves. From being the gaudy darlings of a kind of adoring underworld they were offered seats at the intellectual banquet table. Playwrights ceased thinking of exciting new stage effects and began to train themselves in the social sciences. The matinee idol, with his carefully nurtured personal glamour, disappeared and was replaced by the intensely honest, politically active, socially integrated artist. Nor were these efforts at self-elevation mere fashionable gestures, born of snobbery, sham, or a highbrow hankering to be in the swim. They were sincere, courageous, and back-breaking attempts to do something that seemed, under the urgent proddings of the best minds of the time, desirable and necessary.

The creative people of the theater prepared to do battle—with their audiences. They knew that the battle would be costly, but they were willing to make serious sacrifices. They would have to divest themselves of the enchanting trickery and calculated charm which had won them the sentimental devotion of uncritical hearts. They would have to forego flowers across the footlights, queues in the alley, and enraptured faces in the train windows at whistle stops. They would have to absorb staggering financial losses. They would have to risk involvement with the police, who were suspicious of plays about strikes, syphilis, and the new psychology. They would have to accustom themselves to outraged customers stomping up the aisles, to the hostility of the daily press, to resentment, rancor, and even riot. But they were enduring, in an honorable cause, no more than their prophet and principal playwright had endured before them. Ibsen, alienated from his countrymen, storming about Europe looking for companies enlightened enough to produce his plays, fashioning his next piece in ironic thrust at the fools who had protested his last—Ibsen, the "angry," hounded, and everlastingly rebellious man, was their model.

No one pretended that Ibsen was a "popular" dramatist. By temperament and intention he could not have been. The history of his introduction to America is, by and large, the long, sad story of the "special" matinee. It was not possible to play Ibsen at a profit; to keep going, stars and managers scheduled the popular old warhorses, and a liberal sprinkling of Shakespeare, throughout the body of the week; on Sundays they might pour the profits into an afternoon performance of *Ghosts* for the enlightened.

I suppose every revolutionary form may be said to have hard going at first; usually there is a period of intense and apparently unrewarding struggle, followed by a happier time of acceptance and even triumph. In one sense the Ibsen battle was carried forward to unmistakable triumph: it won the allegiance of an entire generation of dramatists and succeeded in establishing the Ibsen mold as the "accepted" mold of the age. In another sense—in the sense of winning a vast commercial audience for its special characteristics—it never succeeded at all.

Ibsen himself has at no time had a mass following in this country, neither in his matinee beginnings nor in the heyday of his convinced imitators. To this day a repertory company, organizing itself around the usual Shakespeare, Shaw, and Ibsen, tends to make a little money with Shaw, break even with Shakespeare, and break its neck with *The Wild Duck*. The audience resistance that greeted the first propagators of the Ibsen form was not simply the normal resistance to the new and strange; it was a natural and enduring response to a dramaturgy that *meant* to engender resistance, that prided itself on its capacity to irritate, to prod, to unsettle, to disturb. The form itself has not changed over the years; neither has the popular response. How little the intention, tone, and texture of the Ibsen format has altered is clear from Arthur Miller's firm praise, in 1952, of such dramatists as are "rebels insisting on thrusting their private view of the world on others" and in his fiery rhetorical question: "Is it not honorable to have powerful enemies?"

This was a theater that intended to make enemies, and did. In part, it meant to make enemies of the stuffy, the pompous, the recalcitrant, and the retrogressive; since a considerable portion of the population may fairly be lumped under these combined headings, the possible theater audience was nicely decimated with this first stroke. It also, as we have seen, meant to make an enemy, or at least a mute and bewildered stranger, of the shopgirl; the audience was ruthlessly decimated again.

Since the principal dramatist of the new order had not been a popular dramatist, and since most twentieth-century playwrights have chosen to work in a form which was by definition not a popular one, we should not be surprised that we have finally created for ourselves an unpopular theater. If we are caught, from time to time, glancing about us in considerable dismay, wondering why so few people love us, it is only because we have forgotten the premise on which our theater was founded and the process by which it was brought into being.

What is true of Ibsen is equally true of the second, only slightly less influential, model of our time: Chekhov. In some ways we feel a closer kinship with the tenuous Russian than with the turbulent Norwegian. Each man reflects his age: the scientific observation of environment, the social criticism, the sensitively recorded speech exist in both. But Chekhov is not so baldly, so embarrassingly, theatrical. There is less of the residual showman in him: fewer hopped-up climaxes, fortunate coincidences, sledgehammer symbols. There is something closer to the placid, unresolved continuum of life itself in these gentle, ironically perceptive plays. This is still the drama of the significant photograph; but the lighting has been improved.

After Ibsen, Chekhov is the most widely imitated playwright in the contemporary theater, "Chekhovitis" the commonest complaint in the nation's playwriting courses. In recent years the subtler and drier Chekhovian mind has been gaining ground, earning greater allegiance among serious playwrights. Lillian Hellman began life as an Ibsenist: both the theatricality and the (somewhat concealed) social content of *The Little Foxes* stem from the Norwegian school. With

Watch on the Rhine Miss Hellman engineered a beginning compromise: the political intention remains paramount and in strong focus, but the characterization has taken on the more delicate hues of twilight. With *The Autumn Garden* the transition is finally made: the social kernel is almost obscured, the characterization is ruefully Chekhovian, the mood of the play is the principal guide to its meaning. Whenever John van Druten turns serious these days, he turns Chekhov- rather than Ibsen-serious: *I Am a Camera* belongs to the breed. Younger writers are growing up without having attempted the bolder form: Carson McCullers, Truman Capote, William Inge come to mind. The Chekhovian nerve is no longer a nerve that must be located with difficulty; a good many beginners find it native.

Chekhov has never been popular. A difficult "prestige" dramatist in his own country, an "Arts theater" admiration in London, he is almost without peer in his power to chill American audiences. Occasional stars with trusted followings have occasionally sandwiched his work between giddier, and more reliable, ventures. In 1941 a supreme effort was made to carry the day for this admired, imitated, and uncommercial dramatist: Katharine Cornell, Judith Anderson, Ruth Gordon, Dennis King, Edmund Gwenn, Tom Powers, and Alexander Knox joined forces to produce *The Three Sisters*. At least four of these people were independent stars with independent followings strong enough to push lesser plays to success. Together, in Chekhov, they could do no more than eke out a thinnish run in New York and a few disappointing weeks on the road. When London's Old Vic, at the height of its powers under the Laurence Olivier–Ralph Richardson regime, made its first visit to New York in 1946, it suffered the familiar repertory experience: modest success with Shakespeare, disaster with *Uncle Vanya*, salvation with Sophocles' *Oedipus*.

With our eyes open and our fists clenched, we have elected to erect the modern theater on a foundation of unpopularity.

We have dismissed one kind of audience, the mass audience; we have sought out another, the intellectual "class" audience, the audience in which William Morris might feel at home. We now inhabit the house we planned: a house of advanced thought, of social inquiry, and of detached study. The house is supported by contributions—currently large enough to constitute a mild form of endowment—from an intellectual elite. The support is strongest where specifically intellectual life is most abundant, in New York City; it becomes weaker and weaker as we move away from the centers of metropolitan thought. The drama we have fostered seems to have nothing whatever to say to the folk who live in communities of less than 200,000.

Ironically, Shaw escaped the net he cast. In building this new, responsible, and unpopular theater, Shaw behaved with perfect integrity. He tried to do as he counseled others to do, turning out his version of an Ibsen play with something like *Widowers' Houses* or *Mrs. Warren's Profession*, turning out his approximation of a Chekhov play with *Heartbreak House*. But neither vein was really for him. His ebullient instincts outran his advice, and—probably without wanting to, possibly without knowing it—he somersaulted into the arena of pure comedy. Max Beerbohm, then drama critic for *The Saturday Review*, saw what was happening as early as 1901:

> In his serious plays Mr. Shaw was not himself. He was still the youth groping his way to self-expression, and groping, as so many youths do, in the wrong direction, under the wrong master. Hanging on to the coat-tails of even the wrong master is healthy exercise for a youth; it strengthens his muscles, and so forth. But such exercise must not be overdone. Mr. Shaw has loosened his hold on Ibsen's coat-tails not too soon. I admit that his serious plays were exceedingly good *pastiches* of Ibsen, and that in time he could have written serious plays to which one could have given higher praise

> than that. Nevertheless, he was not born to write serious plays. He has too irresponsible a sense of humor. This sense he never could have suppressed so utterly as to prevent it from marring his plays; and, as it is his greatest gift, one does not wish him to suppress it at all.

What we are left with is a joke almost too grisly to bear: Shaw tumbling on, in infectious high spirits, to become the most popular playwright of his time; the while he strenuously taught the rest of us how to be thoroughly unpopular. Because he was a unique personality, we could not follow his practice; because he was a convincing advocate, we followed his precept. We still believe in the dogma he defined.

And, putting aside Shaw's own bubbling behavior, it is still possible to respect and defend the view that the theater *ought* to be unpopular, that it ought to be indifferent to commercial considerations. The Ibsen-Chekhov enthusiasts developed a perfectly straightforward position: catering to the lowest common denominator breeds a shallow, makeshift theater; since the masses are sluggish of mind and devoid of taste, the responsible playwright has no choice but to cut himself loose from them; it is better to have a limited theater of high intellectual standards than a vast theater of low ones.

Furthermore, we may wish to pursue this position for a longer time than we have. We may be unwilling to surrender the particular gains which have been made. We may continue to believe, as Eric Bentley urges us to in *In Search of Theater*, that a "minority art" is necessary. We may see no decent alternative to our present unpopular commitments.

These are candid attitudes. To complete their candor only one thing is necessary: a wholehearted acceptance of the consequences. If we are going to defend the uncommercial theater of Ibsen and Chekhov, we must not be heard to complain when we find ourselves in commercial difficulties. If we are going to carry this theater with us into the indefinite future, we must be prepared to tighten our belts further, to face a continuing shrinkage of theatrical operation.

In the course of constructing an unpopular theater, we have, I think, been guilty of only one dishonesty. Having pushed the shopgirl out of the theater—the movies didn't lure her away; she was in the process of being dispossessed before the movies came into being, and turned to them happily as a dog would to an unexpectedly kindhearted stranger—we proceeded to throw stones at her. Having announced that we didn't want the mass mind in the theater, we took to calling it "irresponsible," "escapist," and "twelve-year-old" when it went somewhere else. It had, indeed, "escaped" from us; but since we had cut the bonds, greased the path, and issued the invitation ourselves, we were in a poor position to resent the jolly departure.

What we had secretly hoped, I suppose, was that although our playwrights were under strict injunction to make no concession to the mass mind, the mass mind would come to us anyway. It would, perhaps, educate itself to the William Morris level. Possibly it would simply recognize our unmistakable virtue and, with furrowed brow and a sheeplike docility, tag along as best it could. Perhaps it might be intimidated into supporting what it was not expected to enjoy. Whatever the unexpressed hope—it seems as though we must have hoped something, considering our present resentment—the spectacle of the dispossessed cheerfully supporting their eviction officers has never been offered us for our serene and deeply gratified contemplation. The "popular" audience has gone elsewhere and stayed elsewhere.

We should remember that a theater may address itself to an intellectual elite, achieve a certain real vitality for that elite, and permanently fail to make that vitality felt on any larger portion of the population. The Restoration theater, for instance, shaped its plays for a given caste and succeeded in producing a superior comic reflection of that caste. Its penalty was to play only to that caste, in its own time, and to go down in history as a special taste, lacking in universality and difficult to revive. During the earlier Elizabethan period London had been able to maintain six or seven theaters, not counting the occasionally used indoor houses. During the Restoration a more populous London could not keep two open. The theater has been unpopular before, without motion pictures as competition.

Legitimate theater was also unpopular in London during the well-bred reign of the talented and articulate Sir Richard Steele. During the early eighteenth century Steele succeeded not only in working out a new intellectual formula for comedy but in imposing it on the playwrights of his generation. Comedy was said to be a matter of sentiment, of noble posture, not of humor. "Laughter's a distorted passion" became the slogan of the age. Proper playwrights, bowing to legislation from above and confident that they were about to improve the stage, eliminated all traces of low farce from their pieces, eschewed the attractive joke, and went on to dramatize little moral lessons in genteel conduct. (The comic dramatist was expected to "steal the pitying tear from Beauty's eye"; his audience was expected to sigh "a social sigh" in return.) The form was imitated and became fixed; it endured for a good fifty years. What did not endure during this period was the audience. The good customers paid polite lip service to the "nobler" ideals of the time, tipped their hats as they passed the theater, and hurried on to the pantomimes, the musical shows, and the coarse farces of the "illegitimate" theaters on the side streets. They crept off, in short, to the competition. The situation is not entirely unlike our own.

Indeed, the degree to which our theater survives at all nowadays is the degree to which it fails to live up to our highest intentions for it. While Ibsen-inspired plays are failing to the right of us, and Chekhov-inspired plays are failing to the left of us, a kind of shameless underground—composed almost entirely of musical comedies, farces, and melodramas—keeps the New York theater in business. Here are the long-run plays—that is to say, the profitable and popular plays—of the past ten years: *Life With Father, Oklahoma!, South Pacific, Harvey, Born Yesterday, The Voice of the Turtle, Arsenic and Old Lace, Hellzapoppin, Angel Street.* As we run over the lifesavers of our generation, we are embarrassed to find *Kiss and Tell* and *The Bat* high on the list. With so few people going to the theater, we wish that fewer would go to these particular things, more to the models we have fought for. In our intellectual climate these are—with the possible exception of *Born Yesterday*—the "illegitimate" enterprises. With a slightly guilty look on their winning faces, they continue to attract such patrons as have not abandoned the theater altogether.

The contemporary British theater offers us a similar irony. The "best" in Britain—the kind of theater that a new William Morris might be willing to go to—survives by means of subsidies from the government Arts Council. The theater that supports itself is a sort of secondary theater in which Agatha Christie thrillers, patriotic tub-thumpers, and family farces draw the good folk from the suburbs into town after dinner. Characteristically, quite a few Englishmen decry this second-level stage as a blot on the national honor; it is a blot, however, that winds up paying the bills.

These tolerated undergrounds apart, we are left with a "serious" theater that always meant to play to a limited audience, a theater for the enlightened few. Now, in its senility, even the few are deserting it.

We must make no mistake about this desertion at the intellectual level. Critic Eric Bentley, a contemporary apostle of the minority theater, cannot contain his revulsion at the theater we built for Shaw and Morris. It is, in his view, a theater of the "sub-intelligentsia." That is to say, we have accepted the responsibility for creating an intellectual's theater and we have created a crude one. Somehow or other our wholehearted imitation of the models Shaw set up for us—Ibsen and Chekhov—has not produced satisfactory work. Whatever intolerable sacrifices we may have made at his behest, the true intellectual will now have none of us. With his back still squarely turned on the popular theater, and with a gesture of contempt for the sub-intellectual theater we have laboriously exchanged for the popular, the theatrical aristocrat moves onward and upward toward an ever more private "minority" playhouse. He is on his way to a subscription performance at the Barbizon-Plaza. There he hopes at last—again in the words of Eric Bentley—to find "the real thing," the genuine dramatic masterpiece.

I don't think he will find it there, any more than he has found it in the antipopular theater of the last sixty years or so. Minority theaters never have produced important work. Every great play we have ever been lucky enough to feast our eyes on has come out of a popular playhouse.

4. *The Moneymakers*

THE NOTION that the common customer might come back to the theater if the theater took some pains to please the common customer is, in our time, a revolutionary one. It is, moreover, shocking. Are we to surrender our obvious gains in literacy to return to *Bertha, the Sewing-Machine Girl?*

Bertha is a sort of macabre race-memory these days, a turn-of-the-century masterpiece we'd all like to live down. The plot, "of which there isn't much," wrote a perfectly straight-faced New York critic in 1906, took up the assorted abductions and rescues of poor little Bertha Sloane and her blind sister, Jessie.

In Act One, Bertha was chloroformed, tossed into a red automobile, hustled to an "uncharted cave in Central Park," and thrown into a lake, the while a gentleman named Slinky Bill crawled up to a second-story window where blind Jessie sat singing to a bound-and-gagged hero. In Act Two, Bertha was tossed onto a moving belt in a sweatshop, carried off to a New York mansion boasting at least one room designed to resemble an Egyptian temple, and there made to watch sister Jessie being suffocated in the mechanical arms of an image of Isis; before the second-act curtain came down, Jessie had also been deposited in a runaway motorboat on the Hudson River. In Act Three, Jessie's room was set afire, a fireman bribed not to answer the alarm, and Bertha herself arrived on the engines to deal with the matter. There was a fourth act, too.

Can an art form flirt with the vulgar mind without sharing that mind's vulgarity? In the nineteenth century Dion Boucicault was a popular dramatist, and a dreadful one. Owen Davis, in 1910, was not a great deal better. The motion picture, rather than the stage, has been popular in the twentieth century; do we seriously want to ape its quality in order to win its audience?

It is perfectly true, by the way, that a craftily popular theater sometimes produces *Bertha, the Sewing-Machine Girl* and nothing more. It is also true that the same kind of theater, consciously catering to the same kind of audience, has at other times produced *Macbeth, Oedipus,* and *Tartuffe.*

This may be a good chapter to skip, since it is going to contain nothing that is not known to anyone who has taken a high-school course in Shakespeare. As our English instructors used to point out, generally with a dryly conspiratorial air, Shakespeare was a man with both eyes firmly fastened on the box office; this was a simple necessity, since the major portion of his income came from his sharing directly in the day's receipts. Shakespeare's competition was the bear-baiting pit, and he was always concerned to meet it: with murders, duels, battles, wrestling matches, suicides, ghosts, witches, clowns, songs, costume parades, explosions, thunderstorms, and plain and fancy eye-gouging.

The plays of Shakespeare came out of a theater dedicated to the proposition that the illiterate was not only welcome but had to be wooed uninterruptedly throughout the performance, at whatever sacrifice in taste. This dramatic pattern—busy, bloodthirsty, unblushingly theatrical—had been set by Kyd, Marlowe, and lesser men; Shakespeare made certain interesting improvements on it, but he was careful not to destroy it.

Molière learned to play the same currently unfashionable game. He learned it, however, the hard way. Having challenged a sophisticated Paris on its own terms at the age of twenty-one, and having gone to jail for his prompt financial failure, he turned to the provinces to pick up the first principles of his trade. By the time he had spent thirteen years figuring out how to please a procession of unruly rustics, he discovered that he was at last able to please Parisian audiences as well.

The plays of Sophocles came from a society which believed in slavery and which believed also that every slave was entitled to a seat in the theater. Because the conventions of Greek drama seem so remote to us now, we hazily imagine Greek performance to have been a sober and high-minded affair. Actually, the performance was garish, musicalized, and shatteringly robust; the audience was a noisy, basket-lunch crowd on a holiday, never above stoning a playwright whose work was not up to par.

No great play has ever come from what might be called a minority theater. All of the work we prize most highly was born of the commercial or at least competitive hurly-burly, and in the presence of a mass audience.

Minority theaters, theaters consciously and carefully fashioned to appeal to the enlightened, have existed. One of the most revealing is the Italian theater of the Renaissance. Here a sharp line was drawn between the popular, or vulgar, theater and the literary theater of the intellectuals. What was fit for the people was one thing; what was acceptable to men of taste was another. The results: the literary drama of the intellectuals was stillborn; the despised improvisation of the common folk—the *commedia dell'arte*—quickly developed the sort of vigor that was to keep it alive on its own slapstick terms for two hundred years and to lead, by a process of natural growth, to the ultimate literacy of Goldoni and Molière.

The contest between the majority-minority ideals existed in Shakespeare's time. John Lyly, for instance, was a man of undisputed talent. He preferred, however, not to soil himself in the public playhouse, choosing to write and stage his work in the purer air of the minority theaters of the court. While his lowbrow friends went on to greatness, Lyly shriveled into the literary-precious. By the time Lyly, aged about forty, wrote his last play, Shakespeare had completed *Romeo and Juliet, Richard II, A Midsummer Night's Dream,* and *The Merchant of Venice.*

The contempt that we feel for the common mind, and that we act upon in writing our plays, was felt, but fortunately less widely acted upon, in the Elizabethan period. Sir Philip Sidney, for instance, found the popular playhouse "observing rules neither of honest civility nor of skilful poetry," behaving "with neither decency nor discretion." As Marchette Chute has recently reminded us in her *Shakespeare of London,* Sidney "had one of the most intelligent and beautiful minds of his generation." When he went to a public entertainment, though, he behaved more or less in the manner that Shaw has ascribed to William Morris: "all he could find there was a gross violation . . . of common sense."

Miss Chute has further reminded us of "the contempt that most young university intellectuals felt for a popular professional writer like William Shakespeare. The plays written by the students of Oxford and Cambridge, or by their teachers, were in every way superior to the crass London product. They were quite untainted by commercialism, they appealed to educated gentlemen instead of London tinkers, and it was undeniable that they were beautifully staged. . . . The students of Oxford and Cambridge were the future hope of the nation and it was not fitting that their minds should become corrupted by watching vulgar productions."

Happily, Shakespeare was fond of money and tinkers, and quite indifferent to this sort of criticism. And, like every other effort to impose intellectual standing on the drama by main force, the Oxford-Cambridge vision produced nothing we care to keep. Even Molière, when he wrote specifically for private performance at the court, wrote less well than he did for the mob.

The experience of the past is there for us to look at. Even if we were to pursue this sort of inquiry into the present, where ultimate values are less certain, we might find ourselves startled and disconcerted by the obvious, by what everyone knows and what everyone pretends not to know. Few arms would have to be twisted to get agreement on the proposition that Chaplin is the finest theatrical artist to have appeared in our time. Yet, once again, the most distinguished artistry has come from the most vulgar roots. Chaplin is not a product of the responsible legitimate theater but of the irresponsible, wholly commercial, film; his beginnings—and his enduring essence—are not to be found in deliberate theory but in spontaneous slapstick; he is a creation not of the higher criticism but of the mindless masses. Indeed, his eventual adoption by the higher criticism has done him the only serious damage of his career. It is in his last few films, as he has begun to cut away his links with the common herd and to speak directly to his newfound intellectual friends, that his artistry has faltered.

These are all home truths, so familiar that repetition would seem superfluous. Yet we have perfected a fascinating technique for dealing with them: we have stored them tidily away in one cranial compartment, swiftly performed a frontal lobotomy, and gone on believing in their opposites. Shakespeare wrote for groundlings, yes; it would corrupt our work to do so. Sophocles was forced to deal with the mass mind; artistry is not possible under these conditions. Molière perfected himself by coming to grips with the common appetite; the common appetite produces nothing better than *Abie's Irish Rose*. Chaplin is the best we know; the popular, pandering motion picture is beneath discussion.

At such times as we *are* compelled to tangle with the facts of theatrical history, we take refuge in the "in spite of" theory. Shakespeare was great in spite of his concessions. Molière was great in spite of his low farce tricks. Chaplin is great in spite of his medium. These men scored personal triumphs *over* circumstances which were in themselves undesirable.

The truth, I suspect, is the other way round: these men found greatness *because* of their communion with the universal audience; the presence of the uncultivated mass in the theater is an indispensable prerequisite for drama of genuine stature; greatness grows out of the very challenge.

The ideal entertainment, no doubt, is one which pleases both the shopgirl and William Morris. (This is not, by the way, the view we hold today—we have dismissed any consideration of the shopgirl's tastes; but it is a view on which we are likely to get at least verbal agreement from the most inflexible aesthete.)

The question is whether you achieve this all-level theater by legislating downward from an intellectual bias, or by building upward from a mass instinct.

The historical evidence, if I read it rightly, is altogether in favor of the latter. A "great" theater comes into existence by first attending to the most primitive passions of its most primitive patrons. By satisfying the race's admittedly childlike—though not necessarily childish—yearning for violence, spectacle, and the broadest of broad comedy strokes, roots are sunk deep into the universal consciousness. (An intellectual will often be found prying into a popular success; a lowbrow rarely exhibits any interest in invading the intellectual's sanctuary.) It would seem that on this broad, firm, democratic base nearly anything can be built. So long as the foundation is secure, all sorts of towering structures can be erected upon it. Drama is by its nature a mass art; the presence of the mass in the amphitheater is necessary not only to the financial stability of so complex an undertaking, but also, apparently, to its artistic validity. The growth of drama is upward from the drunken revel, the shoemaker's holiday, the vulgar farce—not downward from the critical academy. Given time and encouragement, the *commedia dell'arte* does arrive at Molière.

The contrary hope—that a cultivated theater may be envisioned and enforced at the intellectual level and then filter down into the popular mind—has no historical victories to support it. When a "better" theater is sought and established by an intellectual minority it tends to produce a body of work which is literate but bloodless. It finds an understanding audience in the privacy of the court, university, or art theater. To the degree that it is able to invade the commercial theater, it tends to bankrupt that theater. It speaks principally to men of an intensely rational disposition, men who seem to have exhausted the possibilities of simple pleasure and to have moved on to a somewhat rarefied preoccupation with techniques, theories, and theses. Its audience tends to cut off, sharply, below an approximate I.Q. of 130. The earth-bound "twelve-year-olds" do not slowly soak up the visitation from on high. They scamper off—as in the Italian Renaissance or in our own time—to their own devices, where they inconsiderately produce—in the *commedia dell'arte* or in the work of Chaplin—something we all come to value much more highly.

In fairness to the uplift point of view, it must be acknowledged that the popular theater does not always rise to incontestable magnificence, that it frequently finds itself stalemated at a cut-off point of its own. The popular theater has sometimes been frozen at the level of Scribe, of Boucicault, of *Bertha, the Sewing-Machine Girl.* My own guess is that this sort of aesthetic roadblock is the result not of the theater's popularity but of a universal defect in the body politic: the age itself subscribes to a limited vision, to one or another obtuse but tenaciously held sentimentality that successfully paralyzes the movement forward. The groundwork for *Bertha* and *Titus Andronicus,* for *Charley's Aunt* and *The Taming of the Shrew,* is pretty much the same. But the Elizabethan vision was as realistic as the late Victorian was piously muddleheaded. As Alfred North Whitehead has remarked in another connection, "Tennyson was a great poet with a mediocre subject. His subject was Victorian England."

However that may be, the aesthetically stalemated theater that is genuinely popular seems to me in many ways preferable to the more ambitious but deliberately unpopular theater of the minority. The popular theater, whatever its vulgarities, keeps the theatrical structure intact: it commands the loyalty of a large audience, it creates employment for actors, it offers both an outlet and an income for practicing playwrights, it maintains a body of playhouses on a profitable basis. In short, it keeps the conditions for theater alive, just as a minority theater must inevitably diminish, if not destroy, them. At worst, the popular theater holds the fort; at best, it finds its way to *Hamlet.*

It is the popular theater, too, that displays the greater capacity for assimilation. Shakespeare is easily able to absorb the rarefied inventions of Lyly, play with them profitably in such a tentative work as *Love's Labour's Lost,* and then throw away whatever is too special for his audiences. Lyly, working in the polite seclusion of a fashionable boys' school, is unable to draw any vitality from the rude experiments across the riverbank. His conceits are attractive, but they remain mere conceits; the author goes on imitating himself until his private style becomes sterile from inbreeding. When growth takes place, it takes place at the Globe.

One hesitates to develop an anti-intellectual position in an age which is increasingly—and on every front—anti-intellectual. But there are spheres in which the intellectual must be given not only his freedom but a clear authority as well; and there are spheres in which close communion with the common mind is indispensable. We are all agreed that, in the long run, we want something better than *Bertha:* characterization that is both complex and honest; language that is distinctive and revealing; narrative that digs deeply into the truths of human behavior. Our problem is one of approach. For a very long time now we have tried legislating from the top down, with depressing results. It may profit us—even aesthetically—to reverse gears and try for a vulgar popularity.

PART TWO

How to Lose Friends by Influencing People

If we are nervous about the aesthetic penalty we may have to pay for a renewed flirtation with the popular audience, we had best ask ourselves a very serious question. Has our dismissal of the mass audience, and our indifference to its taste, actually helped us produce work of a high aesthetic order?

It is a curious circumstance of our theatrical cycle that imitation has never improved upon, or even lived up to, the first experiments of its founders. To be honest about it, our playwrights of the past fifty years have not done as well with the Ibsen and Chekhov forms as Ibsen and Chekhov did. Each form seems to have reached its peak with its originator and to have declined in subtlety and complexity ever since.

We should remind ourselves that Ibsen himself abandoned the form he had invented long before he was through as a playwright. By 1902 Max Beerbohm was lamenting the fact that the Ibsen style was already "old-fashioned." We have since, both in our practice and our precept, denied that it was old-fashioned, and we have clung to it—but not to our particular profit.

Why was the form exhausted so soon, and why have our continued experiments with it failed to produce the masterworks we hoped for?

I think there may have been an aesthetic defect in it—a defect that led to Ibsen's own dissatisfaction with it, to the audience's instinctive impatience with it, to its imitators' failure to make anything more of it than was there in the first place. The popular audience may not have been behaving boorishly in refusing to support the tradition; it may have been passing a sound and sensitive judgment.

Specifically, the Ibsen tradition—with which we are going to be concerned in the next couple of chapters—did subtle damage to two things: to characterization, and to the thematic organization of what we like to call a play.

5. *A Matter of Opinion*

HOWARD LINDSAY is credited with the thought that if you are going to write a propaganda play, you had better not let any of your characters know what the propaganda is. Sounder advice never came from mortal man. If there is anything to be added to the injunction, it is that things will be better still when the playwright doesn't know what the propaganda is.

A good way to destroy a play is to force it to prove something. Forced it will always be. Life, caught in its complex immediacy, doesn't present itself as a tidy equation.

A large part of modern drama—more than half of it, I'd say—has been built like an equation. We have inherited not the drama of action, of character, of kinetic intimacy with the human condition, but the drama of ideas. This last is a generic term, and there is, of course, a sense in which everything from Aristophanes to George Meredith can be lumped under its banner. It has, however, been given a very precise and limited meaning during the past seventy years, when it might with equal justice have been called the "drama of rational formulation" or perhaps the "drama of the a priori concept." Even within the limited meaning the term has taken on, the form has had its variants. For purposes of illustration, I guess we can safely reduce these to three: the problem play, the thesis play, and the propaganda play.

No one of these is easy to define nowadays; they are all quite closely related and many a playwright has slipped imperceptibly from one to the other. But let's have a try at it. The problem play simply states its problem; it plays fair with both sides; it drops its curtain short of any solution. In John Galsworthy's *Strife* capital has its innings, labor has its innings, the end of the play is neutral. Mr. Galsworthy wanted to set down the phenomena of contemporary social struggle "without fear, favor, or prejudice," with "a certain detachment."

The thesis play takes a further step. It presents the political, social, or moral problem it has in mind and then argues a solution to that problem, or at least a defined interpretation of its meaning. Argument has been added. *Ghosts* and *A Doll's House* are thesis plays: one argues that the inflexibility of the traditional marriage bond is inhuman and, in certain circumstances, disastrous; the other argues that the traditional view of woman's role in society—mother, homemaker, "doll"—is false and unjust. In *All My Sons* Arthur Miller argues that "business is business" is an immoral concept. In *Watch on the Rhine* Lillian Hellman argues that we are all inextricably involved in the political fate of our overseas neighbors and that none of us, however innocent or however persecuted, can evade personal responsibility. In *Tomorrow the World* James Gow and Arnaud d'Usseau argue that an indoctrinated Nazi may be reclaimed by society if he is sufficiently exposed to the democratic way of life. In the thesis play a certain show of fairness, of at least psychological interest in the enemy, is retained; the outcome of the play, however, conforms to—and illustrates—the author's point of view.

The propaganda play takes a third and final step. It outlines a problem, argues the author's solution, and then strives to incite the audience to immediate action. Where a thesis playwright is content to gain intellectual assent for his proposition, the propagandist is satisfied with nothing short of passionate commitment and practical co-operation. He wants you to storm the barricades, whatever they may be, tomorrow. In this form all fairness disappears; a black-and-white case is made as boldly and as baldly as possible; the author eliminates anything that might inhibit your prompt response. George Sklar's and Paul Peters' *Stevedore*, John Wexley's *They Shall Not Die*, and Clifford Odets' *Waiting for Lefty* are propaganda plays.

Each of these forms falsifies its human content in one way or another.

The problem play sets up an opposition of impersonal forces. Here is Force A: it is Capital, or Militarism, or Tradition. Here is Force B: it is Labor, or Pacifism, or Revolt. Force A must have a squad of slightly varied figures to illustrate it: bankers, idle old colonels, white-haired statesmen with their omnipresent secretaries, demure gentlemen of the cloth. Force B must have another squad: working men, mothers who have lost sons in battle, eager young idealists. The forces take turns: the industrialist states his case, the man who has lost an arm in the machinery states his. The events of the play are dictated by the author's desire to clarify a social abstraction. The people of the play are handy types clustering about one of two possible poles. These people are without independence. Psychology is directed not toward the unique personality but toward the cerebral generalization. The problem of the play is everywhere larger than the human forces caught in it; they cannot move it, it moves them. And it moves them, like chessmen on an evenly divided board, toward a preordained stalemate. Small wonder that the problem play has left us no memorable characters, no fascinating narratives. It hangs on the wall like an industrial graph.

As the playwright moves toward the thesis and propaganda plays, anxiety to make a given point, to reach a dogmatic conclusion, takes over. Instead of balancing his opposed social forces so perfectly that they will stalemate one another, he is now out to win the game. As a result, his control over his incidents and characters, his manipulation of these things in accordance with an ideological master plan, must become increasingly firm, indeed almost absolute.

If, in a thesis play, I want to show that a woman who permits herself to play the traditional "wife-doll" role is something less than a woman, and that she can become a true woman only by storming out of her toy house, I must do two things. I must first illustrate the "doll": wife, mother, charmer, intellectual idiot. I must also illustrate the "woman": knowledgeable, dignified, articulate, strong. Suppose, though, that in the course of performing my first task I do my work a little too well: I create a character who is *really* a doll, the very sort of irresistible scatterbrain who needs to be cooped up and cuddled forever in her bric-a-brac world. What happens to my last act? Where does this lovable incompetent acquire the wisdom, how does she get up the nerve, to take to the freer highways? Do I stick to my character and sacrifice my point, or do I stick to my point and sacrifice my character? If I am a good thesis playwright, determined to pursue my intellectual predisposition, I make whatever character adjustments are necessary, even violent ones. I may find it necessary to equip my doll, quite suddenly, with a talent for rational debate and a fortitude of staggering proportions. Given a conflict between a growing imaginative reality and the mathematical proposition I originally had in mind, I must choose in favor of the proposition. The point comes first. I must everywhere be prepared to cut my human cloth to fit my ideological coat.

At the same time, of course, I am as careful as I can be to camouflage what I am doing. I am not honestly prepared to deal with men, because I am committed to an idea. But I must work very hard to give the factors in my proposition the *semblance* of reality. Though each figurehead has an intellectual purpose, I must cautiously play down the purpose. I must slip it in unobtrusively. I must distract attention from it steadily, so that the audience will not catch me at my proselytizing: my malleable mannikins must eat, drink, make jokes, do the thousand little things that genuine people do—all the while that I keep them firmly submissive to my initial diagram. I am really engaging in a kind of sleight-of-hand: pretending to write a play and actually defending an opinion. I am playing a shadow game, and I must not be surprised if all I get is shadows.

My work may be skilfully done. In *All My Sons* the business-man-father, Joe Keller, is very nearly a person. He smokes a pipe, speaks a trade lingo, cries a bit, lies plausibly, engages in a certain amount of hearty backslapping, irritably defends himself when his honesty is questioned. Seeing him in the theater, you try to help the author: you push your belief in Joe Keller because you want to be able to believe in what he has done—profiteered on defective airplane parts during a war. You tell yourself that you *know* men have done just this. But you never quite believe that Joe Keller has done it, or at least not because he wanted to; he has done it because Arthur Miller wanted him to. Here is Joe speaking:

> Listen, you gotta appreciate what was doin' in that shop in the war. The both of you! It was a madhouse. Every half hour the Major callin' for cylinder heads, they were whippin' us with the telephone. The trucks were hauling them away hot, damn near. I mean just try to see it human, see it human. All of a sudden a batch comes out with a crack. That happens, that's the business. . . .

The thoughts are arranged with a plausible logic. The idiom is studiously unliterary. The man doesn't pronounce his final g's, he repeats himself, he inverts sentences, he uses a "life-like" jargon. The key phrase about "business" drops almost imperceptibly from his lips. Yet there is still something of an echo about him; he is not quite speaking from instinct or passion; he is taking his cues from the wings. Though he is meant to be something of a hollow man, he is one degree hollower than a truly convincing character dare be; for all his energy, and for all his jargon, he cannot completely shake off the chill air of the automaton. I'm not sure that his creator has actually "seen it human"; I think he has seen it abstractly and then labored valiantly to give it a humanizing veneer. If we can't wholly get at Joe Keller, it is because Joe Keller is not unequivocally open for inspection.

One of the most fascinating struggles to watch in the contemporary theater is that between the upsurging artist and the stubborn dialectician in the same man. Ibsen was surely an artist, but an artist who stumbled on a dialectical time and a dialectical form. He had an instinct for character, and a passionate determination to make points. The two are in eternal conflict. Nora nearly got away from him; but he hauled her back. Mrs. Alving nearly got away from him; he hauled her back, too—though not without a struggle. Hedda, I think, got away from him. Hjalmar Ekdal got away from him. Increasingly Ibsen found himself puzzled by his people; complexity broke out like a rash. Where he needed a fool to make his social point, he found himself falling in love with the fool. Where he needed a parasite to make his point, he found himself fascinated by the parasite. The more he allowed his people dimension, the less did they fit into the pattern of his thought. As the characters acquire roundness—a perverse, intractable, baffling identity of their own—their precise social meaning becomes ever more ambiguous. In the early *Pillars of Society* the point is unmistakable; but the characters are not especially interesting. In the later *The Wild Duck* the characters are fascinating; but the ultimate point they are meant to make is hopelessly obscure. You can always clarify a thesis by oversimplifying what is human. But the moment you begin to give humanity its due you are bound to destroy the patness of your proposition. (In the end, as we have said, Ibsen rejected the whole sorry struggle and took his characters off to the mystical mountains; the man who had perfected the realistic thesis play abandoned it in mid-career, leaving a subsequent generation to work over its scraps.)

In *Death of a Salesman* Arthur Miller entered the same battlefield. Presumably Mr. Miller started out with a precise social moral he wished to drive home. Mr. Miller has told us, in effect, that this is his principal interest in the theater. It is apparent enough that this moral had something to do with the rightness or wrongness of that American phenomenon, salesmanship. But the play worked out oddly. I have talked with people who regarded it as anti-American propaganda. I have also talked with people who regarded it as a disinterested work of art. There were people who were outraged by it, there were people who were deeply moved by it, there was the man who was heard to mutter, in the men's room during intermission, "Well, that New England territory never was any good, anyhow." So far from leaving a single, didactic impression on its audiences, *Death of a Salesman* seemed susceptible to various, and seriously divergent, interpretations. There was agreement on one thing, though: that the lonely, tormented salesman Willy Loman was a believable, heartbreaking man. Once more a character had taken on stature and independence; in the process he could not help but burst the tidy boundaries that may have been set for him. He is enough of a person to make the play's meaning personal rather than socially prophetic. At the end of the evening, if we pause to work over its "message" at all, we find ourselves asking, "Is this the tragedy of an individual—is it Willy's own fault?" or "Is this a social tract—is Willy the helpless victim of forces outside himself?" We aren't sure. If Willy strikes us as being utterly complete, containing within himself the seeds of his own destruction, we tend to dismiss the peripheral social implications, to allow them a mild function as incidental, and somewhat ambiguous, background. If, on the other hand, we are determined to ferret out the explicit social meaning, we run headlong into further trouble. If Willy is the product of an impersonal force that is evil and destructive, why do we like him so much? And why, as his friends stand over his grave, do they find it in their hearts to praise both Willy *and* his calling? There is a sudden lyricism in their thought that this man has spent his life "riding on a smile and a shoeshine"; we are inexplicably uplifted by it. We feel, somehow or other, that Willy has been justified after all. The truth is, I guess, that Willy has won the chess game; the author, no matter in what contempt he holds Willy's philosophy, can no longer desert the man. He may have all sorts of angry things he still wishes to say; in effect, Willy has silenced him.

As with Ibsen, so with Miller. The earlier *All My Sons* had been crystal-clear in its argument, unmemorable in its characterization. *Death of a Salesman* finds its argument clouded, and Willy unforgettable.

The thesis play breeds this conflict, at least in a man who is in any sense an artist. (A mere editorialist can rattle off broadsides forever.) In the process of putting a humanizing wash on his factors in an equation, the artist has found his imaginative—as opposed to his severely rational—energies aroused. Should he give them any free play, he is headed for ideological trouble. In a still later play, *The Crucible*, Mr. Miller reverted to type and accepted the ideologue's solution: he thinned out his characters in order to make his meaning unmistakable. John Proctor is an "honest" man. William Danforth is a "blind" one. They confront each other, in a climactic trial scene, not as troubled, troublesome, unpredictable people, but as indestructible stone images at the door of a temple. These two can never come to know each other's minds; the author won't let them.

Given the thesis play, the problem will come up; a choice will have to be made. The experience of dramatists from Ibsen to Miller should convince us of one thing: it is better to make a man than to make a point.

In the third and frankest of our familiar forms—the propaganda play—all pretense at human complexity is dropped. The equation is laid bare for all to see. A equals virtue. B equals vice. "Do what I say" equals "health and happiness forever."

The virtuous A does nothing that is not virtuous; the villainous B does nothing that is not villainous; the author's vision is as simple and as urgent as a blow to the stomach. The propaganda play is a play in a hurry; it has no time for the hesitant inflections of the human voice. It is possible to reread *Waiting for Lefty* and still feel something of the author's passion; it is not possible to see its characters as anything other than purposeful cartoons. Placed side by side with the people in the same author's *Awake and Sing*, these obliging mouthpieces have the approximate validity of those good folk in the television commercials who have just discovered a new brand of coffee. (Odets is an artist, too; he has been engaged in a prolonged struggle between superimposed meaning and simply observed life; his later tendency has been toward uncommitted observation, though he is something of a lost soul in an age that has not yet surrendered its hold on the socially significant drama and is therefore unable to give him confident direction.)

The movement of the "drama of ideas"—problem play, thesis play, propaganda play—is always toward greater and greater emphasis on the abstracted idea, the bare-bones equation. It may be asked why the bothersome human baggage was not scuttled altogether, why—for absolute clarity—the equation was not revealed in its nakedness. As a matter of fact, it was. In the 1920s, some thirty or forty years after the drama of ideas had come into being, a form evolved which did just this. It was called Expressionism. In the work of such men as Georg Kaiser and Ernst Toller—Elmer Rice did an American imitation called *The Adding Machine*—the names and faces of men disappeared. The figures who were shuttled about on a kind of dramatic abacus were frankly labeled X, Y, and Z; they inhabited a geometric world in which propositions could be demonstrated without human interference. The hero of *The Adding Machine* is Mr. Zero. The principals in *Man and the Masses* are The Woman, The Husband, The

Masses, The Nameless, The State Official, Bankers, and First, Second, Third, Fourth, Fifth and Sixth Shadows. Man has acquired a capital "M" and ceased to exist.

Expressionism is sometimes regarded as an erratic offshoot of our drama. It was, on the contrary, the logical dead end toward which our drama had been moving. If we pulled back from it rather quickly, it was, I think, in horror at how far we had gone. The intellectual mathematics which underlay our drama had been too candidly exposed, rendered altogether too transparent. If we had to have this sort of thing, we preferred it in diluted form, with a little flesh grafted onto it.

In general, we went back to the thesis play. The strictly conceived problem play had fallen from favor; it was, no doubt, too cool and too inconclusive for the normally energetic theater. The propaganda play has more or less vanished for other reasons, though not necessarily the right ones: the angry desperation of the 1930s was mitigated by an economic upturn; and a new desperation, born of political tensions in the 1950s, created a fear of outspokenness. The thesis play stood roughly at the center of all these forms, offering an idea but discreetly clothing it in human mannerisms, and it must certainly have seemed the best compromise. It is the form that is most with us today.

In fact, it is so much with us that the average young writer at the present time cannot imagine himself writing a play without first having hit on a thesis. The thesis *is* his play. It is his subject matter, it is what the play is about. It is, he will tell you, his "theme."

Under the pressure of a good half century of argumentative drama, "theme" and "thesis" have come to mean one and the same thing. But they don't. A thesis is "a position or proposition which a person advances and offers to maintain by argument." A theme is "a subject or topic of discourse," or, if we may legitimately borrow from one of the other arts, "a melody constituting the basis of variation, development, or the like, in a composition or movement."

Definitions are academic, and I'm sorry to be bringing up Webster. But there are times when semantic confusion can be damaging; in this instance, I think, an ingrained habit of thought stands squarely in the way of the playwright's clearing his head, or of his sensing the possibilities of another sort of procedure.

Ask a playwright what his theme is and he will tell you:

"My theme is that all men of good will must join forces before it is too late."

"My theme is that political witch-hunting must be stopped now or it will engulf our society."

"My theme is that the pressures of modern life have destroyed the family."

"My theme is that Hollywood cripples the creative artist."

"My theme is that materialism corrupts whatever finer aspirations a man may have."

"My theme is that mother-love may become ruinously possessive."

"My theme is that children are people."

I once heard a professor of playwriting announce to his class that he hoped to write a play which had for its theme "the meaninglessness of meaning," a proposition even more advanced in the intellectual order of things than Pirandello's "reality is illusion, illusion reality."

Not one of these, of course, is a theme to be varied; all are theses to be defended. Even where the subject matter suggests possible thematic treatment—it is possible, after all, to write plays about mothers, Hollywood, children, and even politics—it has been attitudinized into a dogmatic pronouncement. "I am," the playwright says, "going to show you that such and such is so; my people are going to prove it." He does not simply say, "I am going to show you my people; I am going to show you the things they do."

Julius Caesar is a play about politics. It has a theme. Call it "political activity" or "political ambition" or what you will. The play is about a group of men engaged in a struggle for power. There is the shrewd, unstable Cassius. There is the pompous, weary, but not unattractive Caesar. There is the reasonable, responsible Brutus. There is the loyal, passionate Antony. There is the excitable Casca. Each enters the struggle for his own reasons, pursues it in his own way, tries to judge and to shape events out of his own understanding. The interaction of these minds is the entire substance of the play.

It has no thesis. So far from adopting or attempting to promulgate an attitude toward this struggle, Shakespeare has been nearly as detached in his treatment of it as the plot summary that appears in *The Oxford Companion to English Literature:*

> Distrust of Caesar's ambition gives rise to a conspiracy against him among Roman lovers of freedom, notably Cassius and Casca; they win over to their cause Brutus, who reluctantly joins them from a sense of duty to the republic. Caesar is slain by the conspirators in the Senate-house. Antony, Caesar's friend, stirs the people to fury against the conspirators by a skilful speech at Caesar's funeral. Octavius, nephew of Julius Caesar, Antony, and Lepidus, united as triumvirs, oppose the forces raised by Brutus and Cassius. The quarrel and reconciliation of Brutus and Cassius, with the news of the death of Portia, wife of Brutus, provide one of the finest scenes in the play. Brutus and Cassius are defeated at the battle of Philippi (42 B.C.), and kill themselves.

So be it. That's the way it was. We are not enlisted in the cause of any one of the conspirators. We are not told that Caesar was, in fact, evilly ambitious—only that Cassius and Casca thought he was. We are not urged to take a moral stand on Caesar's murder; we simply watch it as a terrifying image of actual human behavior. We are not asked to decide whether Cassius was *right* and Brutus *wrong* in permitting Antony to speak over Caesar's body; we know only that Cassius opposed it, that Brutus favored it, and that things worked out as Cassius had anticipated. Because Cassius was "right" about a given issue, we are not thereafter committed to Cassius. We are not even committed to the most thoughtful, upright, and integrated of the play's characters, Brutus. Brutus is, more than the others, an "honest" man. But he is no spokesman. His course is not clearly the course to be taken by all honest men. He too dies of the battle.

Nor is the play a paean of pessimism, cynical and bitter as it counts its corpses. It does not say, in the over-all view: "Power corrupts; absolute power corrupts absolutely." It does not say that ambition is bound to end in failure, that ambition is to be avoided, that political activity is in itself irremediably evil. If it does not say "Go into politics and behave as Cassius, or as Brutus, does," neither does it say "Stay out of politics altogether." Ideologically speaking, it *says* nothing. It simply shows us certain kinds of men, equipped with certain kinds of minds, engaging in a certain kind of activity. And we are fascinated: by the resourcefulness of these minds, by the intricacy of motive, by the interplay of temperaments, by the ingenuity, the passion, the incredible complexity of living men. The author has here given a theme "variation and development," has orchestrated what is truly human; he has not garlanded it with excrescent and highly debatable advice.

A Streetcar Named Desire has a theme. It is, let's say, self-deception. (I don't propose this as an absolute; themes are, almost by nature, difficult to define absolutely; they look to human nature in the round and, like a turning crystal, give off multiple reflections.) The Tennessee Williams play is, in any case, about a girl who deceives herself, or tries to deceive herself, in order to evade a reality which threatens to crush her.

The play has no thesis. We do not disapprove of Blanche

du Bois for what she has done; we understand her too thoroughly for that. Nor do we approve of what she has done; we see that it is destroying her. In her terrifying clash with the "normal" animal, Stanley Kowalski, we do not assign her to the "wrong" corner and him to the "right" one; we do not even assign her to the "unrealistic" corner and him to the "realistic" one. Labels are inadequate; the people are too complex. Stanley is a realist, all right. He can see sham. But he cannot see the sensitivity that is responsible for the sham. He is clearheaded; but he is also bullheaded. She is fake; but almost all of her aspirations are genuine. These two people are in conflict, but they are not in mathematical conflict. We watch them with horror, with apprehension, with anguish, and —very often—with open delight. As they grate on each other like matches on a tinderbox, we see them do "right" things and "wrong" things and sometimes both at once.

The play ends in a certain defined way. Blanche is at last insane. But the ending is not offered as an equation. It does not say, "Deceive yourself and you will destroy yourself." You may take this thought from the play, if you wish. You may also take quite different thoughts from it. You may, for instance, wonder what might have happened to Blanche had she not been caught out by this particularly insensitive man. You may wonder to what degree the boor has been responsible for the destruction of the sensitive. You may feel that there was much in Blanche that was worth saving, that the very things which were most worth saving were the things which made her intolerable. Your reaction may, indeed, be as complex as the life you have been observing.

No two men have yet agreed on the precise "meaning" of the character Hamlet. There isn't really much more agreement, among literary analysts, on the "meaning" of the play *Oedipus the King*. But Hamlet is perfectly real to us; as we watch *Oedipus* in the theater we intuitively accept its narrative. If two masterworks have, after centuries, resisted our efforts to turn them into rational equations, that is our hard luck, not theirs. They do not exist as equations, but as vital, impenetrable images.

It's an old story that Shakespeare so little intruded personal bias and personal belief upon his materials that to this day we cannot say with any certainty what his political, social, or religious beliefs may have been. We know the accuracy of his eye and the honesty of his ear; the rest is silence.

It may seem that I am trying to make a virtue out of ambiguity, even moral ambiguity. I am not; I am trying to make a case for complexity. It is true that in many plays, perhaps in most plays, there is a "rightness" or "wrongness" attached to the actions performed. It is wrong for Macbeth to murder his king; we know that. It is wrong for Othello to allow jealousy to possess him; we know that, too. But these are also things we knew quite clearly before we came; we do not require instruction from the playwright. As Chekhov once said, "You scold me for my objectivity, calling it indifference to good and evil, lack of ideas, and so on. When I describe horse-thieves you would have me say 'Stealing horses is evil.' But that was known long ago without me." Nor is the playwright out to *intensify* our natural moral responses, and so improve us. (Moralists sometimes like to justify drama in this light; it is a left-handed and wholly irrelevant defense.) The playwright is not working at white heat to turn us ever more firmly against murder. He is trying to put us in touch with murder, with the reality of the act and with the strange reality of the man immersed in the act: how he brings himself to it, how he passes through the moment, how he feels and behaves when the moment is over. He is trying to make us intimate with murder as a thing that happens, not trying to revolt us with murder as a thing that is forbidden. The play may follow from, and even rest upon, a widespread moral assumption; but the play is in what follows. A good play does not busy itself trying to enunciate moral values; it assumes them, and gets on with its own work of accurate observation.

William Butler Yeats once pointed out that one of the things dramatic action had to do was "burn up its author's opinions." He pointed it out to Sean O'Casey, who had just abandoned the earlier style of *Juno and the Paycock* and *The Plough and the Stars* and begun to experiment with his later, intensely didactic style. *Juno* has no thesis. A great deal of suffering is mixed with a great deal of laughter; the people who bring about the suffering are funny and endearing; irresponsibility exists, but it is never attacked; the conclusion of the play is no more than a tipsy ne'er-do-well's assertion that "the world's in a terrible state of chassis." The texture of the play is thick and multicolored, patterned after the coherent contradictions—the vices and virtues inseparably bound together—of mulish mankind. In subsequent plays, however, O'Casey not only took sides in the sociological, philosophical, and political arenas; he scrawled giant slogans in bright-colored chalk. His talent for language did not desert him, but his love of the actual went down before his prophetic apprehensions about the future. To read the work of O'Casey in sequence is to wish that Yeats, speaking to him in mid-career, had been more persuasive.

What is intrinsically wrong with the thesis play is that it puts the drawing board before the drama. It begins at the wrong end of the creative scale. It begins with a firm, fast premise, achieved in the intellectual solitude of the study, and thereafter proceeds to make all life dance to a quite debatable tune.

This is not to say that the rational mind should play no part in the shaping of a play. Obviously it must always play a very large part indeed. The author observes this or that brilliant facet of life; he catches a glimmering here, a fugitive gesture there. Once caught, these must be nursed, coddled, carefully pared, gently joined. The rational mind does the last-minute weaving, makes all sorts of judgments about what is, and what is not, to be retained. But it does its work as a scalpel, not as a die press. It shapes, but it does not stamp. It does not originate the process, killing the spirit before the spirit can be born; it arrives late, and tidies up.

Though the terms "theme" and "thesis" are now used interchangeably, there is an enormous difference between them. In the one, the playwright—uncommitted to any a-priori view—is forced to go out and *observe;* he must look to life for his materials. He may know, in general, that he wishes to write about jealousy; but he must first see what jealousy looks like.

In the other, the dramatic mansion is prefabricated. The playwright comes equipped with an agreeable syllogism, complete in all its parts. He clothes his major premise, and his minor premise, in a semblance of human flesh; but they are only premises after all, pointing to a planned conclusion. What we call the drama of ideas is just that: a drama in which the people are digits, adding up to the correct ideological sum.

Our drama of ideas is also a drama in which only the dramatist is allowed to have any ideas. What is "correct" is determined by the playwright. The audience sits in humble tutelage, not so much loving the characters as being lectured at by them, not so much enjoying the varied patterns of life as submitting to their rigid organization by a puritan with a stick.

6. *The Visitation from on High*

A LONG TIME AGO it was customary to introduce a new play with a little rhymed prologue. One of the actors would step before the curtain and, speaking for the author, beg the indulgence of the audience. He would point out, winningly, that the author made no special claims for his work; that he knew he was completely dependent on the generosity of all present; that it would be awfully nice if they could find it in their hearts to overlook the appalling defects of the enterprise and to applaud such small successes as might accidentally turn up; that he had no true object but to please them; and that, win or lose, he was their humble servant.

It is doubtful whether any author, at any time, felt quite so humble. The man who made this pretty protestation, however, had quite a realistic sense of his role in the theater, and of the audience's.

The practice of the prologue has been discontinued—rather fortunately, I think. For the playwright who attempted one today would be obliged—if he had any sort of candor in him—to speak pretty much as follows:

"Now if you will all just sit up straight in your seats, be perfectly quiet, and at least *try* to understand what I am saying, I will brush you up on quite a few things you sadly need to know. It is possible that you did not come here tonight for instruction; in which case it is necessary for you to be lashed into a sense of your responsibilities. It is possible that you have come here in some rude quest of pleasure; in which case you have come to the wrong place. I do not offer you pleasure; I offer you a memory of pain. You have a moral obligation to attend closely, and to endure much, for the play is an excellent one. It is excellent because, in the process of composing it, I have given no thought to commercial considerations, I have made no compromises with any of you; I have been steadfastly true to myself. I have worked long and hard on this play, and I love it. Since I am, as a person, both sensitive and well informed, it would become the rest of you to love it, too. Should you not like it, we can have little doubt in which of us the defect lies. Furthermore, should you not like it, I shall not hesitate to attack you in the press for the dunderheads you are, and I may even decide to withdraw my talents from the theater that needs me so sorely."

This sounds rough. Yet very little of it is invented.

The "memory of pain" phrase, for instance, comes from a letter written to *The Saturday Review* by a young playwright whose first production had just opened—and closed—on Broadway. George Tabori, noting that the reaction to his *Flight into Egypt* had been one of uneasiness, explained as follows: "It was my intention to create uneasiness. . . . I did not want to 'please.' I wanted to irritate, disturb, and shock; to leave the audience in a state of tension; to send them home unpurged, with a memory of pain."

Here are portions of a letter from a talented young man whose collaboration with another talented young man had just opened—and closed—on Broadway:

". . . we loved it. It has meant a very great deal to me; working on it has made me re-examine my own life. . . . We had a fine time; one of the happiest times of my life. But all the time, I know that each of us felt we were taking part in an experience that was, for us, a religious one. . . . We wanted to do something, and we did it in the very best way we could, and we're proud of what we've done, and we'd do it again. I am sorry that what we thought we had (and think we have) did not communicate itself across the footlights . . . because I think that out of feelings like ours, and effort like this, good things for the theater can come."

Fragment of a letter from one of our most distinguished playwrights, shortly after a failure:

". . . we are so few, among so many. . . ."

One of the troubles with the modern theater is that the playwright no longer has to die to reach Parnassus. He starts out there.

In some strange way he has come to conceive of himself, rather than the audience, as final arbiter. Since he is better informed than the folk on the benches, he is obliged to become their instructor. Since they are, at heart, a sluggish crew, he must become their prod, their irritant, their gadfly. And since the theater is something of a temple—Maxwell Anderson is fond of the phrase—he cannot very well avoid assuming the mantle of high priest.

Instructor, gadfly, high priest—these are the roles that the modern dramatist most frequently chooses to play. And because he is all of these things, because all truth is in him, he need strive to please only himself.

This is a creative state of mind which has, consciously or no, become quite commonplace. It is, I suppose, a state of mind that merits a certain limited sympathy. The good dramatist *is* an exceptional human being. His powers of insight *are* probably greater than those of any single spectator out front. He *does* deserve rather more respect than that originally allotted to Shakespeare, soiling himself in the bankside mud, or to Molière, who found it necessary to slip in the back way when he was invited to lunch with the King. It is, in addition, asking an awful lot of a talented man to pretend that he is not so talented.

But a man who hopes to make something of a success in a social situation might profitably indulge in a bit of false modesty, and be forgiven the deception. An attractive shyness, and an apparent reluctance to pontificate, might go a long way toward helping him win friends and—if this is what he wants to do—influence people. Grace is every bit as winning as a righteous aggressiveness. It might also become the dramatist to put off playing the elder statesman until the audience has actually voted him the title, or at least until he is a little elder.

Quite apart from the need for a trace of false modesty—in order to dispel that vague aura of the "word" being handed down—the playwright may very well need some real modesty. He has not troubled to conceal his sense of superiority to the mass audience: it has the mental capacity of a twelve-year-old, it is interested only in noisy musicals and noisier farces, it must be instructed rather than served, it cannot be trusted to recognize quality.

What if none of these things is true? None of them would seem to be true. Shakespeare's twelve-year-olds admired not only what was lowest but also what was highest in his work. Far from insisting that he endlessly repeat the crude excitements of *Titus Andronicus* or the rowdy horseplay of *The Taming of the Shrew*, they stayed with him through *Othello*, *Lear*, and *The Tempest*. If Shakespeare was at pains to solicit their favor, they responded by conferring their favor on some remarkably good plays; it cannot seriously be said that they stood in the artist's way. Sophocles' audiences seem to have loved him very much. Molière's were notoriously loyal, even in the face of the displeasure of church and court. Nor did they paralyze this artist at the rough-and-tumble level of his roadside farces; they made a success of the intensely sophisticated and theatrically difficult *School for Wives*. So far as I know no genuine masterpiece has ever been rejected by the common audience before which it was first performed. (I'm skipping some politically rigged opening-night demonstrations here; in spite of extraordinary pressures, good plays have always been quickly recognized.)

There is a legend to the contrary that is hard to kill. Almost anyone you meet at a literary salon nowadays (cocktails, five to seven) will tell you solemnly that all great artists have had an unhappy time of it, that they have suffered at the hands of the vulgar, that they have had to be rescued from oblivion by astute critics and imposed upon the general culture by generations of intellectuals. The public never knows what it is getting—or, more likely, in this view, missing—until it is too late; it must be told about it a long time later.

The legend, I think, derives from other, more privately conceived art forms. A painter working in solitude may wait some years for recognition; but he must also wait some years for simple circulation. Whereas the dramatist writes for an assembled populace and an immediate verdict, another kind of artist may be at the mercy of the gradual manner in which he is exhibited. Even here I doubt that the chain reaction is as slow in igniting as garret romancers like to think; but what may be partially true of one art form is not necessarily true of the socially conceived theater. Response in the playhouse is closer to spontaneous combustion. It also seems to be incredibly accurate. Since we have no known instance of the mass audience brutally dismissing a first-rate play, it is time we abandoned the canard.

What history suggests to us is that the audience can rise to any heights of which the playwright is capable, that it can go anywhere he can take it. The working phrase here, though, is "take it." In order to take the audience somewhere, the playwright must first embrace it. He must know it intimately, must honor its intelligence, must welcome its partnership. He is never going to manage the joint ascent unless he has shown the audience clear affection and honest respect. It is not going to trail after him on a lonely and privileged solo flight.

Humility is not only an attractive posture; it is—even in the theater—a positive virtue. "Respect for the audience" is not simply a sly, calculated conniving with a great beast's lowest instincts; it is a due obeisance paid to a powerful and just universal intelligence.

In our concern over the artist's personal integrity, we have wandered far from this sort of respect. Personal integrity is a splendid thing. One is delighted with a dramatist who steadfastly refuses to throw in a dishonest line just because he is not up to the moral effort of finding an honest one. One can have only praise for the playwright who makes no compromise with what he knows to be cheap, or seriously feels to be false. Insincerity is, sure enough, a vice.

But its opposite, "sincerity," is no automatic guarantee of theatrical validity. We've all been to plays where we had no trouble whatever in recognizing the author's sincerity—and where we had a great deal of trouble recognizing anything else. The dramatist had been true to himself but not to any objective world with which we were honestly familiar.

And I'm not speaking here of the radically experimental play, the play of deliberate distortion. I'm speaking of the sort of play in which a character clearly meant to be sympathetic never engages our sympathies, in which a moral act meant to elicit our support leaves us oddly indifferent, in which a motive or a deed seems unintelligible as human behavior. Though the playwright has seen his characters doing these things, we cannot. He may be an honorable man; but he is, in one way or another, inhabiting a private world.

The danger in making the individual psyche—even the gifted dramatist's—the last court of appeal, the sole determinant of what is and what is not "true," is that the individual psyche may at any time cut its moorings; indeed, the more it comes to rely exclusively on itself the more it tends to cut those moorings.

To this hazard a decent respect for the audience mind may stand as a corrective.

I'd say to the playwright:

Allow that the audience, too, has an intuitive capacity for recognizing what is true. Allow that this truth exists not in the dramatist's mind alone, nor even in the audience's mind alone, but, so to speak, in a third place outside both—in human behavior itself. Conceive of this truth about human behavior as something objective, concrete—something that can be caught, reflected, recognized. Think of it as public property, not private income. Turn your integrity not inward upon yourself but outward upon this shared reality; work very hard to make your image accurate. It is never enough to say "I have written honestly, by my own lights." It is necessary to say "I have written accurately, by everyone's lights."

Try to see what the audience sees—and is inarticulate about. Your job is simply to articulate a common experience of life.

And be assured that once you touch this common core, once you stumble upon a truth that can be universally recognized for what it is, the audience will know and applaud what you have done. A prominent playwright recently lamented the early closing of one of his shows with the thought that it had been "too true" for his audience; its truth had been ugly, and the audience had resolutely shut its mind to anything so uncompromisingly honest. When you are in this frame of mind, remind yourself that the audience has never exhibited any reluctance to deal with the injustices wrought upon Lear or with the punishments visited upon Oedipus. In our own time, it has not been unwilling to share the anguish of a Willy Loman or a Blanche du Bois. The audience does not reject an unpleasant truth because it seems unpleasant, but because it seems untrue.

A good play is a meeting of minds, not the thundering imposition of a superior mind upon a lesser one.

As far as that goes, the Ibsen-inspired dramatist has too much on his mind to begin with.

7. *Act Before You Think*

THE PLAYWRIGHT in our time has become a thinker. It often seems to me that the best thing a playwright can do is put off thinking as long as possible.

Everybody tells the playwright that he must have a theme before he can begin to write his play, and so, by heaven, he promptly manufactures one.

I have known young writers to sit back and run through all the available themes—pride, covetousness, lust, anger, jealousy —with the intention of picking the one that appealed most.

I have even known some to survive this deliberate bout with the universals, fasten on a likely generality, and fashion a story to fit.

To someone who has never tried to write a play this must seem wholly absurd. To someone who has given over his life to the business it may bring back memories: of the anguished search for a subject, for a starting point, for *anything* to set the creative machinery going. There are many times in a playwright's life when he is passionately intent upon writing a play, and hopelessly without a play to write. It is reliably reported of one of our brightest new dramatists that he never *can* invent a subject; it must be assigned to him. Shakespeare seems to have gone his entire life without having hit upon an original plot. The dilemma is frequently real enough; if we cannot always approve the playwright's procedure, we can at least sympathize with his pain.

The writer who behaves in the desperately well-intentioned manner outlined above is a little better off than the writer who shapes his play to a thesis, but not much. The man with a thesis has served notice on his materials: behave yourselves; I have something in mind. The man who has plucked jealousy out of the blue is somewhat less fettered; he may look around him for samples of that jealousy at work, he may stumble upon an actual one, and, if he does, he is free to follow it wherever it leads him. But he has begun his work arbitrarily; he has been cool and considered at the very time when his imagination might have been given its freest and most spontaneous play.

I sometimes think we do the dramatist a disservice in urging a premature clarity upon him. "Pin it down to a word," we say, "or at least to a simple sentence; you must know precisely where you are going before you dare write so much as a line." Our intentions are good; clarity is, ultimately, a virtue. And temperaments vary; some writers can work only in this way. But in a time when formulas are rigid with age, when most of what we do is the result of habit rather than inspiration, when fresh exploratory contact with the basic materials of drama is imperative, I think we might be a bit more generous.

Suppose we say to the playwright: "Determining your theme is not necessarily Step Number One in writing a play. It may be, at the very earliest, Step Number Two. It may also be a step to be taken with extreme care, lest you freeze your material before it has begun to send off shoots."

I doubt that good drama, any more than good work in the other arts, ever begins in generalities. More likely it begins in a specific image, in something actually seen or actually heard. There may have been a young couple, shoulder to shoulder and grimly silent, on the subway. A maiden aunt, fingering her necklace and defensively insisting that "all the men were killed in the war." A worn doctor, speaking rapidly and mechanically as though in constant dread that he might hear what he is saying. An unsuccessful young husband, with a vacant smile, spending all his time with his children. An effusive diner who has tipped heavily and is staring directly and warmly into the waiter's face for a sign of appreciation. A bandaged man, across from you on a train, talking on and on about the blood he has lost. A snarl of drunken voices coming from a slow-moving automobile on a Sunday morning in Manhattan. A habit of blinking the eyes for quick control. A laugh. An embarrassed paleness. A radio suddenly snapped off.

This accidental brush with the texture and timbre of unclassified life may not register at once. It may graze the writer so gently that he overhears it, and forgets it. A long time later it may return to consciousness, as something inexplicably remembered. But when it does come back it will come back exactly—as though a tuning fork had just been touched, a tingling reverberation, alive, dimensional, immediate and intimate.

Once more, I'd say to the playwright:

Get it down while it's still alive—before you have thought too much about it. Resist the temptation to analyze, to abstract, to generalize, to codify. Never be in a hurry to cerebrate. Cerebration is not your business. Imagination—the seizing and reflecting of images—is.

The philosopher F. S. C. Northrup has pointed out, in *The Meeting of East and West*, that an "aesthetic" truth and a "theoretical" truth are different kinds of truth. They are, in fact, opposites; each is an ultimate, "irreducible to the other." The fact that you know the theoretical wave length for the color blue does not help you to make a person born blind see blueness. Conversely, seeing the sensed color blue does not automatically lead you to any knowledge of its wave length. Both are descriptions of the same phenomena, but the descriptions are not interchangeable; worked out, they do not produce the same effect.

If you are in the process of discovering a play, don't worry too soon about its wave length. The critics will get that for you later. (They will get it wrong, too.) Get the color.

W. H. Auden on the subject of the beginning artist:

" 'Why do you want to write poetry?' If the young man answers 'I have important things to say,' then he is not a poet. If he answers 'I like hanging around words listening to what they say,' then maybe he is going to be a poet."

A play, like a poem, is something to be discovered. Auden again:

"A poet writes 'The chestnut's comfortable root' and then changes this to 'The chestnut's customary root.' In this alteration there is no question of replacing one emotion by another, or of strengthening an emotion, but of discovering what the emotion is. The emotion is unchanged, but waiting to be identified like a telephone number one cannot remember. '8357. No, that's not it. 8557. 8457, no, it's on the tip of my tongue, wait a minute, I've got it, 8657. That's it.' "

Wait a while. Let life do the talking. Listen to it. Let it

move. You may be surprised—and quite possibly delighted—at the odd and interesting way it does move. Hold that busy brain of yours back; it wants only to label life, and is bound to limit it. Work by touch as long as you can.

If you are going to write a play, be sure that you begin with something concrete: a phrase you have heard, a gesture you have seen, a face that has disturbed you. If you are working from memory, tease the memory until it has brought detail back to you; don't transform the first vagrant echo into a featureless formula. Detail, detail, and more detail is what you are after. A summary can be made after you have gathered the material. Gather it first. If the lifelike fragment seems to have come out of the blue, seems unrelated to any actual experience you can recall, thank God and go fishing. Don't leap at it analytically like a double-entry bookkeeper. It has actually been stored in an echo chamber you didn't know you had. Don't start locking up. Leave the door open; there may be more where that came from. If you are desperate and culling the daily newspapers for possible inspiration, don't read the editorial page. The editorial page is full of conclusions. Don't read the front page, either. The front page is merely recent. Read the two-inch items that turn up at the bottoms of pages 3, 4 and 5. These are here not because the people involved are automatically newsworthy, or because the abstract issues in which they are involved are the major issues of the day. They are here because some otherwise unimportant people did something inherently interesting. What took place is interesting because it does not fit into our overly neat notions of the sequence of human behavior. Truth stranger than fiction? It is infinitely stranger than theory. If you are ransacking the library in the hope of hitting on something—this is a perfectly legitimate device, by the way; the response that one temperament has made to a given body of material may set off a quite different response in another temperament—try not to steal from the author's ultimate *rationale* of his work. Steal from the work. Don't borrow from the last chapter of *War and Peace*. Borrow from the third, sixth, or twelfth.

Wherever your first fragmentary image comes from, look to see that it has eyes, ears, nose, teeth, five fingers on each hand, and an odd way of breathing. Arland Ussher speaks of James Joyce as a kind of "scavenger" of the ready-to-hand world. He had "an almost canine receptivity to all its sounds and smells." This is a virtue that few of our dramatists possess.

I have no way of knowing how Tennessee Williams works, but it seems to me that, more than any other contemporary playwright, he works by touch. You feel, as you watch a Williams play, that the author has seen, somewhere, a shaken, fastidious, unbearably pretentious young woman, that he has not only listened to her but let her go on in her own intolerable, destructive, heartbreaking fashion, that he is determined to spare her nothing and yet to honor her for exactly what she is. You feel that Williams is willing to pursue an elusive inflection forever, that he is loath to interrupt it for fear it should cease to be heard.

Blanche du Bois greeting her sister in *A Streetcar Named Desire:*

> Stella, oh, Stella, Stella! Stella for Star! Now, then, let me look at you. But don't you look at me, Stella, no, no, no, not till later, not till I've bathed and rested! And turn that over-light off! Turn that off! I won't be looked at in this merciless glare! Come back here now. Oh, my baby! Stella! Stella for Star! I thought you would never come back to this horrible place! What am I saying? I didn't mean to say that. I meant to be nice about it and say—Oh, what a convenient location and such—Ha-aha!—Precious lamb. You haven't said a *word* to me. . . . Well, now you talk. Open your pretty mouth and talk while I look around for some liquor! I know you must have some liquor on the place! Where could it be, I wonder? Oh, I spy, I spy!

Stanley Kowalski, rummaging through Blanche's belongings, in the same play:

> Look at these feathers and furs that she come here to preen herself in! What's this here? A solid-gold dress, I believe! And this one! What is these here? Fox-pieces! (He blows on them.) Genuine fur fox-pieces, a half a mile long! Where are your fox-pieces, Stella? Bushy snow-white ones, no less! Where are your white fox-pieces?

Tom Wingfield, in *The Glass Menagerie*, screaming an answer to his blindly nagging mother:

> I'm going to opium dens! Yes, opium dens, dens of vice and criminals' hang-outs, Mother. I've joined the Hogan gang, I'm a hired assassin, I carry a tommy-gun in a violin case! I run a string of cat-houses in the Valley! They call me Killer, Killer Wingfield, I'm leading a double life, a simple, honest warehouse worker by day, by night a dynamic czar of the *underworld, Mother*. I go to gambling casinos, I spin away fortunes on the roulette tables! I wear a patch over one eye and a false mustache, sometimes I put on green whiskers. On those occasions they call me—*El Diablo!* Oh, I could tell you things to make you sleepless! My enemies plan to dynamite this place. They're going to blow us all sky-high some night! I'll be glad, very happy, and so will you! You'll go up, up on a broomstick, over Blue Mountain with seventeen gentlemen callers! You ugly—babbling old—*witch*. . . .

The best of Williams' work is filled with lightning flashes of things instantly recognized, with echoes that cannot be pushed away, with figures that slip about the stage with the unmanageable impulsiveness of loosed quicksilver. You feel, too, that the method is fragmentary, that it comes in flashes with little conscious control; that is why, I think, the Williams endings are so often either inconclusive or, as in the case of *The Rose Tattoo*, desperately patched together in the struggle to shape things up. I think it is better, though, to have touched Amanda Wingfield in the inconclusive *Glass Menagerie* than to have built Joe Keller for the perfectly conclusive *All My Sons*. It is better to have given us two acts of that volatile Serafina Delle Rose who eludes control in *The Rose Tattoo* than to have supplied us with the half-dozen deadheads who populate, and perform most co-operatively, in tidier plays.

Give your people a sporting chance to get away from you.

After you have watched and listened for quite a long time, after you have tried to get down exactly the look of the thing you have seen and exactly the sound of the thing you have heard, after you have let that original image summon up all the associate images of which it seems capable, then you may want to rough out a theme.

Why? At this stage, largely as a reminder. You are not now trying to put a clamp on your initial image; you are trying to jot down a clue to it in case it should wander off somewhere during the course of your later work.

A painter, seeing something, very often reaches for a scratch pad—in romantic movies, he uses a tablecloth—to dash off a hasty line. This is by no means his painting; it is only a detail; it is not even complete as an outline; it may never be referred to again. But there is always the chance that the precise curve, crease, or curious juxtaposition of shapes in a structure may not be seen again, may be faultily recalled, or may, if seen again, fail to produce in the artist the same astonishing illumination. He tries to make a quick memo of what has dazzled him.

I think a dramatist's theme might well be such a line: a rapid, responsive thrust at the heart of the work, a fragment of radiant reality which opens outward in a dozen as yet undetermined directions, a kind of mnemonic device for dredging up—again and again—that first essential excitement. Only by implication does it contain the final form of the work; that will have to be found, gradually uncovered; having a theme should not end, or circumscribe, the process—it should simply set it in motion.

The painter, of course, is luckier than the dramatist. He can draw an actual line. Since the dramatist works with words, he is likely to jot down a word, a phrase, or a sentence.

When he does so, he should be careful about the word or phrase he chooses. It ought not so much represent his considered thought about his material, as some aspect of the material itself. Corral a dozen young playwrights, ask them what their themes are, and, if you are lucky enough not to get a barrage of theses, you are still likely to get some rich, rolling sonorities: "brotherhood," "integrity," "man's inhumanity to man." We are quick with a "brotherhood" nowadays. In part, we have been taught to write "significant" plays and so are avid, all too early in the game, to latch onto "significant" words. We also inherit, from the scientific bent of the past hundred years, a habit of abstraction. We live in the time of the "common man," the "family unit," the "ethnic group," and the "human factor." We like to talk like this. We cannot help it. We tend to think like this, too, even when we are writing plays. But when, having seen a man instinctively reach out to pull another man back from the edge of a subway platform, we leap grandiosely to the concept "brotherhood," announce that "brotherhood" is the theme of the play inspired by the incident, and begin to build our play backward from our lofty pronouncement, we are in imminent danger of producing a faintly pompous, if not distressingly hollow, play. The vitality of drama is not in any key word that can be deduced from it; it is in the crackling reality of the original image.

When you are working out a theme, stay close to the image. Don't look for a word that simply *includes* your image: "brotherhood" includes practically everything, and suggests nothing. What if your theme is the image itself, the impulsive lunge you actually saw? Are you sure that you need anything more?

In a play called *Harriet*, Helen Hayes made use of what was, for me, an unforgettable gesture. As the placid, businesslike, devoted Harriet Beecher Stowe, Miss Hayes passed the evening in grave but gentle tolerance of her incompetent husband. Once, caught suddenly off balance, she let her hand fly halfway to his face in clawlike savagery. The moment was quickly over; there were no more moments like it. I have always supposed it to have been the invention of the director. But there was, in that single graphic and aborted gesture, more "play" than in the remaining two and one half hours of dreary verbalization.

Such a gesture, supposing that you have seen one, might be a more reliable index to the entire content, structure, and "meaning" of your play than any amount of logical formulation. It might do very well for a theme, containing, in a concrete fusion of muscle and will, all that will ever be essential to your play—at the same time that it leaves all sorts of room for expansion and variation.

You may need no more theme than a line of dialogue. I'm not thinking now of the sort of line that consciously summarizes the play and comes into being—if it ever does—relatively late in the creative process. I'm not thinking of George Kelly's dialogue synopsis for *Craig's Wife*: "People who live to themselves, Harriet, are generally left to themselves." (In fact, it's a good idea to throw away this sort of line, once you have thought of it; it's a lot like that joke in which a man on the telephone keeps loudly addressing "Bill" and, when he is finished, brightly announces that "That was Bill.")

The kind of dialogue fragment which might easily serve as a theme is that which has lodged in your memory, its inflections intact, and which has just now summoned up the very associations which have impelled you to write. Without having the faintest notion of how Tennessee Williams worked out *The Glass Menagerie,* I would not find it difficult to believe that the whole structure of the play had grown from, say, the remembered, monotonously repeated phrase "gentlemen callers." Suppose that you have heard the phrase used, in a certain odd and compelling tone of voice; it sticks in your ear. Listened to, it brings the speaker to mind: she uses an idiom that has vanished, uses it as though it were still in vogue; she has, at one time or another, been very much preoccupied with the matter, it loomed large in her own background; she is insistently preoccupied with it now. Do I follow the preoccupation that rings interminably in the phrase? Does it lead me to a mother who puts a high value on "gentlemen callers," to a daughter who is in need of "gentlemen callers," to a son who is expected to provide "gentlemen callers," to, at last, a "gentleman caller"?

The play may not have been written in this way. But the dialogue fragment might easily have provoked every moment of it.

A theme may be anything that *helps* the playwright to remember, and to nurture, his materials. It is a convenience, not a moral obligation. The playwright is under no injunction to explain his working processes; he is not bound to offer the critics a convenient analysis of his work; he does not owe the producer a ten-word caption that can be printed alongside the Cast of Characters; his publisher does not demand a slogan on the flyleaf of the book. The theme may, in fact, remain the author's well-kept secret until doomsday, and no one need ever be the worse for it. The play is expected to be intelligible on its own terms, without textbook marginalia.

For the playwright, and in due time, the theme may very well become what we have always held it to be—an organizing principle. Let's say that you have begun with a concrete image. In the process of recording its lifelike pulsations, companion images have been suggested to you. A remembered phrase suggests another remembered phrase. A gesture suggests a face. Phrase, face, and gesture come together and begin to move of their own accord. You see them in relations you had not previously imagined. After a while, whether by progressive recall or by associative improvisation, you have a good bit of material at hand. You have a dozen, or two dozen, fragments, all of them related to an initial stimulus, all of them somewhat different. There is now a danger that you have accumulated, or may accumulate, more than you need; some of the recall, some of the improvisation, may be irrelevant. A decision may be necessary. You look into your multiplying scraps for a clue. Which of them seems to have had the greatest vitality, for you? Which has evoked the largest number of companion images? Which has had the greatest generative power? Which evokes most accurately the impulse that set you off? Which, more than any other, seems to reach out and embrace most of your remaining material?

In order to have some basis for selection among proliferating images, and in order to keep a finger on the vital pulse of your work, you may now settle upon a single word or phrase. But notice what you have done. You have drawn your organizing principle from the material itself, you have let your first fragment lead you to your final form. You have *not* established the principle, or premise, first and then contrived material to fit.

By the time you have reduced the essence of your play to a concept, you have already gathered all that is truly important to it. It has its own fertility, its own energy, now; you are not so likely to kill it with calculation.

A writer's critical power should be held in reserve as long as possible, so that his creative power will be able to act freely. As Aristotle once said, "The moving principle seems to become stronger when the reasoning power is relaxed." Beware the theme too soon conceptualized. It may anticipate the movement of life, and intercept it. The easy generalization may act as a short circuit, cutting off observation, clear attention, direct response to the peculiar universe around you.

Be swift to see and slow to identify.

Repeat, with Auden:

"*How can I know what I think till I see what I say?*"

PART THREE

How to Spoil a Good Story

One of the unpopular traditions of our time has, with perfectly good intentions, transformed theme into thesis, character into mouthpiece, playwright into high priest. If none of these transformations has had much appeal for the onetime theatergoing public, neither has it produced for us the enduring art we sought. It has, rather, helped to circumvent art.

The other important—and equally unpopular—tradition of our time has come to us with just as good, or even better, intentions. It meant, in a sense, to correct some of the Ibsen-inspired defects, notably the defect in characterization. But in going about its work, it attacked and laid waste still another traditional popular value, the value of Story. It did not think it could make its own peculiar improvements without first sacrificing the attractions of narrative, and the sacrifice of narrative, I believe, became an act of sabotage from within. Once more the denial of a popular value ended in the denial of a quite necessary aesthetic value.

For the next few chapters we shall be talking about the plays we are still writing in imitation, or semi-imitation, of Chekhov.

8. *It's a Very Small World*

A YOUNG STUDENT who keeps turning up at my office has a great idea for a play. It's about his aunt.

The little old lady has lived in a third-floor room for fifteen years. Her family cannot remember when she last came out of it. She has a rocker, and can be heard rocking herself to sleep right after lunch. She is an avid reader, and has a vast collection of magazines dating back to 1907. She will chat agreeably enough when her sanctuary is invaded, but her eyes cloud over whenever it is suggested that she take a day in the sun. The children come up to see her on their birthdays, and she gives them little homemade presents on which she has worked long and hard. Ask her about her private life and you will get a sharp glance that says you must go now. No one has ever known her secret. No one will ever know. She lives, as I understand it, on shredded wheat.

Now I have nothing against this student, and I have nothing against his aunt. If, in talking to him, I occasionally feel a pang of alarm, it is because I am morally certain he will write that play; I am morally certain it will be produced; I am morally certain it will fail; and I am morally certain that, immediately it has failed, there will be a handful of angry letters in *The New York Times* denouncing a barbarous public for its inability to see beauty where beauty is. The play will be ruefully remembered by twenty people for twenty years. In time it will be revived at City Center, where it will fail again. The tears of the twenty will be shed anew.

You can see the play. There will be a setting designed in evocative browns by Boris Aronson. Perhaps Lillian Gish will be persuaded to inhabit it. The performance will be a fragile, and strangely perceptive, one. The little old lady will putter about doing odd and interesting things. The children will come, and we will have a scene of gaiety broken by the youngest's thoughtless suggestion that she come down to see his bicycle. The oldest, glancing back, will shepherd the tumbling crew away. There will be a significant pause, as the old lady leafs a magazine, not seeing it. A knock on the door. Her brother, the father of the family. They both know why he has come, but neither will speak of it. He has come to make amends, and to make one more effort to lure her from the room. But he must circle the subjects, letting an inference waft across the room as she wafts one back. His wife appears. There is an ugly silence. They go. The old lady rocks.

As the play goes on, there will be one cruel effort to shock the recluse into life. It will fail. Then the oldest daughter will come quietly one twilight, seeking help. The mother and father are driving her toward a certain way of life, their way perhaps. The girl needs a champion. The old lady is sharp with her, fighting down her own impulse to help. The girl leaves, in tears. The old lady is terribly disturbed.

Eventually there is a scene in which the aunt, after a profound inner struggle, bestirs herself. She will come down. She dresses. She does all the little feminine things she did fifteen years ago. She steels herself. She walks, haltingly, to the door. Her hand touches the knob. There is a breath of air from the window, and the curtains stir slightly. There are sounds of children's voices from the street below, perhaps the sudden shrill sound of a mother calling them. The trembling hand falters. The old lady does not go.

Sometime later, in the dusk, the door opens. The girl enters, slowly. She has given in. She will lead the life that has been planned for her. When it is ended, or nearly ended, she too will be a recluse. These two stare at each other in understanding. The old lady rocks. The girl leans against the window. Curtain.

It must be understood that all of this will be sensitively done. When a saddened reader writes to the *Times* of the sorry, sorry waste, the waste will have been real.

What might have made a small, noncommittal sketch for *The New Yorker*, a fragment for *The Partisan Review*, or perhaps the central image for a twenty-line poem has been wasted on the theater. Talent is talent; but not all talent is theatrical talent.

We are in the habit of making demands on the theater. We say that it *ought* to be open to the penetrating mind; that it *ought* to embrace the clear signs of inspiration; that it *ought* to make room for any and every sort of literary value. We say, further, that the audience *ought* to support such tenuous work as may show flashes of such value; that it ought to support it in preference to specifically theatrical work that does not possess such value.

We rarely suppose that the theater makes demands of its own. Or, if we do, we suppose them to be casual ones: the character revelation must be cast in the form of dialogue; some allowance must be made for chairs and tables; our observation of character must be sectioned into parts, so that a few curtains may fall (though none need fall dramatically). Literary value transposed to the theater is simply literary value enclosed in quotation marks.

The theater is a somewhat ruder place than this. It is, and we are appalled to discover the fact, quite a primitive place. A great many seats have been lashed together in an outsized building so that a great many people can come together for a robust and companionable outsized experience. The audience is not confused about the kind of experience it is looking for. When it wishes a private experience, it makes suitable arrangements. Intending to pore quietly over a delicately wrought character sketch, it snaps on one light in the living room, settles into the most comfortable armchair, murmurs a silent prayer that the telephone won't ring, and shuts out all thought of company. When it comes to the theater, it comes looking for company. It comes looking for noise—it takes a loud play to fill a large building. It comes looking for color—it takes bold hues to hit the top of the second balcony. It comes looking for activity—it takes a lot of activity to spellbind this on-the-town and out-for-the-evening band. An arena has been erected so that an event may take place.

Whatever is uneventful dies peacefully in the arena. Whatever is soft or slow or small shivers and expires in this busy barn.

Once upon a time there was a theatrical requirement known as magnitude. When Aristotle tried to pin down the essentials of tragedy, he described the form as "an imitation of an action that is complete in itself, as a whole of some magnitude." And he quickly added, "for a whole may be of no magnitude to speak of." When Aristotle spoke of Beauty, he called it a "matter of size and order." Finally, he ventured so far as to say that "the longer the story, consistently with its being comprehensible as a whole, the finer it is by reason of its magnitude."

In general, we distrust scale nowadays. Certainly we distrust spectacle. We know that the audience yearns for extravagant event; but we are inclined to think of the yearning as one of the least attractive of the audience's characteristics. It is a superficial desire for thrill; it is a primitive fondness for excessive color; it is a fairly shoddy form of escape, of sublimation, of vicarious romantic experience. It constitutes an unrealistic attitude toward life.

I'm not sure that we understand this passion for excitement correctly. It may be a passion for reality, especially that reality which cannot be grasped in any other way.

Extravagant things, violent things, events of notable magnitude, do from time to time touch the outer edges of our lives. I suppose most of us have known suicides. A good many of us have married friends who do one another physical damage. People do cut one another up in bars. Each of us has heard a screech of brakes and some sort of thump, and then moved cautiously toward the crowd at the curbstone.

At this point, though, something happens to us. We are drawn toward the scene of violence by an immediate, unquestioning impulse. But the closer we approach it the more intense does a counter-impulse become. Having shouldered our way to the edge of the spectacle, we are overcome by a powerful urge to turn away. We are simultaneously fascinated and repelled.

We are fascinated by something that is real. We are repelled because it *is* real. Whatever charity we may have in us, whatever sense of the ugly, whatever awareness that the victim is a man like ourselves, casts a veil over the event—over our clear sight of the event. Because we are humane, we deny ourselves a direct vision.

Should the disturbing event come closer, should it strike with shattering force either family or friends, our vision of it, our grasp of it, is hazier still. We are, quite literally, blinded by emotion; we cannot see the event for the intensity with which we feel it. Yet there is something actual and meaningful and perhaps majestic to be seen.

Our art forms are often concerned to show us with clarity those events that are much too tremendous to be seen clearly in life. Intense passion, at close range, involves us too much; in the theater we may watch it without that direct involvement which obscures its meaning. The larger the event, the more likely are we to lose hold of it in life; and the more necessary does it become for the theater to seize and to shape it for us. If the greatest plays of the past are plays in which characters tear out their own or one another's eyes, in which characters kill or are killed, in which sons turn violently upon their mothers or husbands upon their wives, it is not because audiences once asked for cheap stimuli but because audiences did ask to have their experience, their clear knowledge of life, enlarged.

The contemporary theater insists that a play, to be true, must be small and casual. And there are small and casual truths. They are, however, the truths we are best able to deduce for ourselves from the daily round. We pin them down with a reasonable accuracy as we listen to the children at the breakfast table, overhear our neighbors on the commuters' train, or watch our fellow workers at the office party. We make some mistakes; but not too many. To have small-sized truths confirmed in the theater gives us a mild pleasure; we recognize, we nod, we smile. But the experience cannot exhilarate us; it has not added notably to our knowledge. We remain grateful to the play that shows us more of the truth than we dared to face by ourselves. We are also excited by it.

The dramatist is, if he but knew it, a fortunate man. The audience tells him very clearly what it expects of him. If he pays some sort of attention to his audience, he is likely to become quite popular. And in the process of becoming popular he will find himself plunged into the most passionate—and potentially the most profound—materials a violent universe affords. He need only be honest to the bitter end.

In the contemporary theater we are extremely honest about trivia, and extremely indifferent to any activity more pronounced than the rustling of a leaf, a dress, or a newspaper over coffee. Indeed we are hostile to the idea of activity.

9. *Anything Happen Next?*

I ONCE SPENT an extremely pleasant evening walking the streets of Washington, D.C., from the Willard Hotel to the White House and back, in the company of Thornton Wilder. Mr. Wilder is exceptionally good company. In fact, he is such good company and is therefore in such demand that he rarely has time to finish writing a play.

What I remember most clearly from the conversation is Mr. Wilder's insistence that the theater of story—the theater of "what happens next?"—was in deep discredit, had outlasted its usefulness.

The author was in part explaining his latest play, *The Skin of Our Teeth,* which had just begun its Broadway run to considerable critical acclaim. Mr. Wilder is one of the most genuinely observant men now not working for the theater, and *The Skin of Our Teeth* is in nearly every respect a fascinating play.

As the season wore on, though, it picked up an odd reputation. Taxicab drivers, who normally head for the theatrical district around eleven o'clock, took to lining up at the Mansfield a great deal earlier. *The Skin of Our Teeth* became known as the hit with the largest number of people leaving after the second act. The play was the talk of the town; but a lot of the talk was shrill with outrage. The production did not get its expected run in New York, and was a sudden failure on the road.

The usual explanation for this strange state of affairs has always been centered on the liberties Mr. Wilder likes to take with dramatic convention: the bold leaps in time, the practice of addressing the audience directly, and so on. The audience, it was suggested, stubbornly resists this sort of innovation. But Mr. Wilder had already done most of these things in *Our Town,* without enraging anybody.

It later occurred to me that perhaps the real reason for the curious reception given *The Skin of Our Teeth* lay in the fact that nothing happened next. The play was built circuitously: the same thing happened over and over again. In Act One the human family survived physical disaster; in Act Two the same human family survived domestic disaster; in Act Three it survived military disaster. Each act was joyously illuminating; but each act was complete in itself, built to a recurring pattern, no one of them requiring the others to fulfill its meaning.

Mr. Wilder was, of course, quite right about one thing. "What happens next?" has, as a compelling principle, been thoroughly discredited in our generation. We no longer believe in the importance, and certainly not in the primacy, of narrative. Story is something we make halfhearted concession to; action is a quality suitable for Western films; plot is no more than a monstrous artifice, abhorrent to men of taste; situation is the province of hacks.

Arthur Hopkins said it all:

"Plays of the future will be more concerned with character than event. This is in line with other art forms as well as with scientific research which is seeking the essence of being rather than dwelling on details of its manifestations. . . . Certainly there is a greater and richer variety of expression in character revelation than in the altered application of long used situations. Someone once took the trouble to enumerate the basic situations available to the dramatist. I doubt if anyone would attempt to catalogue the number of character facets that are employable. It would be like counting fingerprints. That the inner man is a richer field than his outer manifestations is evident in much classic literature. One of Hamlet's soliloquies unfolds a more exciting panorama than all of the frantic killings in the last scene."

We are repeatedly told that character is primary. If not character, mood. If not mood—mood sometimes sounds a bit romantic—then the objective study of environment. These are not only the dramatist's sources, the wellsprings for his creation: they are the actual ends toward which he is working; they fulfill, in themselves, the requirements of drama.

If one half, or something better than one half, of our drama has been dedicated to the illustration of intellectual opinion, the remainder has been devoted to the dispassionate examination of character, mood, and milieu—to plays in which these things are the predominant, when they are not the exclusive, content. We are now in the realm of Carson McCullers' *The Member of the Wedding*, Truman Capote's *The Grass Harp*, John van Druten's *I Am a Camera*, Paul Osborn's *Morning's at Seven*, Jane Bowles's *In the Summer House*, William Inge's *Picnic*.

We have come to this second strain, I think, in two ways. In part it stems from our rebellion against the souped-up narratives of nineteenth-century melodrama. The theater that preceded ours had made action everything, character nothing. Horrified by the garish hues and cardboard humans of this "insincere" theater, we have hastened to invert the process, to make character everything, action nothing.

I suspect that we were further—though perhaps subconsciously—distressed by our experience of Ibsen. Ibsen gave us our social format, our impulse toward the drama of purpose. But he gave it to us in a sham narrative context, a context that seemed to be telling us a story while it was really telling us off. An orphanage might burn down for a second-act climax, but we were to understand that it wasn't an orphanage burning down; it was a corrupt way of life. A wife might dance a tarantella in the living room to keep her husband from answering the postman's ring, but the dance wasn't really a dance; it was part of a diagram. We sensed the uneasy relationship between the concrete thing that was being acted out and the abstract intention that made it impersonal; in time we began to titter at the juxtaposition. The idea and the illustration were self-conscious in each other's presence: too pat when they fitted, too puzzling when they didn't. We felt that something was wrong. Either the thesis was out of place, or the story was. An age committed to thesis made a natural deduction: the story was the interloper. Story now had a second strike on it.

At the same time that we were making wry grimaces at *Bertha, the Sewing-Machine Girl* and worrying over the unresolved element in Ibsen, Chekhov flickered faintly on the horizon.

More than any other available model, Chekhov has appealed to whatever is "sensitive" in the contemporary playwright. Here is humble, patient, perceptive, even poetic work; and its focus is character. Such action as it contains is known by its absence, like a day that is clearly remembered because no mail came. In *The Three Sisters* the principal characters wish to go to Moscow; they do not go. In *Uncle Vanya* an old man brings himself to the point of firing a gun at the nonentity on whom he has wasted his life; he misses. In *The Cherry Orchard* a charming incompetent makes inadequate gestures toward salvaging a way of life; the way of life vanishes. In *The Sea Gull* the members of a family grapple, in John Gassner's phrase, with "their inability to realize themselves in a static environment."

To any writer it must always have been clear that the value of Chekhov is not in what is done. It is not even in what is not done, though this is admittedly more important to the Chekhovian scheme. The value is in the many-sided character revelation—now an impulse, now an inhibition, now a moment of exhilaration, now a moment of despair—that takes place in the narrative void. In one sense it is the very existence of the void that makes so much revelation possible: because the people are suspended, they may be examined with infinite patience. The void itself comes to seem desirable; it allows more time for portraiture.

To the writer who had no special urge toward ideological billposting, the Chekhovian vision must have come as a godsend. The form was free from argument and open to artistry. Remembered moods might be explored indefinitely. Attractive characters might be examined under a dozen different lights, turned slowly and gently before the connoisseur's eye. This was a drama of nuance, of overtone, fragile perhaps but filled with shimmering images. It was worth the attention of a poet.

Let me say at once that the Chekhovian manner does seem to me preferable, in a great many ways, to the Ibsen manner. It takes its origins from life, it respects life, it imposes little that is mechanical upon life. The man who uses it has unquestioned creative freedom in certain directions: in the direction of character, of atmosphere, of environmental evocation. The movement of the form is toward the concrete and three-dimensional, not toward the theoretical. The creative processes that it employs seem to me—so far as they go—wholly valid.

Yet the form is shatteringly unpopular. Chekhov, as we have said, cannot be played here. The plays to which the Chekhovian tradition has given birth—plays such as *I Am a Camera* and *The Member of the Wedding*—sometimes earn a relative popularity through the interest of their stars. But we must pause to consider how relative that popularity is.

I Am a Camera, with an extraordinary performance by Julie Harris in its principal role, was able to last out a season in New York. It at no time played to capacity. It was not popular in the sense that *A Streetcar Named Desire* was popular: 855 performances. It was not, of course, popular in the sense that a successful motion picture is popular. It was, at best, popular with that very small, very dedicated band of die-hards who continue to attend the New York theater and whose support is not sufficient to maintain that theater.

It is not difficult for me to enjoy what is good in a play like *The Member of the Wedding*. I know the sort of play I am going to see. Seeing it, I recognize it for an excellent example of its kind, the best that is available to us. Because I am professionally concerned with the theater, and interested in its survival on any terms, I find myself liking it. But I cannot, let's say, make my mother-in-law like it.

My mother-in-law, like most mothers-in-law, is not personally concerned with the survival of the theater. She is personally concerned with her personal satisfaction. (She is, I must add, a born playgoer and no dolt.) When I took her to *The Member of the Wedding*, by way of a dutiful treat, she was willing to grant the virtues that had been pointed out to her. Yes, the acting was interesting. Yes, the children were very real. Yes, the stage pictures were lovely. But, after all, "there really wasn't very much to it, was there?"

She came away in vague dissatisfaction, as much irritated with herself for failing to succumb to the play as she was with the play for failing to make her succumb. All that quality, and why don't I care?

In addition to trying to point out the merits of *I Am a Camera* through the columns of the newspaper for which I work, I urged a number of friends to see it. I never found one who thanked me. Again the tentative, rather sorely tried agreement: yes, it's well done; yes, it's literate; yes, I suppose I should admire it. "But it didn't honestly hold me; I certainly wouldn't go back; I couldn't in conscience tell a friend he'd enjoy it." These were non-professionals, and intelligent non-professionals: people who read fairly widely, listen to a certain amount of music, go to a selected number of movies. They are, quite simply, the audience that has disappeared from the theater and cannot, even after a couple of honest tries, be lured back.

Both *The Member of the Wedding* and *I Am a Camera* displayed unmistakable values, and pretty much the same ones. Characterization in both cases was sensitive and complex. Each created a sustained atmosphere. The language of the one was gently poetic, of the other ruefully perceptive. These plays lacked only one thing that the more popular *A Streetcar Named Desire* might be said to possess: a strong clash, a vigorous narrative.

What has crippled the drama descended from Chekhov is its calculated inertia.

We have made ennui almost a point of honor. The ennui originates, naturally enough, in our model. Chekhov was specifically concerned, as he clearly announced, with "disappointment, apathy, nervous limpness and exhaustion." What we forget is that these special characteristics were derived from, and intended to mirror, a given time, place, and state of mind: the moribund Russia of the nineteenth century. Russia itself has long since thrown off Russian inertia; only we continue to cling to it.

We have supposed that the creative method and the content to which it was first applied were inseparable. Chekhov comes to us all of a piece; ergo, we must keep all of the pieces. That the method itself is open to new uses, to dramatic extension, seems to me clear from the career of Tennessee Williams. *The Glass Menagerie* is quasi-Chekhovian in both method and content: the play ends in universal frustration. The later *A Streetcar Named Desire* retains the method but moves on to a more virile content: the play ends in the brutal triumph of one of the contending forces.

This aspect of our heritage—the conception of the content as stagnant—has, I think, been more or less unconsciously assimilated. But however we have come to it, we have now come to the simple belief that character is best pursued in the absence of action. We have, therefore, been very careful to minimize the activity that takes place on stage, to hustle unavoidable activity into the wings, to apologize profusely for the faintest intrusion of vulgar event. If a little boy must die in *The Member of the Wedding,* he must die during the intermission. To play the death scene on stage would expose us to a charge of theatricality.

We are now embarrassed by the dramatic gesture. We do not wish to be thought capable of so gross and unliterary a lapse. Since event is suspect, our plays must be cautiously uneventful.

We make our chaste intention clear at the beginning of the

evening. Our plays—of the Chekhovian tradition—open in a timeless twilight, announcing at the outset that nothing will change. Characters move in longing, recoil in inhibition, freeze into paralysis. They dart at the universe in feeble exploration, make fainthearted protest, resign themselves to final frustration. The curtain falls on the twilight we knew at the first, on a world in which the promise of action has never existed, a world of perpetually suspended animation.

Arthur Laurents' *The Time of the Cuckoo* presents us with an American spinster on European holiday. The girl is given a fleeting chance at illicit romance. She is aching for the experience. She is hopelessly bound, though, by the conditions of her upbringing. She cannot act. She goes home.

Elmer Rice's *The Grand Tour* presents us with an American spinster on European holiday. The girl is given a fleeting chance at illicit romance. She is aching for the experience. She is hopelessly bound, though, by the conditions of her upbringing. She cannot act. She goes home.

Lillian Hellman's *The Autumn Garden* presents us with a spinster who runs a boardinghouse. To that house come any number of former friends, all of them exhausted by the tormenting emptiness of their lives. One of the guests is a onetime suitor, now edgily married elsewhere. There are faint stirrings of old fires. Each member of the party, though, is, in the end, a prisoner of himself. None can act. The gathering disperses.

William Inge's *Picnic* presents us with a Kansas back yard full of women—a spinster, a woman whose husband has deserted her, an adolescent crying for maturity, another youngster who is ready for life but hasn't come across it yet. All sense that they exist in a vacuum; they sit on the back porch and wait for fulfillment. A muscular lout passes by. Fires are fleetingly stirred. In the original ending, the male went his errant and inconsequential way. The women returned to a timeless waiting in the fading sun.

The Dorothy Parker—Arnaud D'Usseau *Ladies of the Corridor* presents us with a hotel full of women, older women. Most are widows; all are aching with loneliness. For one, a man comes briefly near. Because this forlorn soul is a prisoner of her lifelong habits, she succeeds in driving him away. Life goes on in the hotel—as before.

Terence Rattigan's *The Deep Blue Sea* presents us with a middle-aged woman who has broken with her husband in order to attach herself to a much younger man. She is unable to conquer her possessive emotional habits, and succeeds in driving the man away. She tries suicide, twice; she fails, twice. At the end she stands in an empty room, without husband or lover.

Robert Anderson's *All Summer Long* presents us with a mother who would like her family to be happy together but is too ineffectual to do anything about it; a father who would like to be on good terms with his sons but is too ineffectual to do anything about it; a daughter who tries to bring on an abortion in order to preserve her figure, but fails; an older son who loves to play basketball but who is unfortunately crippled; and a younger son who would like to preserve the family homestead, on a riverbank, from the steady erosion that is undermining its foundations. The house is washed away.

Truman Capote's *The Grass Harp* presents us with two spinster sisters, one of whom can no longer bear an arid and unloving existence. This sister takes flight in a memory of childhood: she goes to live in a tree. A man comes by; fires are fleetingly stirred. The other sister persuades her to return home. At curtain the two are ascending the familiar stairs again, companion shadows in the dusk.

Horton Foote's *A Trip to Bountiful* presents us with an old woman whose barren life is passed in a bleak city apartment. Outside the neon lights blink fitfully. Inside an intolerable daughter-in-law shrills away. The old lady, in despair, takes flight in a memory of childhood. She returns to her home in Bountiful, Texas. It is a tangle of rotted timbers and matted weeds; it no longer exists. She returns to the city apartment, over the neon lights.

John van Druten's *I Am a Camera* presents us with an attractive, desperately rattled young sophisticate who brandishes her cigarette holder against a pointless and unpromising future. There is a fleeting relationship with a pleasant young man; it cannot come to anything. The young man tries to persuade her to take hold of her life; she tries and fails. She is a prisoner of her nerve ends. She cannot act. She goes away.

Carson McCullers' *The Member of the Wedding* presents us with an ugly duckling who longs to go on her brother's wedding trip. She is not, of course, permitted to go.

Stand close to these plays and they seem remarkably varied in style and background and feeling. Move back just a bit and you can begin to detect their common ancestry, their common inspiration.

What binds them together is their commitment to stasis. To observe life carefully, you must make it stand still. To make life stand still, you must deal in the stillborn—in characters who are unable to change themselves, their relationships, or the world about them. You must, perforce, deal with Chekhov's disappointed, apathetic, or nervously limp.

So far from realizing the splendid variety of Arthur Hopkins' vision—an "uncountable" number of characters, as different from one another as "fingerprints"—we have reduced the possibilities to a very few: to just such characters as are incapable of creating, or coping with, a situation.

We have, in fact, restricted our character types to two: the exhausted and the immature. Neither is likely to involve us in serious activity.

Sometimes we become a shade nervous about our preoccupation with impotence. We suspect, rather vaguely, that the audience may find us enervating. If the suspicion nags long enough, we may make a slight concession: we may interpose a delicate note of hope toward the end of the evening. The old lady in *A Trip to Bountiful* announces that, though Bountiful itself has disappeared, she has found renewal in the soil and the air of the Gulf, and that she is now willing to rejoin her terrifying relatives. The principal matron in *Ladies of the Corridor* announces that she is no longer going to be lonely because she has simply decided not to be. In production, *Picnic* was provided with a last-minute event: one of the girls went off after the boy.

Whenever this sort of suggestion is incorporated into a play—the suggestion that something has happened, that something has changed—a difficulty crops up. No one believes in the change. The "upbeat" ending invariably seems contrived. The true Chekhovian takes comfort in this. "You see," he cries, "what a price you must pay for flirting with audience pleasure, with the desire for a 'plot'!" And, in a way, he is right. The character of the play—its essential immobility—has long since been perceived by the audience. Stasis is inherent in its very texture, a texture that ought not to be tampered with, halfheartedly, at eleven o'clock. A true paralysis is not so easily cured.

As for our preoccupation with the immature, Henry Popkin, in a *Commentary* article for September 1953, advances the notion that we are engaged in a mass flight into infantilism, a flight prompted by the terrors of our time. I don't know that we need be so hard on ourselves. The problem may be merely a dramatic one. Once in a while the dramatist may feel the urge to have some sort of event take place. (It gives him a third act slightly different from his first, for one thing.) Forbidden any indulgence in willful activity, he may look around for a happening that cannot be helped. No one can help growing up. There's nothing flagrantly theatrical about the process. It involves no decision, is pleasantly imperceptible. A fleeting moment of lonely awareness and it's all over. The girl may step out in her new frock, the boy in his new manhood. No voice need be raised, no twilight violated. Something has happened, but nothing deliberate has happened: an uncompromising compromise has been reached. In any case, a good many awkward, baffled, tongue-tied youngsters do grow up on our stages.

We leave these youngsters beating their wings hesitantly against the thinnish night sky. In general, we don't pick them up again until they are sufficiently exhausted to appear in *The Autumn Garden.*

If our more sensitive playwrights scrupulously avoid entanglement with what may be thought of as the active middle-life, it is no simple oversight. We take a special pride in the tenuousness we have managed to achieve. It was not surprising to find a star actress, in a recent newspaper interview, speaking thus warmly of her incoming play:

"I thought [the producer] was so brave. Here was a script with no murder, no crime, no great sex story, no real psychological problem. It was just a drama of the human spirit, a drama of human values."

The play closed in short order. I suspect that the interview may have helped it on its way. Let us gracefully pass over the implication that murder, crime, sex and psychology are lacking in human value. There remained a curious promise to the potential audience: the promise that nothing of any conceivable interest would happen all night. Mothers-in-law the country over could be heard making other plans.

10. *Fine Tailoring*

We know that the audience would thank us for livening things up, for incorporating in our otherwise tender and touching apostrophes to twilight a dash of theatrical suspense. We can read the box-office figures, too. It is perfectly clear that the superficial excitements of *Dial M for Murder* will outrun *The Time of the Cuckoo* every time. The melodrama of *Stalag 17* will bring more people into their seats, as well as to the edge of them, than *I Am a Camera*. The motion picture, telling repetitive and paper-thin stories, will—even in these dull days—continue to command a larger loyalty than we dare hope for.

But we know also—or think we know—that any flirtation with story value will automatically bind us to the superficial content of *Dial M for Murder* or the latest M-G-M film. Excitement may be desirable as a commercial come-on; it is never desirable if we are serious about producing art.

The idea that interesting plotting interferes somehow with the patient pursuit of truth has recent, and even current, evidence to support it. The last kind of plotting we knew in the theater—just before we threw narrative out and settled for stasis—was plotting of a highly artificial kind. It was called "well-made-play" plotting.

In this sorry school, a playwright might assemble four or five or ten or twelve isolated situations that in themselves would provide "good scenes." He would then piece them together in so crafty a fashion that they would *seem* to belong to one another. But this skillful fellow was not really engaged in imaginative development; he was up to his ears in conjuring.

A letter might be lost; a cloaked figure might be mistaken for someone else; the juxtaposition of the lost letter and the mistaken identity might lead to the severe embarrassment, or to the felicitous triumph, of the principal characters. Unfortunately, the juxtaposition could only be clever; it could not be taken for an accurate imitation of action that had been observed. A house had been put together out of odds and ends, then painted to resemble solid brick.

The French dramatist Scribe was praised for this sort of plotting, eventually identified by this sort of plotting. In turn, we have—rather witlessly, I think—come to identify all plot with Scribe.

Remembering Scribe, plot scares us.

Nor is the well-made-play wholly a thing of the past. When a modern dramatist does turn his hand to story, he tends to reach for the tool nearest at hand; unconsciously, he reaches for Scribe. The formula may be disguised a bit in its twentieth-century dress; but we sense that it is really a formula—that it brings something false into an otherwise honest theater —and we remain distressed.

Robert Anderson's *Tea and Sympathy*, for instance, is, I think, an up-to-date variation of the species. A young student in a boys' school is falsely accused of homosexuality. He attempts to prove himself and, presumably since it is his first such experience, fails. The failure causes him to doubt his own virility. This sequence of events is leading to a "big" scene: one in which the headmaster's wife, certain that the boy is innocent, offers herself to him.

The play would seem to have been built backward from the final scene: the boy *must* be shown as innocent; the woman *must* seem generous. (She could very quickly seem otherwise.)

To meet these conditions, and to bring them into perfect balance for the closing sequence, Mr. Anderson arranges the following circumstances. The boy is accused of homosexuality because he has ignorantly accepted an invitation to swim in the nude with a suspect instructor. His innocence is such that, even when he is accused, he cannot understand what he is being accused of. He has hitherto been accepted as more or less normal by his fellow students, he has been a casual member of their bull sessions, nothing has been made of the fact that he has been assigned a female role in the school play. Distressed by the accusations, the boy makes a hurried date with the town tart; when this proves a fiasco, he succumbs to his new fears.

Each of these circumstances does pave the way for the boy's participation in the key scene. But each of them—if my sense of probability is not lulled to sleep by Mr. Anderson's craftsmanship—leaves me with an unanswered question about the boy's character. He has horned in on college bull sessions; why has he never heard of homosexuality? He is privy to school gossip; why has he heard no word of the instructor's habits? He is sensitive, intelligent, imaginative; why does not an invitation to a nude swimming session at midnight stir any faint chord of alarm in him? He knows enough about his friends' sexual habits to be able to go to the telephone and call the one girl in town who is likely to co-operate in his experiment; why has he never heard of the traditional experimental failure? (In musical comedies starring Bobby Clark, this is a joke.) And why, if he is seventeen, well-informed, and—the playwright insists—perfectly normal, has he had no active stirrings of any sort, why is he so entirely passive throughout the play? He must, of course, be thus passive to serve the final situation; but does he exist at all, along the way, as a character I can recognize? He may be necessary as a peg in a situation; isn't he ambiguous as a person?

The boy's essential ambiguity is shrewdly sustained in the play. At one point in the action—after the accusation has been established—we find him trying on feminine clothes for a role in the school play. The scene is theatrically graphic—it makes a picture of the boy's problem. But the picture is irrelevant. We have been given to understand that the boy is not effeminate, that his being cast as a girl is without special meaning. At the same time that this irrelevance is insisted upon, we toy with such implications as may be derived from seeing him in skirts. An effect—a deliberately ambiguous effect—has been inserted for its usefulness in sustaining the situation. Mr. Anderson is not above dallying with the principle of mistaken identity.

Preparing the woman for the final scene poses a different sort of problem. She must never seem to be taking advantage of the boy; she must be both sensitive and honorable. How make her seem sensitive? Give her an insensitive husband—not because she is likely to have married such a man, but because being married to such a man will set her own qualities in bold relief. More than that. Make the husband particularly intolerant of the boy, aggressively inclined to believe in the accusation.

But the woman now has a husband, and she ought not be unfaithful to him. How make her infidelity honorable? What better than to have her discover in her husband an incipient homosexuality, the very reverse of the boy's problem? Behind the lad's passive façade lies an inherent virility. Behind the husband's masculine façade lies an inherent effeminacy. Honor now compels the rejection of the husband and the rescue of the boy.

All values have fallen into perfect balance. The play is airtight. But it really *is* airtight. No character can breathe here. The virile boy cannot behave as virile boys behave; he must mark time until the plot is ready to make use of him. The sensitive wife cannot marry as sensitive women marry; she must swiftly explain away the oddness of her choice. And into the same woman's life, at the same moment in time, come two males who counter each other precisely. Coincidence is as surely at work here as in Scribe.

Not so transparently, it is true. We are removed from Scribe now, and can see through his deceptive graces to the ground plan beneath. We are closer to Mr. Anderson; he makes use of a casual diction that is close to us. We are introduced to his immaculate balances in so easy and plausible and unsensational a manner as to make it difficult for us to recognize them as balances, or calculations. The New York production of his play was, furthermore, so brilliantly served by the urgent and lifelike stage direction of Elia Kazan that we were carried from moment to moment with momentary assent. Even as we watched it, though, and even as we admired its patent skill, we were conscious of a faint reluctance in our responses, a faint nagging at the bases of our skulls. The action was moving forward with a fluid logic, but—wait a minute; was that last passing gesture precisely true?

That well-made play plotting takes a certain toll of honesty, accuracy, and unfettered observation is perfectly plain. It takes a smaller toll, I think, than thesis plotting; the situation that shapes the characters may in itself be lifelike; the thesis is pure cerebration.

But is it story itself that has imprisoned these people and limited them to a handful of convenient responses? Or is it only one kind of storytelling, one particular set of outdated mechanics?

The well-made play does its building backward, tooling every tidy moment to fit a prearranged pattern of "big" scenes. Surely there are other ways to build.

One rarely has the feeling that Shakespeare is building anything backward. He must have had, as we know, a fairly decent idea of where he was going; he generally worked with someone else's story, or some historian's chronicle, in mind. The business of getting where he was going, however, remained rough indeed—loose, flexible, open to impulse. The plays are a riot of inventive plotting—but they contain very few neat or "well-made" scenes.

It has been said—correctly, I think—that Shakespeare so far recognized story as primary that he never hesitated to sacrifice character to it. But there are two ways of sacrificing character to story. One is to manufacture story in tight detail—far in advance of any other process—and then shape the characters to fit. The other is to grasp the story in general terms, to set the characters in motion with a certain gay independence, and then—if by some mishap the characters take to the fields and refuse to come home—to drop them from the play. The second was, of course, Shakespeare's constant method. Mercutio is wonderful, and he is given his head. Mercutio, wonderful as he is, gets out of hand. Mercutio is run through. (And his passing is made to help the plot.) The Fool in *Lear* is a magnificent Fool. There comes a time when he can only tag after the story. The story promptly forgets about him.

The results may be, from time to time, decidedly sloppy. But the method does accomplish two things: the characters are developed; and the story gets told. I'm not sure that, in our heart of hearts, we ask anything more.

Molière, being French, is thought of as being more rational, and therefore better organized. And Molière is neater in the sense that he uses fewer characters, fewer subplots, fewer backgrounds. But the manner in which he completes a tale while encouraging his characters is remarkably similar. He begins a play with some sort of situation in mind: a good-for-nothing is going to pose as a learned doctor; a hypocrite is going to use his reputation for piety as a means of seducing his benefactor's wife. Molière knows—and so do we—approximately how it is all going to come out. But between these two story points—the beginning of an action and the end of it—he leaves a great deal of elbowroom. The characters are committed to the situation because it is the situation that concerns them. But they are free to attack it in their own way, to dodge and feint and boldly advance as only they would dodge and feint and boldly advance. They are given narrative boundaries, but no explicit instructions. Sganarelle is free to mock doctors, and to escape detection, in any enchanting way that occurs to him. Tartuffe can be pious, and fraudulent, in a thousand different ways; let's see which scenes he chooses to play.

These inspired and exuberant figures are anything but docile. And sometimes, sure enough, they arrive at a point where they've exhausted the story without having tidied it up. Loose ends clutter the stage; the characters have been busy with essentials. At such points Molière is cheerfully unconcerned. There is always a "little box" that can be discovered upstairs, the while the author shrugs and smiles. It will explain everything. Or a message can come from the King, a long-lost father from somewhere, to solve what needs to be solved. The really important things have long since been taken care of; there has been a story to give the piece its theatrical vigor, there have been characters to tell it true.

We can, if we are patient purists, do better than this. No one has ever called *Oedipus* a sloppy play. But no one can, in conscience, call it a well-made play, either. It is perfectly conceived; but it is not ever contrived. Messengers may arrive; old shepherds may be persuaded to speak. But it is not Sophocles who has sent for them; it is Oedipus. The revelations that stun Oedipus are not coincidental revelations; they are revelations that Oedipus has longed for, sought out, commanded. They are the revelations that this man's character—with its pride, its intelligence, its resourcefulness, its determination—must bring about. Oedipus initiates everything, is responsible for everything. He needs no help from a cunning author.

It would be a mistake, though, to hold up the *Oedipus* as a really useful model. Let genius create the perfect play when it can; let the rest of us see what our talents naturally produce. The *Oedipus* is perfect. But recognize this about it, too: it is unique. Not even in Sophocles' own library do we find its like again. The *Antigone* is looser, the *Electra* a great deal looser. If we tend to think of the Greeks as having written exceptionally compact plays, we had best subject ourselves to some of the more curious improvisations of Euripides.

And the taste for tightness may come with experience, as a final refinement of rougher, freely robust processes. If so, well and good; the dramatist is inching his way to an *Oedipus*. Maturity is almost bound to bring an intensified control of the materials at hand, a heightened organizational power—and the dramatist who waits for maturity is apt to find himself cultivating his *own* organizational pattern, a personal rather than a borrowed or superimposed one. It is wise, I think, to inch toward *Oedipus;* the taste for tightness developed too early is almost certain to end in creative constraint.

Compactness is not the essence of plotting. Movement is. The movement must have some generally defined direction. But it need not advance on regulated sprockets, at the unalterable rhythm and on the controlled causeways of the assembly line.

The best modern plays have been flexibly plotted. *A Streetcar Named Desire* has a plot. Blanche du Bois finds herself in a situation and she deals with it by descending upon her sister and by assuming intolerable airs. Her activity creates, in turn, a situation for Stanley Kowalski. He deals with it by trying to expose and destroy Blanche. As these people engage in fiercely active contention, they force one another into crisis after crisis. But the forcing is theirs, not the author's. Mr. Williams does not so much guide the play as follow it. To follow it, he must be prepared to make certain elisions of time and place, to forego a certain neatness of pattern, to move almost as erratically as his characters do. The play is in a good many scenes; it has no rigid shape. When Blanche is ready to do something we quickly move to her side; when Stanley is ready to act we move to his. The play tends to take its structure from the activity of the characters; it does not set a structure and ask them to inhabit it.

Death of a Salesman is more restless still. The play is

plotted: Willy Loman does certain concrete things to cope with the situation in which he finds himself; because his responses are stubborn and unintelligent ones, they destroy him. But to catch Willy Loman in the act of making his characteristic gestures, Mr. Miller takes enormous freedoms, leaping backward and forward in time, snatching an essential moment here and another there, accepting his character's deeds as a structural determinant.

The best work of Williams and Miller indicates fairly clearly that honesty need not be confined to character drawing, or to atmospheric evocation. As a writer, I may be as honest about my story, my situations, my unfolding plot as I am about the first faint glimmerings that suggested the play to me. I don't have to settle for the glimmerings, the poetic fragments, and call them the completed work; I can go on into active complexity without the least loss of integrity.

I may start with a character, as Chaplin always did. Each of Chaplin's early films was based on the same shambling, but by no means simple, figure: the tramp. What can he do *this* time? Is it reasonable to send him to the Klondike, seeking gold? It is. Is it probable that he should crawl into an abandoned cabin for the night? It is. Is a snowslide unlikely in the Klondike? Not at all. Next morning I find the cabin perched over a gorge, and teetering giddily. I have arrived at a very broad farce situation—one of maniacal magnitude—but I haven't really falsified anything anywhere. I haven't denied the background; I have made the most of it. I haven't destroyed the character; I have given it a spectacular opportunity to reveal itself.

I know a man who cannot tolerate the thought that he has made a mistake. Is he, in the long run, likely to make one? It would be most improbable if he didn't. Confronted with one, what will he do? If I know him, he will deny it and insist on vindication. Granted my knowledge of the man, is the frantic activity and final terror of *Oedipus* so very far away?

Plotting may be as much a process of discovery as characterization is a process of discovery. Good plays will still be written the other way round, I am sure; but I am equally sure that it is the hard way. It takes enormous patience to begin with a situation and then make certain that characters enter it honestly. In a time when all situation is suspect, when the only plotting we remember is well-made play plotting, when we need to rediscover the relationship between character and story experimentally, I'd run the risk of a certain sloppiness.

And I would certainly try to get over the fear that pursuing my people into active excitement must automatically involve me in thinner portraiture. It doesn't work out like that.

11. Men at Work

We are especially interested in Hamlet these days. Of all the figures out of the classic past, he seems closest to us. It is very easy to make Hamlet over in our own image; our actors have labored mightily to show how "modern" he is. Hamlet, you see, doesn't want to do anything.

We are proud of Shakespeare for having so shrewdly anticipated Chekhov. We are pleased with ourselves for being able to read into an Elizabethan melodrama the latest fashions in neurasthenia. We like to analyze Hamlet as a "man of inaction," to see him, in the familiar commonplaces of *The Oxford Companion,* as a man whose "melancholy, introspective, and scrupulous nature makes him irresolute and dilatory." Here is someone we understand.

Of course, we're a little bit embarrassed, along with Arthur Hopkins, by all those "frantic killings" in the last scene. Indeed, we are embarrassed at other points. In the course of

Hamlet, here are some of the things Hamlet does: he courageously pursues a terrifying ghost; he swears vengeance on his sword; he sets into motion a detective-story investigation that includes a re-enactment of the crime in the presence of the criminal; he manufactures a disguise, by feigning madness, in order to go on with his work unmolested; he casts off his sweetheart, in part for the same purpose; he turns violently upon his mother; he kills the spying Polonius; he escapes from a guard that has been set over him; he fences with Laertes and kills him; he stabs the king; he dies (on stage).

For an inhibited fellow, he's a fairly busy one.

There is some justice in singling out the soliloquies, as Arthur Hopkins has, for special admiration. Any one of them, as an isolated excerpt, is more poetic and—it's true—more profound than the lines that accompany the killings.

But suppose you took away the killings. Suppose there weren't going to be any, and everyone knew it from the beginning. Suppose Hamlet were truly a paralyzed soul, constitutionally incapable of any decisive act. Suppose he were simply "irresolute" and his "irresolution" were to become the entire character content of the play. Would anything happen to the soliloquies?

I think they would cease to exist. The soliloquies are about the killings. They spring into being out of a very urgent need for violence, a need that cannot be ignored. They exist because the killings are contemplated and because the killings are certainly coming.

More than this, it is the threat and the fear and the inevitability of the killings that prompt Hamlet to the precise definition, and complete revelation, of his character. The soliloquies do not record the torment of an impotently introspective man. They record the torment of an active man compelled to perform an act that is loathsome to him. The scar on Hamlet's psyche is not something he was born with, something he is now imprisoned by. It is a new scar, one that is being freshly carved during every moment of the play, and with a perfectly real knife.

Hamlet does not wish to act but he *must* act. (This, by the way, is what is known as a situation.) Action may be undesirable, but action is necessary. Something is bound to happen next, and the certainty that this is so not only moves the play; it shapes the man.

Hamlet is by no means alone in acting. Macbeth, a hesitant man in his own way, is embroiled in murder most foul and murder most multiple. Falstaff may be something of a philosopher, but he is a philosopher on a battlefield. Othello's introspection rises from a snarl of intrigue.

We are pretty well agreed that a great deal happens in *King Lear*. ("Too much," we say, in characteristic despair.) Lear chops up his kingdom. He drives from his sight the one daughter who loves him. He banishes Kent. He is driven into a thunderstorm, where he goes spectacularly mad. Edmund tells lies to sunder a father and son. The son turns up in the storm disguised as a lunatic. The father has his eyes put out. An old fool dies. A villain is stabbed in a struggle. Edmund pursues two illicit love affairs. An army from France comes crashing across the countryside. Goneril poisons Regan and kills herself. A battle is fought on stage. Cordelia is hanged. Edmund is slain. Lear dies.

Lear is drenched with plot, all but swamped in plot. That any sort of characterization should emerge from this maze—that the busy playwright should have a moment left for personal portraiture—is beyond belief.

Yet there they are, the whole parade of them: Lear, Edmund, Edgar, Gloucester, Kent, Regan, Goneril, Cordelia, the Fool. If few plays have ever attempted this degree of narrative complexity, few have ever given birth to quite so many memorable people.

But Shakespeare was a genius, we say, and Shakespeare was an exception. He may have catered to the simple-minded demand for excitement; he may have overstuffed his plays in his anxiety to give pleasure; he was simply extraordinarily fortunate in having a peculiar and towering talent that enabled him to make these unsuitable compromises and still get on with his more important work.

It may be true, as Donald Clive Stuart has remarked, that Shakespeare's "point of departure was a story," that "he sacrificed the study of character to the presentation of his story," that he "would have agreed with Aristotle that the action is the most important element of a play, while character is secondary."

But Shakespeare was lucky, we go on saying, luckier than most men. His gift for portraiture survived his bent for pandering. His results are unrelated to his method. If you will gently separate his people from his plotting, you will have something worth studying. There is no profit in the plotting as such.

There is profit in Molière, though. Here was a character playwright—a man so steeped in personal values and so indifferent to storytelling that he was finally accused of having written an "actionless" play.

This is the actionless play he wrote:

A lovely girl is kept under lock and key. She engages nevertheless in a secret romance with a young stranger. She is forced to prepare herself for marriage to an old fool. The young man unwittingly confides every detail of his romance to the old fool, who is using an assumed name. The old fool pretends to help the young man in his suit, while taking great care to thwart him. The girl ingeniously continues to deceive the old fool. The young man attempts to abduct the girl but fails, whereupon he pretends to have been murdered. In the confusion that follows, the boy and girl elope. The boy, still unaware of the old fool's identity, asks his help in secreting the girl. The old fool retrieves the girl and draws up a marriage contract. The boy's relatives—together with the girl's long-lost father—arrive and agree to the May-December marriage. At the last moment it is discovered that the girl is promised to another from infancy, and that her true betrothed is the boy. The old fool is routed. Between times, a couple of comedy servants deceive the old fool and even push him around physically.

Molière's reasonable defense of his "actionless" play was that the piece was perfectly active, but that the action was mainly psychological. And the psychological action is, of course, there—dazzlingly so. But there's a fair amount of vulgar suspense in the brew, too.

Molière's character plays rest squarely on the slippery deceptions, the outrageous mistakes, the thumpings and thrashings and flights by night of traditional French farce. If Shakespeare has, out of the street brawls and blood baths of his kind of play, produced Juliet, Mercutio, Beatrice and the various Richards, so has Molière, out of plays that find the characters hiding in closets and dodging under tables, produced Arnolphe, Harpagon, Tartuffe and M. Jourdain.

In fact, the moment we begin to dig into the plays that have given us the characters we most admire, we suddenly break open a beehive of activity. We admire Electra; and a murderous girl she was. We love Hotspur; and remember his ruinous temper. We are delighted by Sganarelle and Martine; and we notice the stage direction, "He takes a stick and beats her."

The bustling, complicated, and sometimes absurd plotting of the past does not seem ever to have inhibited character. It would almost seem that there is some correlation between the range of a play's activity and the size of its characterization.

Is this possible? I think so.

It takes a certain number of psychological responses to enable a man to stir a cup of tea. It takes a good many more to enable him to kill his father.

If my man is simply going to stir tea, or fall into a way of life that has been thrust upon him, or fail to pass his entrance examinations at college, or marry the girl next door, or not marry her because his mother doesn't want him to, I shall need to know exactly enough about his responses to enable him to do, or not do, these things. I may pin down these responses perfectly; I may find every nuance, every minute shade of decision and indecision, every trait, every tic, every torment that plausibly belongs to him. But I do not need to know him beyond his capacity for action. I am not invited to explore resources that are never going to be used. I am not compelled to mine him for motives and powers and perceptions that are beyond the limited behavior patterns I have set for him. To do so, to allow him to grow indiscriminately, would be to engage myself in a gross disproportion.

If, on the other hand, my man is going to kill his father, or betray his brother, or cast off his daughters, or wantonly destroy the woman he loves, I am going to have to know a great deal more about him. I am going to have to go into the human labyrinth, into that intricate chain of impulses that has led him to so large and abhorrent and final a deed. I am tracking down something far more complex, something darkly buried in the subterranean recesses of the human personality, and I must work in infinite depth. I have an enormous span to cover: from the most secret wish to the most extravagant act. And I must know every inch of it intimately. As Lessing pointed out: "The poet finds in history a woman who murders her husband and sons. . . . But history tells him no more than the bare fact, and this is as horrible as it is unusual. . . . What therefore does the poet do? . . . He . . . will endeavor to define the passions of each character so accurately, will endeavor to lead these passions through such gradual steps, that we shall everywhere see nothing but the most natural and common course of events." The range of character response is now very great; the character, supposing him to be thoroughly known, becomes "great" accordingly.

If Oedipus is one of the titans of the stage, it is in large part because there is so much he must do. He must rescue the country he governs from its present distress. He must contend with the news that he is himself responsible for that distress. He must defy the most powerful authority that could be pitted against him—the divine voice of the oracle—and outrage its most venerable representative, Tiresias. He must set into motion an investigation that may destroy him, must steel himself to the blow that may fall, must fanatically whip up his pride in order to keep himself from believing that the blow will fall, and must meantime endure, fear, and desperately lean upon that wife who may be his mother. He must stand, shattered, when the unthinkable truth is known, must tear out his eyes in expiation, must accept the suicide of Jocasta, must take leave of his children, and must at the last reconcile himself to the justice of a world that has destroyed him.

Oedipus is never free of a "situation." Nor is he ever impotent in the face of one. As each arises, he acts. With each action, his stature and complexity increase.

It does require the genius of a Sophocles to make so staggering an array of improbable situations at all tenable. But what part have the situations played in drawing out the genius of Sophocles?

The degree to which situation itself may stir the fires of creative characterization is clear from a commonplace practice of the Greeks: the endless, taken-for-granted reworking of old narratives. (We'd call this "the altered application of long-used situations" today, and dismiss the practice as profitless.) Aeschylus, Sophocles, and Euripides made use of the same stories, yet the people who inhabit their plays are as distinctive as Mr. Hopkins' fingerprints. It is as though Sophocles had looked at Aeschylus' handling of the Orestes-Electra confrontation and said "Yes, it could have happened that way. But look. Electra might have felt differently. There are other states of mind possible here." And as though Euripides had come along and said in turn "All very well. But I can show you a psychology for Electra you haven't yet thought of, a psychology that will explain what she does more clearly still." The facts of human behavior become an interpretative challenge; but first you must have facts that are challenging. Surveying a handful of Electras at a later date, we tend to cancel out the common narrative and concentrate our interest and respect on the character variations; but none of these variations would have come into being if a given piece of behavior—an action—hadn't needed explaining. So far from being the death of character, situation would seem very often to have been the source of it.

In the modern theater we hold that character must be divorced from situation, if character is ever to amount to anything. The past indicates, at the very least, that no such divorce is necessary.

I wonder if it is even possible.

It is possible, of course, in the technical sense—as many a contemporary playwright has labored to prove. I can write a play that is devoid of narrative, or deficient in narrative, and still attend to my characterization quite honorably. But can I make such a play survive in that very particular art form known as the theater?

The best test I know of is the twin-Oedipus test. Sophocles wrote two plays about this titanic figure, one of which we have—for all practical theatrical purposes—forgotten. It's quite an experience to take the *Oedipus at Colonus* off the library shelf and set it beside that other *Oedipus* everyone remembers.

What is the difference between the two plays, both masterworks of one of the two or three master dramatists of all time? Read them in succession. The characterization in both pieces is fully formed, everywhere superb. The psychology of the *Colonus* is actually more difficult of realization than that of the *Oedipus*, yet it *is* realized. The language is, if anything, more exalted in the *Colonus*. (You are, by the way, likely to be staggered by the profundity and lyric power of this unfamiliar play.)

The *Oedipus at Colonus* is in complete possession of all the values we now prize most highly; yet we do not prize this play enough to read it or to produce it. If it has failed to live in our memories, and if it has failed to hold the stage as the *Oedipus* continues to hold the stage, it is because of a single lack: the lack of the breath-taking theatrical tension that derives from the detective-story plotting of the *Oedipus*. There is only one important difference between the two plays, a difference in narrative strength, in narrative coherence. The robust health of the play we cherish must derive from its suspenseful activity.

A comparative study of the successes and failures of theatrical history would, I think, indicate that narrative strength is required not only in thundering tragedy and flamboyant farce but in the most fanciful and featherweight flights of wit. There is no wittier play in the English language than Congreve's *The Way of the World*. In addition to its unsurpassed verbal grace, it contains two of the most enchanting comic characters ever to have been designed for the stage. Yet *The Way of the World* does not play on the stage; it was a failure when first presented and it has never been able to establish itself as part of the permanent repertory. Again, it possesses the values we hold to be supreme; but it lacks the one value necessary to carry a play forward in the theater. Its narrative is a mere makeshift, confusedly roughed in. Because it has neither interest nor authority *as narrative*, it is too feeble to support the undeniable brilliance of the play's language and characters. For want of a plot, the play is lost to us.

Oscar Wilde's *The Importance of Being Earnest* is something less as literature, and a great deal less as a vehicle for character, than *The Way of the World*. Written nearly two hundred years later, it has already outperformed the Congreve showpiece and is likely to go down in history as its theatrical better. Its sturdiness lies, as Oscar Wilde knew, in its narrative. There is a story to the effect that, at the play's first performance, Wilde paced in agony backstage, refusing to take comfort in the audience's delighted response to individual lines. He was waiting. Not until the second act, and the explosion of laughter that went up at a development in the play's action—Jack enters in mourning for his brother, who happens to be alive and amorous in the next room—did Wilde begin to take heart. He had to be certain that the audience was following the plot, and finding the plot itself substantially funny, before he would allow himself the hope of success. It is easy enough for us to recall five or six of the play's best quips and to imagine that its success was due to them; but no play has ever survived on the strength of five quips, or five characters, or five variations on a mood. These other values must rest, apparently, on a strong theatrical foundation; the narrative may be preposterous, but it must be ruggedly present.

It would seem that story and character are not the enemies we sometimes suppose them to be. Situation and event have not, of themselves, prevented character from flaring into life. From situation-riddled plays have sprung the largest and most lifelike people we know, larger and more lifelike than the people we produce in our chastely conceived character plays.

It would seem, too, that the absence of situation and event has prevented certain otherwise magnificently equipped plays from enduring in the playhouse. The audience's thirst for story may be a sound one; a simple-minded instinct may be simple-mindedly right.

And, while we're at it, let's stop worrying about story as a kind of sugar plum thrown to the kiddies, a pretty little confection designed to conceal the truth about life. Life is the damndest thing.

12. *House Rules*

I WISH THAT MY LIFE were as free of situations as the character playwright likes to tell me it is. I wouldn't mind spending a couple of years in the timeless twilight of *The Member of the Wedding*; I think it would rest me. I have no real aversion to sitting on a back porch more or less indefinitely, waiting for a pretty girl to pass by.

My problem is that I can't get out of bed in the morning without getting all fouled up by circumstance. I have, for instance, four sons, each of whom is perfectly capable of presenting me with a situation by ten o'clock in the morning. I have a wife who is pretty good at it, too.

Let's take an example. When my oldest son was two, he spent a great deal of his time in the back alley breaking milk bottles. I am a philosopher at heart, and I was not content with simply thrashing him and confining him to his room. I had to know *why* he liked to break milk bottles. I still have a certain amount of college psychology rattling around loose in my head, and I kept remembering such phrases as "The impulse to break things is essentially an impulse to create *new* things" and "The child is delighted with the variety of shapes that can be produced by breaking down a single shape." I went out into the alley to examine the variety of shapes that my son had produced, telling myself that this was very good creative training, that I was learning to see things with the eyes of a child. It was while I was learning to see things with the eyes of a child, and holding two interestingly jagged milk bottles experimentally in my hand, that a policeman arrived, sent by our neighbors to discover just who was making the alley unfit for driving.

I thought of it as a situation at the time. If it had been Lou Costello playing with the milk bottles, and Bud Abbott towering over in a policeman's uniform, the whole thing might have been cheerfully dismissed as a gagman's contrivance for a lowbrow two-reeler. Unhappily, the policeman was real. Unhappily, so was I.

Not long ago my wife returned from a shopping spree with something over two hundred dollars' worth of costume jewelry that she had certainly not bought. The pieces were bundled cozily together in a neat little bag, the price tags still on them. Possibly my wife had swept the treasure off the store counter, along with her legitimate purchases, without noticing it. Possibly someone had snatched the loot, become frightened, and dumped it into our car. Possibly my wife has not told me the whole truth to this day.

In any case, my experience with the police has taught me caution, and the need for quick, citizenlike decisions. I promptly called our local station, explained that we were in possession of valuables not belonging to us, and asked that an officer be sent to retrieve them. In short order a modest, unassuming, very noncommittal plainclothesman arrived, hat in hand.

Naturally, he asked questions. Naturally, we answered them with many a merry jest about the light-fingered Kerrs—jests designed to make him realize that we knew ourselves to be under suspicion and that we were innocent enough parties to be jolly about it all. He remained noncommittal.

In due time he put away his notebook, gathered up the jewelry, and permitted himself to be ushered to the door amid heartier and heartier jocularities. At this point, however, the detective was unable to leave because someone had stolen his hat.

We do have a four-year-old who is adept at this sort of thing—he is unable to pass through a room without lining his pockets, and we are utterly unable to catch him in the act—

and after a twenty-minute search we were successful in reclaiming the hat from beneath a panda in a second-floor closet. I do not know what report the detective made to his superiors. We were never offered a reward, though.

I sometimes have visions of a gag conference in which that slick character who is traditionally known as Manny bounces in, eyes ablaze, and bubbles over with: "Listen. This guy's a dramatic critic, see? So his wife writes a play. He's *got* to review the play. Take it from there."

I regret to say that something like this happened to me recently. (I didn't like the show much, and *that* led to several situations.)

If I am fond of farce, it is because I have learned to believe in it.

We have a bad habit these days of regarding *every* arrangement of circumstance as mechanical. It is mechanical to put a man in an embarrassing comic situation. It is mechanical to trap a hero in an ironic complex of events. I would be performing a merely mechanical chore today if I were to invent a scene in which a man who had arranged a murder prepared to unveil the corpse before the paramour who had urged him to the deed, only to discover that the hitherto concealed corpse was in fact the corpse of that paramour. I would be obliged to apologize for such calculated nonsense, to use it—if I used it at all—in the frankly light, sophisticated, and ephemeral context of a *Dial M for Murder*. But it was Sophocles' favorite scene.

The truth of the matter is that circumstance is with us. It acts as a pressure on all our lives. It is not unrelated to character. Some of this pressure originates in character—the stubborn character of other people. And all of it influences our own character—shapes it, exposes it. Character is best revealed by the response it makes to circumstance.

Between the pressure of circumstance and the response of character a tension exists.

This tension—this opposition of forces so powerful that one or another must give way—is the distinguishing mark of what we have come to call story. The story may be very simple. Scheherazade will be beheaded if she does not enchant her husband. Robin Hood will be hanged if he does not defeat Prince John. Jack will be eaten alive if he does not outwit the Giant. Charlie Chaplin will starve to death if he does not steal a small child's hot dog.

A story is the record of a pressure and a response. By driving story out of the contemporary theater, we have taken the pressure off, we have made response unnecessary. As tension has disappeared, so has character of any stature.

In practice, we are not confused about the necessity for narrative tension. We are bored by a book, and we put it down, when tension is not present. In the theater we sit back, glance at our watches, hope for an intermission, and remind ourselves not to bother coming the next time.

But our boredom is not—as it is often said to be—the boredom of a spoiled child peevishly demanding spectacular new distractions. It is not the boredom of the foolish in the presence of the first-rate. It is the boredom of the experienced adult who has found life itself to be more complex, colorful, contrary and challenging than the pale and passive literary artifice that is presently set before him.

We are all involved in stories—in love stories (what will she do if I try to make her jealous?), in father-and-son stories (did he start the fire in the garage, or didn't he?), in success-and-failure stories (do I dare to insist on more money?). No day is free of decision, and no decision is free of danger.

Each of us finds himself standing—all too frequently—on the threshold of action. The course that is best for me to take is rarely crystal-clear. I must choose between uncertainties. If I think my son is lying to me, I must punish him. If I punish him for something he didn't do, I am damaging our relationship and possibly his character. If I do not punish him, and he is in fact guilty, I am surely damaging his character.

I cannot evade acting. I must choose between alternatives (I am caught in a situation), and whichever alternative I choose is certain to have continuing effects (new situations). Short of total exhaustion, I am not free to defer decisions indefinitely; I do not inhabit a timeless cocoon. My life is a jumble of stories in progress, and, though I cannot know in advance the pattern each will finally assume, I am unavoidably engaged in the shaping of many patterns during my every waking moment.

"Story" has been variously defined. Perhaps the definition most frequently quoted nowadays is the one E. M. Forster has given us in his charming but audience-baiting *Aspects of the Novel.* Mr. Forster is, in many ways, a representative spokesman for our age: he regards the story-eager audience as "cave men . . . or their modern descendant the movie-public"; he wishes that story weren't necessary because it is a "low atavistic form"; holding these beliefs, he is eager to define story in its minimum terms and, if possible, get the whole thing over with. A story, he tells us, is "a narrative of events arranged in their time sequence." Whenever one happening is simply followed by another happening, whenever two statements are connected by an *and*, a story exists. " 'The king died and then the queen died' is a story."

My initial difficulty with this is an instinctive one. "The king died and then the queen died" does not seem to me to be a story, not even a bad one. It is not a story in the sense in which I normally use the word. If a friend bustles up to me with a bright look in his eye and says "I've got a great story for you—listen to what happened to me today!" and then follows through with "I went down to the office and the boss wasn't there" I am not so apt to congratulate him on his narrative powers as I am to terminate our acquaintance at the earliest opportunity.

Even if he expands his narrative, I am no better off. "I went down to the office today *and* the boss wasn't there *and* I went out to a bar *and* I got very drunk *and* I went back to the office *and* the boss still wasn't there *and* I went home" does continue to pile up events in their time sequence but brings me no nearer the story I had expected to hear.

That boss had better show up somewhere—quick—if I am to endure this conversation further. Mr. Forster expects that the *and* construction will lead the lowbrow listener to inquire "and—then?" But I do not find myself saying "and—then?" to this fellow. I find myself saying "Good Lord, I have an appointment and I'm five minutes late for it now."

I do not find that the simple *and* construction holds my attention or satisfies that taste for story which I do possess. There is a mental level at which the *and* construction is useful, but in my own experience I find that it disappears abruptly at the age of four. If I wish to entertain a three-year-old before putting him to bed I will tell him "Once upon a time there was a little boy and his name was Johnny Kerr and he lived in a white house and he had a mommy and a daddy and a twin brother and when he got up in the morning he ate eggs and toast and orange juice and cereal." I am entertaining him with his own experience; at the age of three his experience is a pressureless time sequence in which certain concrete familiarities recur. I am deliberately not telling him a story because he is unable to grasp any sort of complexity working against that time-and-object sequence. At the age of four, however, he will no longer be satisfied with an unreeling catalogue. He will demand that a wolf be incorporated into the narrative. Somewhere outside that white house there is now a wolf to threaten the white house and the twin brother and even the egg for breakfast. The child's experience has altered; he is conscious of instability, of possible alternatives to the way things are now. (He is, by the way, shiveringly pleased with all these possibilities.) He is growing up.

He is now conscious of change—of the possibility of change, of the threat of change, of the excitement of change. So long as he lives he will never lose that consciousness. He will spend the rest of his days wrestling with change, encouraging it or resisting it, but he will never return to the security of what is changeless.

He will, as he grows older, fight very hard for certain kinds of stability. But to gain the very stability he desires he will first have to change a thousand things that stand in its way. The moment he has completed his first thousand changes, and achieved the particular stability he has been fighting for (in his marriage, in his home, in his social life, in his job) he is directly aware that his hard-won victory is in itself unstable. There has never been, in fact, a moment when he could count it firm. Pressures descend upon it immediately, avid to change it, and he must now do daily battle to change the pressures if he is to protect his uneasy and trembling triumph. The surest condition of his life is that no condition is sure.

Because he has a passion for permanence, he will use certain of his art forms to reflect that passion, to pin permanence down. He will, of course, have to use a form that is divorced from time, free from the possibility of change. Painting is a space art, divorced from time and free from change. Here he may freeze the moment he wants to remember, the face that will not change before he has loved it enough. (Neither the moment nor the face need be sentimentally conceived; these are truths, caught before time has altered them into other truths.) Sculpture is a space art. Here form may be imprisoned long enough to be known enough.

The moment out of time is perfectly real, and its reality may be preserved. But so is the contest between time and the moment real. To mirror this other reality we have developed other art forms.

Drama is one of the time-and-space arts invented for the purpose. Drama does not try to capture Macbeth, fully formed, in any one of his isolated postures. Nor does it present Macbeth as the sum total of a series of tableaux: one in which he desires the kingship, one in which he shrinks from murder, one in which he commits murder, one in which he regrets the deed. Macbeth is known to us by his *movement* from one state of mind to another. He *is* movement—he exists only as something fluid, restless, passing, elusive. He does not add up; he slips by. He does not stand still to the view; he changes before our eyes.

Compare the method with that of a recent Chekhovian dramatist. Jane Bowles's *In the Summer House* presented us with a variety of fascinating characters: a woman tyrannically dominating her daughter because she is herself secretly terrified of being dominated; a daughter rebelling violently because she secretly longs to be dominated; another mother submitting piteously to a daughter's tyranny because she knows that to alter their relationship would be to expose it as worthless and so leave her with no relationship at all.

In the five scenes of this play the characters were observed in constantly altered circumstances. In Scene Two Mrs. Eastman-Cuevas was taking a stick to all about her; in Scene Five she was clinging wretchedly to her daughter's gown. In Scene Two Mrs. Constable was incapable of speaking above a whisper; in Scene Five she was roaring out drunken commands. In Scene One young Molly Eastman-Cuevas was hiding shyly in a vine-covered summerhouse; in Scene Five she was turning her back on her private world and courageously flying into a difficult future.

By the end of the evening everyone and everything had changed. But we had not been permitted to observe a single change in progress. After four of the scenes there was a time lapse of a month, after one of them a time lapse of ten months. All movement, all change, took place during the lapses. When it was time for us to meet these interesting people again, we met them in a state of momentary rigidity—a new state each time, but a rigid one nonetheless. We were offered one still life, then another, then another.

The play failed, I think, for this reason. Its incidental virtues were extraordinary. The language was far more evocative than what Broadway is accustomed to. The characterizations were fresh, bold, patently truthful—in every way superior. In production, each of the five moods was imaginatively sustained.

The play simply refused to make use of, or even to take cognizance of, the medium in which it was presented. It was never shaped to move forward in time; it was shaped to stand still, while time moved forward elsewhere. It might as well have been cast in the form of a series of haunting water colors, or—to be a little more reasonable about the matter—a series of isolated character sketches in a literary quarterly.

Drama is what it is—human figures moving through large spaces over longish periods of time—for the precise purpose of mirroring, exploring, illuminating, and in general tipping our hats to the fact of change. Change is both a terrifying and an exhilarating condition of our lives; this is the tool we have devised to honor it.

Because the change we choose to mirror is not simply an involuntary change (not a vegetable or chemical change over which we have little control) but a human change involving the living intellect, the malleable emotions, the power of choice and the exercise of will, we prefer to call this change an "action." But the two terms—change and action—are as nearly synonymous as terms can be, as a glance at the dictionary definition of "action" will suggest: "The act or process of producing an effect . . . the effecting of an alteration."

Put it this way: there can be neither change without action nor action without change. (We are surely badgering the obvious here, but the distressed state of modern drama stems largely from its defiant denial of the obvious.)

And, to pursue the obvious just a little farther, there can

be no change without conflict. I cannot change the landscaping in front of my house without getting good stiff resistance from the earth beneath me. I cannot change my wife's habits without stiffer resistance still. I cannot be made to change my clothes for visitors without physical and moral effort, and nothing is tougher than getting me to change my mind. Nature insists on change and opposes change at the same time—is always in a state of conflict.

The notion that a play must incorporate a conflict is often discredited nowadays as the audience-baiting showmanship of crude and conscienceless melodramatists. Someone once discovered, so the legend goes, that you could sell more tickets if you threw in more fights—and hacks have made the most of mayhem ever since. Shakespeare's wrestling matches, fencing bouts, even his murders are sops to silence the mob in the pit, and so on. Today's honest dramatist—even though it might be to his financial advantage—refuses to compromise with the irrelevant.

But there is nothing irrelevant about conflict: it is the unvarying condition of change. Once you have granted that a play has anything to do with activity, you have already granted its status as a contest. The concept of opposed forces meeting and doing battle does not derive from the habitual panderings of third-rate dramatists to thrill-drugged cretins; it derives from that accurate observation of nature which is supposed to be the good dramatist's business.

This trinity of old-fashioned terms—action, change, conflict—has not come into being, then, as a haphazard accretion of devices that were seen to work. It is a tight trinity of related—in fact, inseparable—values, bound together not by logic alone but by everyman's immediate experience.

Again, the old Aristotelian suggestion that a proper play have a "beginning, middle, and end" is not the tidy, and somewhat insufferable, rule-of-thumb it is thought to be. We are generally outraged by its transparent patness. Why should I falsify life by coming to a conclusion? Why cannot I drop my curtain on continuing life? Why must I force my observation into an arbitrary shape—rising action, climactic action, falling action? Must I really reduce my materials to George Cohan's "In the first act, get your man up a tree; in the second act, throw stones at him; in the third act, get him down"?

Or we cry out with George Tabori:

"Almost everything in our culture is calculated to 'please' by pandering to current prejudices and myths, by giving the audience an easy catharsis as if to say: 'It's all right. We have given you some laughter, some suspense, some tears. You've got a little involved, but it's all over. The problems of the play have been neatly solved: the protagonists are married or crazy or dead. You may go home and forget about the whole thing.' This undoubtedly is the way to 'popular' success. I am neither contemptuous nor envious of it, but the nature of my play demanded a different approach. The stage need not be reduced to a confession-box or the analyst's sofa. The problem of the uprooted (or any other social problem) will not be solved by the audience, and the audience will obviously remain indifferent or paralyzed if it feels that the problem has been solved for them on the stage."

But the notion of completeness—and the audience does demand a *kind* of completeness—has virtually nothing to do with the soothing resolution that is manufactured at the expense of truth. Completeness—beginning, middle, and end—requires only that that change which is essential to the nature of drama should actually have taken place. The terms are merely descriptive of such successive stages as are seen to occur in life when any true change is under way.

There is a beginning stage in any change: a stage at which motivating pressures are beginning to clamor for a response. There is a middle stage: a stage at which the response is given and the inevitable conflict joined. There is an end stage: a stage at which the contest between pressure and response has resulted in a different relationship between these two things, a new state of affairs, a *changed* state of affairs.

The new state of affairs need in no sense be cheerfully complacent, neatly contrived, or craftily commercial. (All of the principals may be dead; that is a new state of affairs.) It need not bundle up the problems of the world in a miraculously manageable package, nor need it even resolve all of the issues that are deviling a few individual souls. All that is asked of the dramatist is that he show the beginnings of some one particular change, that he trace it through its natural turmoil, and that he bring the contending forces into a different—though not necessarily a perfect—balance. Things were one way; now they are another; we have seen them move.

It is scarcely necessary to illustrate the point. The pressures that drive Hamlet into motion are the conduct of Gertrude, the conduct of Claudius, and the appearance of the ghost. From the time that Hamlet takes an oath to act we are embroiled in the strains and tensions of movement that is everywhere resisted (because the movement itself is repugnant to Hamlet, some of the resistance comes from within himself). At the end everything is changed: for Gertrude and Claudius, and for Hamlet. In *The School for Wives* the pressures that work upon M. Arnolphe are his general fear that so young and desirable a woman will be whisked away from him and his particular fear that Horace will do the whisking. From the time that he pretends to be assisting Horace in his suit in order to gather such confidences as will enable him to thwart that suit, we are immersed in the middle tug-and-pull. At the end Arnolphe has lost his Agnes and Horace has won her. The pressures that force Oedipus to act are the destitution of his community and the suggestion that he himself is responsible for that destitution. From the time that Oedipus furiously rejects the suggestion and determines to get at the truth we are again caught up in the central anguish of a change in progress. At the end, what was said to be true is discovered to be true; the discovery destroys Oedipus.

There are different kinds of changes. Aristotle, studying the practice of Greek dramatists, laid emphasis upon two: reversals and discoveries. ("The most powerful elements of attraction in Tragedy, the Reversals and Discoveries, are parts of the Plot.") That is to say, there are changes of circumstance (an uncle dies and leaves the hero a million dollars; Richard is killed at Bosworth Field). And, though circumstance may stand still, there are changes in our knowledge of it (Electra discovers that her brother is alive; Willy Loman discovers that he is not his image of himself; Oedipus discovers that he has not escaped stain).

But the most laborious illustration may be of some use if it helps convince us that certain traditional by-laws of drama—such as the "beginning, middle, end" bugaboo—are neither strait-jackets on the dramatist's invention nor commercial conveniences designed to degrade it. *Hamlet*, *The School for Wives*, and *Oedipus* are alike in charting a change through all its important stages. In almost every other way they are notoriously dissimilar: in tone, in structure, in the emotional effect that the completed change has on us.

The so-called rules of drama—there are precious few of them—have not been handed down to us, then, in the interests of "neatness." They do not of themselves produce that peculiar neatness that strikes us as false; Shakespeare never wrote a "neat" play in his life. The few standard notions that have echoed down the ages—action, change, conflict, completeness—are only rough descriptions of the nature of a medium, rough approximations of what an audience may expect from actors acting in a large space over an extended period of time.

For the dramatist, the door remains wide open; he may explore any terrain, in as personal a manner as he wishes. But he does have to find the door. It is the door to an amphitheater, not one to an art gallery, a concert hall, or a library in which literary quarterlies fill chaste and silent shelves. The simplest and boldest prescriptions of the past—most of them indebted to Aristotle—discuss the location, and the shape, of the door.

If we are going to get through it, and out into that theatrical country which is all freedom, excitement, and exhilarating momentum, we are probably going to have to do business once more with the age-old concepts of activity and change. And if we do decide that this is what the theater was intended for, we are going to find ourselves telling stories. The wolf (the witches, the ghost, the oracle, the truth) is hammering at my door. I must do battle, or die. I do battle. The wolf is routed; or I am.

I think, too, that we must get past the rather faint and apologetic definitions of "story" that have become characteristic of our time, that we must bring our understanding of "story" into line with our actual appetite for "story." We are not really interested in *and* constructions. We are interested, let's say, in *if* constructions. *If* Scheherazade does not enchant her husband, she will be beheaded. *If* Macbeth wishes to become king, he must murder Duncan. *If* Hamlet wishes to see justice done, he must perpetrate a dozen injustices. *If* Clarence Day's soul is to be saved, he must be firmly baptized.

Our instinct for story is aroused whenever we scent difficulty—the hard choice, the crippling alternative, the threat and the necessity of change. *If* I act in a certain way, what happens next?

Above all, our dramatists must rid themselves of the superstition that "story" is the irresponsible invention of profiteering mountebanks. Most of them, nowadays, are inclined to lump "story" and "fairy tale" into the same grandmotherly handbag, and to toss away the handbag as trash.

But there is a sense in which the wildest fairy tale is truer than some of the timeless, pressureless plays the modern theater finds "honest." A good fairy tale is always a primitive and fantastic mirror of the way things are. It may be advisable to try to bring the mirror more sharply into focus; it is never advisable to break it.

That "if" of the fairy tale is an "if" that haunts all of us, day and night. "What happens next?" is a permanent whisper inside us.

PART FOUR

Arthritis in the Joints

Between them, the two most respected models of our time nipped steadily away at freedom of characterization, flexibility of theme, and the long-standing fascination of narrative. These models—Ibsen and Chekhov—were in part unpopular because they meant to be, because they pursued an intense personal vision which was felt to be superior to the common vision. They were also unpopular because their respective visions, however honestly attained, were limited ones, employing the theater at less than its capacity and offering the audience less than it demanded.

If the audience has been shrinking over a period of time, so has the stage been shrinking—in its activity, its excitement, its size—over the same period of time. Ibsen and Chekhov carved out niches for themselves at the edges of what had once been called theater; their imitators shrank the whole theater to the size of the niches. As a result, the theater has for some years been removed from its own center, and from the audience that lives at that center. The stage has had heart trouble.

It has also suffered from a stiffness of the joints. This stiffness is really older than Ibsen or Chekhov. It comes from certain practices—realistic practices we call them—that had been developing in the theater since the eighteenth and early nineteenth centuries, that were seized upon by Ibsen and Chekhov as eminently suitable to their new purposes, and that have by now become the fixed habits of the unquestioning dramatist.

From the eighteenth century we have inherited a drama that is stubbornly prosaic. From the nineteenth we have inherited one that is scientifically painstaking.

Both inheritances once had the appeal of novelty, of experiment. But each had an enervating malaise within it, and each has visited upon drama its own form of muscular atrophy.

If our theater has been unpopular at heart, it has also been irritating in its extremities—sluggish of foot and faltering in its speech.

13. The Slow Boat to Nowhere

A FAMILIAR NIGHTMARE is that agonizing one in which you are desperately anxious to get somewhere but can move only at a semi-paralyzed pace. The mind darts ahead; the body lags as though deep under water. I don't know what precise waking experience is supposed to set this nightmare in motion; but I can imagine its taking place after almost any visit to the contemporary theater.

Our theater might easily have been invented for the delectation of snails. We are accustomed to the slow-motion photography of the realistic stage and so do not suspect that there is anything unduly sluggish about it or that it in any way accounts for our undisguised boredom. This is what the theater should be—an imitation of life. And this is the way life goes. What else should the playwright do?

Well, here is Shakespeare setting a scene:

"But, soft! What light through yonder window breaks?"

And here is John van Druten:

"Olive!"
"Sally! Darling!"
"Come in. How are you?"
"Couldn't be better. (*Looks around.*) So this is it! It's very grand."
"Do you think so?"
"Very. How long have you had it?"
"Six weeks."
(*Inspecting; impressed*): "Um!"
"Do you want to see it all?"
"Sure."

"Well, this is the living room. It's sunken. Kitchen's in here." (*Opens door. They go through.*)

"Darling, it's enormous! You could feed the whole army. Do you have a maid?"

"Colored. Daily. *When* she comes. Which isn't very often. I think she's got a complicated love life."

"Don't we all? (*They return to living room.*) How did you find this?"

"It's Claire Henley's. Claire's on the road with the Lunts."

"I don't know how that girl gets the breaks she does. I was sick about *your* show. Did you get my message, opening night?"

"Yes, I didn't know where to thank you. You were jumping around so."

"Darling, I *know*. Split weeks and one-night stands. It's heaven to be through. How long did you run, actually?"

"Five days."

"Did you get any notices?"

"A couple of mentions. (*Opening bedroom door*): Here's the bedroom."

(*Going in*): "Very saucy. (*Flippantly*): Luxe."

"What?"

"Luxe. French, darling. One of those untranslatable expressions. It means luxury. And beds like that!"

"Bathroom and dressing room in there."

"Dressing room! (*She peeps in.*)"

(*Excusing it*): "Well . . ."

"Darling, it's the cutest place I ever saw in all my life. (*Going to window*): Where do you look out?"

"Onto the summer garden of the 'Bonne Chanson.' That French restaurant next door."

"What's that like?"

"Lovely. But terribly expensive. You know, no menu. The man just comes and *suggests*."

"Put yourself right next door to temptation, eh? Or is it

for the boy-friends when they come to take you out? (*Acting*): 'Where shall we eat?' 'Wherever you say.' 'How about the place next door?' 'Okay.' (*Back to her own voice*): I know. I once thought of taking an apartment over the Colony, myself. What are you paying Claire for this?"

"A hundred and a quarter."

"Have you got another job?"

"No."

"No! And there's nothing in the offing, this late in the season, for any of us."

"I know. But I still have a little money left over from that radio serial I did. And it's when you're out of work you need a place to live. When you're *in* work . . ."

"You live at Sardi's—if you can get in. Yes, but all the same! What did you want to move for, anyway?"

"I was tired of a hotel room. And there were reasons."

"What?"

(*Evasively*): "Not now. Come and have a drink."

One might have thought that in Shakespeare's sceneryless theater a great deal of time must be devoted to descriptive dialogue, to "setting the stage." Logic would also have suggested that in our own thoroughly detailed theater the scenery must speak for itself, be taken for granted, be dismissed in favor of the action. But things don't seem to work out that way.

My memory is by no means all that it used to be, and I really did expect, on looking into Shakespeare's *Romeo and Juliet*, to find four or five introductory lines describing the Capulet orchard. But there are no more. Romeo makes quick mention of a window, and that's that. With the next line we are hurried off into Romeo's passionate feeling for Juliet; the emotional content of the scene is quick upon us.

By the time Mr. van Druten's heroine has hinted that "there were reasons" and then parried any prying questions with the offer of a drink we are verging on emotional content, too. But we've been a long time verging; and we've still got to make that drink.

Let's allow for the fact that Mr. van Druten, expert craftsman that he is, has subtly insinuated certain other values into his scene-setting. When he has a girl speak of her maid's "complicated love life" he is distantly preparing us for the subject of the play. When he digs out the fact of a show's failure, he is telling us something about the professional and financial status of the girl, slipping in bits of information that may conceivably prove useful. When he makes a joke about "untranslatable expressions" he is amusing us by the way. When he lets an actress invent an imaginary conversation with a boy friend he is planning the arrival of an actual boy friend. And so on.

But even when we have allowed for these underground thrusts we are left with twenty-five lines directly concerned with the arrangement of the apartment. Add five to ten lines that have no purpose other than moving the characters through the apartment ("Come in. How are you?") and you have a ratio—between Shakespeare and van Druten—of approximately thirty to one. That is to say, Shakespeare moves about thirty times as fast as van Druten.

Mr. van Druten, by the way, is entirely aware of this. In his interesting *Playwright at Work* he remarks that "every playwright has his own speed, and mine is slower than I wish it were."

Let me have Mr. van Druten take over for a moment here: ". . . There are slower writers still. George Kelly is one of the slowest. When I saw *Daisy Mayme* on my first visit to America, I was amazed at the time it took over almost nothing. . . . I can remember thinking that I would not be able to bear it, and then as the performance moved on, it had established the tempo for the whole play. The characters became endearing, because one knew them so well, and the whole *rallentando* speed of the play was essential to its mood. . . . A slightly similar mood, keyed to a sharper, though still gentle mood of comedy, comes from Paul Osborn's enchanting *Morning's at Seven.* Here the reluctant forty-year-old Homer, his fiancée, Myrtle, aged thirty-nine, and his mother are sitting together in the back yard.

> "I love your back yard, Mrs. Bolton. It looks cool. It's simply heavenly."
> "Yes, we like it very much."
> "All the trees and everything. I bet you sit out here all the time."
> "We sit out here a good deal of the time."
> "Well, I should think you would. It's simply heavenly. I don't know when I've seen a more attractive back yard."
> "Yes, we're very fond of it."
> "Well, I should think so. It's so nice and wild, too. Like being in a forest."
> "I'm glad you like it."
> "Well, I certainly do. It's simply—heavenly, that's all there is to it."
> "Well, it's nice of you to say so."
> "Well, I mean it."
> "Have mosquitoes sometimes?"
> "Yes, there are mosquitoes sometimes."
> "How dreadful!"
> "But I don't think that we've had quite so many this year as usual. Have you noticed that, Homer?"
> "Not so many. That's right."
> "Isn't that interesting the way those things go? One year you'll have a lot of mosquitoes and the next year not so many mosquitoes. Or a lot of caterpillars one year and the next year not so many caterpillars. I wonder why that is."
> "I don't know why that is. Do you, Homer?"
> "No, I don't know why that is."

"It's very interesting, isn't it? Anyway I suppose the mosquitoes and the caterpillars and all those things have some purpose. They wouldn't have been put there if they hadn't."

"No, I don't suppose they would have."

"Don't suppose so."

"It's all a part of some big plan. Some big—plan of some kind."

"This is slow playwriting, too [we are still with Mr. van Druten] but it is exquisite. The repeat of the word 'heavenly' is like a delicious chime. . . ."

Now it wouldn't be fair to use this scene as a symbol of *all* contemporary dramaturgy; Mr. van Druten has offered it as an example of extreme lassitude. Nor would it be especially relevant to point out that the play was a failure; there have been successes that moved at something near the same pace. I think we must also acknowledge that the sequence has a certain charm; it is the drowsy charm of the mosquito, but a charm nonetheless.

What may, perhaps, be said is that the passage stands as an extreme example of a theatrical style that has no other extreme. The play is remarkably slow; but we have no plays that are remarkably fast. We have many playwrights who write a bit faster than this. We have a few playwrights who write two bits faster than this. We have no playwrights who write thirty times—or twenty times, or even ten times—faster than this.

It is not really a question of every playwright having his own rate of speed. It is much more a matter of a time in history, and a style in structure, setting an over-all rate of speed, and allowing for minute individual differences within it.

The contemporary playwright is committed, pacewise, to the second hand of the clock. The age in which he lives has long since agreed to respect the scientifically measurable surface of life. If there is a door, it must be opened as doors are opened. If there is a meeting, it must be made as meetings are made, with a "How do you do?" and a "How have you been?" and a "What have you been doing since I saw you last?" What things take time must take just that time, and no less. Should they take a shade less, they must never seem to.

Shakespeare can write "*Enter Romeo*" and let Romeo be challenged at once. He is under no obligation to say where Romeo has been, how long it has taken him to get there, or, for that matter, just where he is now. If an exciting scene ensues, that is enough justification for his presence.

The realist must work otherwise.

A doorbell must ring. It must ring long enough for someone in another part of the house to hear it, drop whatever he or she is doing, and take a few steps before appearing in the living room. Greater haste would seem implausible and suggest contrivance. The maid, answering the door, must cross the stage at normal speed; if she is a comedy maid, she may cross it at subnormal speed. The door must be opened. Romeo must identify himself, say who he has come for. The maid must reply that Juliet may or may not be home and offer to "go see." Romeo's coat must be taken—and hung up. Romeo must be asked to step into the room. He must look around it as he does. He must be asked to sit down. He must sit down. He must wait. He may, if he wishes, pass the time by lighting a cigarette, leafing a magazine, or toying with articles on the mantelpiece. He may, of course, adjust his tie before the mirror. In time—reasonable time—footsteps will be heard on the stairs. Juliet? Perhaps. More likely the maid. Miss Juliet will be down in a moment, and wouldn't he care to make himself a drink?

We are, in effect, eternally writing the scene before the scene, asking that the drama wait while the milieu is inventoried. But our torpor is not ended with the arrival of Juliet, or with the arrival of that drink. Though the scene proper may have begun, the drama itself may still not move faster than the normal rhythm of the milieu.

Romeo must offer Juliet a cigarette, suggest that he make her a drink. He must ask for her father, admire her dress, inquire about a painting on the living-room wall. He must make pleasant little jokes to show that he has nothing urgent in view for the evening. Juliet must take time to make a telephone call. Romeo will speak of his day at the office, Juliet of the movie she has seen that afternoon. There will be sudden, brisk discussion of a mutual acquaintance, and light laughter. Romeo will offer to go. Juliet will say that it isn't at all late—yet. Romeo will sit down again, thoughtfully picking at his socks. In and around the believable badinage will scurry little meaningful glances between them. At last he will take her hand. (The scene is over now, for that doorbell is ringing again.)

Van Druten's Romeo and Juliet meet:

> "Sally, this is Bill Page. Sally Middleton."
> "How do you do?"
> "How do you do?"
> "May I take your things? (*She takes his cap and bag and puts them on desk.*) Let me give you a drink."
> "Thanks."
> "Scotch?"
> "Swell. (*Looking around*): This is very pleasant. I haven't been in an apartment like this for quite a time. . . ."

They are left alone for the evening:

> "Did you get your number?"
> "Yes, thanks. Well . . ."
> "Won't you have another drink?"
> "You're sure you're in no hurry?"
> "None at all."

"Well, then, thanks. I'd like to."
"Help yourself, won't you?"
(*Going to drink table*): "Will you?"
"I don't think so, thanks."
"Are you and Olive old friends? . . ."

They come back to her place after dinner:

"What a night! (*Closes the door behind him.*) Did you get wet?"

"Running from next door? No. Come in and sit down, won't you?"

(BILL *shakes out his cap, and puts it down. He helps* SALLY *off with her coat. She switches on the lamps.*)

"Would you like a drink?"

"Not after all that brandy. I must have had five, waiting for the rain to stop."

(*After a moment's pause, going to the radio*): "Would you like the news?"

"I don't think so. Unless you would."

"I don't think . . . really. (*She starts to wander purposely.*) Have a candy?" (*Offers box.*)

"No, thanks. You don't have to entertain me, you know. Relax. What are you fussing about?"

"Was I fussing? I didn't mean to. (*Pause*) That was a lovely dinner. Thank you."

"You were right. It's a good place. . . ."

Enough of baiting Mr. van Druten, who has entertained us rather more consistently than most of his contemporaries. Nor need we look only into offhand comedy or the deliberately sleepy play of mood for examples of retarded movement. Take a snatch out of an exceptionally good character-melodrama, William Inge's *Come Back, Little Sheba:*

"There's still some beans left. Do you want them, Doc?"
"I had enough."

"I hope you got enough to eat tonight, Daddy. I been so busy cleaning I didn't have time to fix you much."

"I wasn't very hungry."

"You know what? Mrs. Coffman said I could come over and pick all the lilacs I wanted for my centerpiece tomorrow. Isn't that nice? I don't think she poisoned Little Sheba, do you?"

"I never did think so, Baby. Where'd you get the new curtains?"

"I went out and bought them this afternoon. Aren't they pretty? Be careful of the woodwork, it's been varnished."

"How come, honey?"

"Bruce is comin'. I figured I had to do my spring housecleaning some time."

"You got all this done in one day? The house hasn't looked like this in years."

"I can be a good housekeeper when I want to be, can't I, Doc?"

"I never had any complaints. Where's Marie now?"

"I don't know, Doc. I haven't seen her since she left this morning with Turk."

"Marie's too nice to be wasting her time with him."

"Daddy, Marie can take care of herself. Don't worry."

"'Bout time for Fibber McGee and Molly."

"Daddy, I'm gonna run over to Mrs. Coffman's and see if she's got any silver polish. I'll be right back. . . ."

The characterization is touching. Careful preparation is being made for a scene to come. This is, furthermore, a play that will ultimately erupt into a violence unusual for our time. Its rhythm, like the rhythm of all realism, is essentially lazy.

Realism imposes a completeness of detail and a casualness of deportment that does not deny the possibility of drama but that does postpone its appearance interminably. I may wish to convey a certain piece of information to my audience. I must not, however, seem to be offering information. I must seem to be respecting the random and inconsequential rhythms of life, of a life that accomplishes nothing directly. I must force my characters to pretend to be interested in everything else under the sun: the time of day, the shape of a shoe, the best way to scramble eggs. Under no circumstances must they exhibit interest in the information *I* wish to convey. This information may, if I am clever, pop out accidentally. It may be inferred, in bits and pieces between the stretches of polite patter. After every fourth line I may inch my way forward, offering one snatch of essential evidence for every four snatches of plausible window-dressing. I am allowed to advance my story so long as I advance it surreptitiously, without cracking the placid surface. I become a specialist in the hint that is dropped in passing, the meaningful remark that is never noticed, the implication that may be drawn from my silence on a subject. The drama may be heard as an occasional echo; only the idle foreground may be elaborately developed. If drama is my business, it is a shady business, and I must let it in the back door while everyone else is at tea. My play, as a result, moves with the caution of a man who is trying to get up a flight of stairs without squeaking any of the floorboards. I am a dramatist on tiptoe.

My first obligation is to total reality. My story and my characters together do not, of course, constitute total reality. I must therefore suppress them until I have paid my respects to whatever is real outside them, around them, or near them —to whatever is irrelevantly real.

I want to take my characters into a bar, let's say, for some dramatic purpose. I cannot simply take them there and let them get on with the purpose. I must first prove that I have been in a bar, that I know what bars look like, that I know the kind of people who come into bars, and so forth. I must write, with Eugene O'Neill:

FIRST LONGSHOREMAN (*as they range themselves at the bar*): Gimme a shock. Number Two. (*He tosses a coin on the bar.*)

SECOND LONGSHOREMAN: Same here. (JOHNNY *sets two glasses of barrel whisky before them.*)

FIRST LONGSHOREMAN: Here's luck. (*The other nods. They gulp down their whisky.*)

SECOND LONGSHOREMAN (*Putting money on the bar*): Give us another.

FIRST LONGSHOREMAN: Gimme a scoop this time—lager and porter. I'm dry.

SECOND LONGSHOREMAN: Same here. (JOHNNY *draws the lager and porter and sets the big, foaming schooners before them. They drink down half the contents and start to talk together hurriedly in low tones. The door on the left is swung open and* LARRY *enters. He is a boyish, red-cheeked, rather good-looking young fellow of twenty or so.*)

LARRY (*nodding to* JOHNNY—*cheerily*): Hello, boss.

JOHNNY: Hello, Larry. (*With a glance at his watch*): Just on time. (LARRY *goes to the right behind the bar, takes off his coat, and puts on an apron.*)

FIRST LONGSHOREMAN (*abruptly*): Let's drink up and get back to it. (*They finish their drinks and go out left. The* POSTMAN *enters as they leave.*)

O'Neill was, by contemporary standards, a rapid dramatist. It should be noticed, though, that the First Longshoreman, the Second Longshoreman, Larry, and Johnny are not participants in the play's action. They are participants in a life that goes on apart from the play, that brushes shoulders with the play most briefly and accidentally, that does not influence the play. The time they take is, strictly speaking, lost time. But the contemporary dramatist is obliged to lose time. He dare not pursue his people, or his events, from one room to another without pausing to do a picture study of the flora and fauna.

Under these conditions, Shakespeare would have been in serious trouble. It was Shakespeare's habit to move with his people, perhaps to twenty or thirty places in a single play. If he had felt the obligation to identify each background, to smooth out each transition, to illustrate the life and times of every passing extra, the first performance of *King Lear* would undoubtedly still be in progress. There are a good many Messengers in Shakespeare's plays, but they do not appear except with messages. There are no scenes in which we study three or four Messengers sitting around waiting for the next call to duty; we do not have to be convinced that there is a waiting room for Messengers somewhere. It is probable that Messengers do eat, drink and speak to one another; but they do not do it on our time.

The problem of co-ordinating a naturalistic rhythm with a dramatic rhythm has, nowadays, been solved by suppressing the dramatic rhythm, or, at best, by introducing the dramatic rhythm as a subtle counterpoint to the dominant naturalistic beat.

We have been unwilling to trim, or to skip, time. We have therefore trimmed, and in some cases skipped, the dramatic action. Today we allow so much action as is compatible with an hour or two in a living room; should one of the characters have something more vigorous in mind, he had best leave the room to attend to it. (He may give us a careful accounting of what he has done, and of the time it has taken him to do it, in a later act.) Not only the pace of the play but the extent of its activity is dictated by the physical room and by the clock on its mantelpiece.

Julius Caesar covers, quite coherently and without a lapse of tension, a period of two years.

The average contemporary play covers:

ACT ONE: An afternoon in early spring.

ACT TWO: Late that evening.

ACT THREE: The next morning.

Each act will be continuous in time, unless the dramatist has been notoriously careless and sent one of his characters off to accomplish something he cannot possibly accomplish in time for the act curtain. In this case the dramatist will notify us, in a line on the program, that "the curtain will be lowered for one minute to denote a lapse of one hour." We have, indeed, become so scrupulous about the implausible passing of time that the producers of *The Seven Year Itch* were impelled, with malicious glee, to provide *their* program with the helpful note that "the curtain will be lowered for thirty seconds to denote a lapse of thirty seconds."

Our minutes are all accounted for. And it rarely occurs to us that, like most people who indulge in total recall, we are bores. The knack we have for duplicating the dawdling that goes on in the world fills us with pious satisfaction. We are accurate. We do not cheat. We do not indulge in unrealistic convention. Marlowe may have thought, in his primitive way, that it was acceptable for Doctor Faustus to pass the whole of his last hour on earth in a bare forty-eight lines. We do not demand of our audiences such barbarous imaginative leaps.

Conventions are, in our view, the youthful indiscretions of playwrights who knew no better. It is a pity that Richard III should tell us so baldly what he is going to do, that Iago should be so outspoken about himself, that Lear should have divided his kingdom before we have had time to seat ourselves in the theater. We have, after a great deal of work, managed to bring ourselves to a nearly conventionless theater, a theater in which the surface of life and the surface of the stage are virtually indistinguishable from each other. We do, of course, have a few conventions: the suggestion that the audience can see through one wall of an actual room is a convention; the notion of a curtain falling over continuing action is another; there are a few more. But they are the fewest possible. We have bested convention, and thereby *perfected* the mirror.

It never occurs to us that the conventions used by our primitive forbears were very often ingeniously devised short cuts—short cuts designed to get us past whatever was irrelevant and inconsequential and on to everything that was vigorously relevant and of serious consequence. A Greek chorus puzzles us and seems an excrescent weight on the play; actually it was the fastest way then known to rough in an involved background, keep us in touch with extracurricular developments, and outline for us the moral and philosophical profundities that might be deduced from a difficult narrative. In a play like Charles Morgan's *The Burning Glass* it takes us two and one half hours simply to state a philosophical position: science has made us so comfortable that we have become morally rotten. A Greek chorus would have polished off the thought in three minutes. We are not interested in this particular method now, nor need we be; but we ought not to deny its virtues.

The Elizabethan soliloquy was, in part, a short cut. It was the fastest way of getting to know a character, the fastest way of sending him about his business. The conventional endings of many of Molière's plays were short cuts. The essential content was exhausted, we had had all the important fun; why nod ourselves to sleep over a casually convincing windup?

A short cut is helpful in several ways. It relieves the monotony of familiar terrain ("Come in, how are you?" is familiar terrain). And it takes you to the heart of the place you want to be.

Speed is not its only virtue. Speed is, I think, a perfectly desirable quality in a play; the audience is quick-witted (how often the audience is ahead of us in the contemporary theater, whispering the developments before they take place!) and it is always delighted to be transported swiftly from crisis to crisis.

But a much more substantial gain is ours for the hurrying. The practice of eliding whatever is obvious or familiar or drearily routine leaves twice as much time—and twice as much room—for the basic dramatic content. If I do not spend three minutes getting my characters on stage, I have three minutes to give them for more significant purposes. If, over the course of the evening, I pare away forty-five minutes of realistic small talk, I can pack forty-five minutes' more substance into the play.

In *Our Town* Thornton Wilder wishes to take his boy and girl into a drugstore. If Mr. Wilder were a thoroughgoing realist he would first have to change his set. That in itself would take, say, a minute. Opening his curtain on all of the necessary counters, mirrors, tables and chairs, he would be required to fill his accurate background with accurate activity. There would be other customers, some at tables, some at the counter. The play would pause while some of them order, thus giving a familiar locale its familiar rhythm. The druggist would josh an old customer. After a moment, the boy and girl would enter, hesitantly. They might, if Mr. Wilder were an absolutely insistent realist, have to wait their turn for a seat at the counter. ("You take the empty one," says the boy; "No, I'll wait for two," smiles the girl.) Perhaps they examine a display of candy boxes while they wait. In time, they are seated, and they order. However long the scene is to be, it must be long enough for their sodas to be made—realistically —and consumed. They dare not leave until naturalism has had all its rites. By way of authenticity, their conversation will be interrupted from moment to moment as other customers enter, as the druggist attends to them. When the sodas have been plausibly downed, the boy and girl are free to go. But there must be a last fillip to the drugstore rhythm: a newcomer enters and we hear him giving his own order to the druggist before the curtain slips down. A scene that is intrinsically worth three minutes' playing time might easily have been extended to eight or ten.

But Mr. Wilder, in *Our Town*, has invented for himself a

jovial stage manager and a sceneryless stage. The boy and girl are walking along a Main Street that has no shops to be accounted for, no strolling friends to be met. The boy suddenly says, "Emily, how would you like an ice-cream soda, or something, before you go home?"

The stage direction now reads "They come into the drugstore and seat themselves on stools." The stage manager has created a counter by placing a plank across two chairs, and we are promptly engrossed in the scene proper. The rhythm of the *scenes* in *Our Town* is a gentle one, and the play never seems to scurry. But because there is no extraneous rhythm delaying the scenes, because Mr. Wilder's conventions cut through such factual detail as is inappropriate to his story, *Our Town* is able to encompass, in the customary two and one half hours, the childhood, adolescence, romance, marriage, and death of at least one of the principals. There is, in fact, enough time left over for Mr. Wilder to offer us an after-death passage in a graveyard. The scale of the play is in proportion to the structural speed of the play. Mr. Wilder has saved time in order to use it, and use it magnificently.

The conventions that please Mr. Wilder are relatively stylized ones. Shakespeare, apart from one or two uncharacteristic instances, uses nothing so formal as stage manager or Chorus. The soliloquy, the suggestiveness of verse, the short scene in the unelaborated or even unidentified locale, and the small formality of the rhymed-couplet exit are enough for him. Arthur Miller, in *Death of a Salesman*, merely shifts his lights and tosses in a line to let us know what time jump we've made. Conventions need not seem unreal. They are simply agreements, of almost any sort, between author and audience. "We agree," say these two parties, "to accept this or that short cut as a substitute for certain uninteresting segments of reality; our agreement is for the purpose of spending more time on the more interesting segments." If a convention falsifies some minor portion of life, it does so in the happy expectation of cramming more life into the play.

I think we need to invent a few conventions, enough to get us past "How have you been?" and "What'll you have?" anyway. The kind of convention does not matter much; the audience is swift to make profitable bargains. Our conventionless theater, rejecting whatever cannot be fitted into the box set and the daily routine, is by now so undernourished that it can barely drag itself around.

14. *Elbowroom*

WE FURROW OUR BROWS over the problem. If we are going to overleap the confining and clockbound conventions of realism, where are we going to go? It's clear enough that we can stretch dramatic structure a bit beyond the mechanical compactness of the well-made play—Williams and Miller have given us strong hints about this—but how far dare we stretch before illusion snaps? At what point do we run the risk of losing touch with reality, and landing in the no man's land of the ostentatious amateur?

The point, I think, is a great deal farther ahead of us than we imagine. We have lately advanced a discreet inch or two; our freedom may extend for miles.

The most inhibiting concept we have labored under, and a concept that has conditioned nearly every aspect of twentieth-century playwriting, is our peculiar notion of what constitutes an Imitation. The term "imitation" has belonged to the arts since the dawn of time. Aristotle defined a play as "the imitation of an action." Since Ibsen, Hauptmann, Chekhov and

Zola we have broadened the definition, and we are now in the habit of saying that a play is an "imitation of life."

With the coming of realism, we began to take extraordinary care that our imitation be accurate. Earlier playwrights seemed to us to have been most cavalier with the observable facts of life; they had been remiss in their reporting, had allowed distortion and dishonesty to invalidate their work. If art was an imitation, we were now going to make the best imitation that had ever been made by the simple process of sticking as close to the subject imitated as possible.

We began, then, not to paint flickering fires on canvas fireplaces but to build structures solid enough to contain real fires. We looked at the floorboards and found them unrealistic; we quickly covered them with genuine carpets. Running water became a matter of honor; if a play called for faucets, they were going to be practical faucets and the water that flowed from them had best run hot and cold. By the time of *The Voice of the Turtle* we were able to scramble real eggs on a real stove and really eat them.

We are a bit superior about Belasco nowadays, though considering our continued preoccupation with on-stage practicality, I don't know why we should be. Belasco's style of imitation was almost miraculously literal. If a man was supposed to enter the stage from a dusty dirt path, a dusty dirt path was strewn from wings to dressing room. Producing a play that took place in a Child's restaurant, Belasco went to Child's not only to observe but to buy. He bought spoons, knives, forks, cups, steam tables—and deposited them on the Belasco stage. Imitation became more and more exact. Legend has it that for a play taking place in a boardinghouse the master went shopping for a real boardinghouse, bought it, tore it down, and reconstructed its second floor within his theatrical proscenium arch.

As I say, I don't know why we sneer at Belasco. The Moscow Art Theater we continue to admire sometimes worked in much the same way. One of Stanislavski's productions is said to have called for an actor who could play a beggar. No actor realistic enough could be found. The byways were then scoured for an actual beggar and an actual beggar was persuaded to impersonate himself professionally. (I am happy to report that he was a failure.) We burrow just as close to character fidelity in our current semidocumentary films; much of the early work of Rossellini, for instance, mixed professional actors with men hauled in off the streets.

Our passion for reproducing reality by adopting the original reality continues to earn a kind of automatic applause from our audiences. Two or three years ago Lindsay and Crouse introduced the first practicable television set to be seen on the stage in a play called *Remains to be Seen*. Everyone had seen a television set, everyone knew how television sets worked. Yet the miracle of seeing one work *on the stage*—the astounding realization that an electric cord could be plugged in somewhere other than in a living room—caused the audience to gasp and to beat out an approving salvo. We remain convinced that the stage is at its most remarkable when it is doing something that we do thoughtlessly all day long in our homes.

The anxiety to make the theater imitatively correct was not, of course, confined to stage settings, or to the sort of characterization that brought us the Moscow Art beggar. It was a consuming anxiety, affecting every department of dramatic life. The actor's conduct—even when he was truly an actor—became geared to the accuracies of the candid camera; players lounged and lighted cigarettes so naturally as to seem to be really lounging and smoking. And the words that the actor spoke were words that might have been spoken anywhere. It was uncanny how the stage could, in every way, approximate the usual.

Every once in a while some critic, or scholar, or uncomplicated playgoer would feel a slight distress in his bones at all this. Something, his sleeping taste told him, was wrong. If he brooded about it, and tried to put a name to his dissatisfaction, he would generally conclude that the notion of imitation itself was wrong. The theater wasn't meant to be like this; it had fallen into error because docile dramatists had slavishly submitted to a fantastically wrong premise as old as Aristotle. If we were going to get away from an exasperating literalism we would have to get away from imitation itself.

Thus, John Hospers in his *Meaning and Truth in the Arts* feels compelled to say that "to continue to use the term 'imitation' as the departure from exactness increases is misleading and dangerous." Imitation means exactness; anything that is not as exact as we can make it is less and less of an imitation, finally no imitation at all.

It may seem irrelevant to go poking into learned dissertations on the subject, to worry about the precise meaning of a tired term. But our supposition that abandoning exactness means abandoning imitation itself has very practical consequences in the theater. The dramatist, fed up with tape-recorded speech and hot-and-cold running water, is led to believe that he can improve himself and his craft only by abandoning the recognizably human altogether. He cannot imitate the world of men because imitating it means copying it with a dreary and mechanical accuracy; therefore he must throw over the world of men and invent his own world. Having made the decision, he writes something like Tennessee Williams' *Camino Real*—and is injured to find that his effort to improve an art form has led only to his quick rejection by the admirers of that art form.

Imitation, then, has led us into a double problem. If we continue to practice it, we are literal dullards. If we revolt against it, we are unintelligible anarchists.

The two-pronged dilemma need never have come up. Imitation does not mean scrupulous exactitude. It means something very different indeed.

Our naturalistic imitations have not, as a matter of fact,

been imitations. Or, to put the matter a little more carefully, they have not moved toward imitation but toward a quite different thing, Identity.

When Belasco tears down a boardinghouse and mounts one of its rooms in the theater, the on-stage result is not an imitation of a boardinghouse. It *is* a boardinghouse. When a young couple in *The Voice of the Turtle* scramble eggs on the stage they are not imitating the scrambling of eggs. They *are* scrambling eggs. When Stanislavski hires a genuine beggar to join his acting company, the man hired is not imitating a beggar. He *is* a beggar.

In each of these cases imitation has disappeared and identity has been substituted. (It should also be noted that in each instance the artist has disappeared, imagination has disappeared. Belasco has dismissed the art of scene design; *The Voice of the Turtle* has dismissed the art of pantomime; Stanislavski has dismissed the art of acting.)

The struggle toward Identity is not a struggle toward more and more perfect imitation but a struggle away from the very idea of imitation. Imitation cannot be defined in terms of similarity alone, though we have supposed of late that a greater and greater similarity to the thing imitated was its natural and inevitable tendency. An imitation cannot even exist without being profoundly different from the thing it is imitating.

Let's be strict about the matter for a moment. An imitation that is wholly similar to the thing imitated is identical with it, and therefore not an imitation. Conversely, an imitation that is wholly dissimilar to the thing imitated has lost all contact with it, and is therefore not an imitation.

Imitation must be defined as a similarity *plus* a dissimilarity. It must in part be like its subject, in part very much unlike it. Both conditions are indispensable if the term is to have any distinctive meaning—if, for instance, an imitation is to be distinguishable from an identity—and the two conditions must be held in more or less perfect balance.

There is no way in which precise mathematics can be applied to the problem, but a hypothetically perfect imitation of something would be about fifty per cent like it and fifty per cent unlike it. A fifty-one per cent dissimilarity begins to move us toward chaos; a fifty-one per cent similarity begins to move us toward that inartistic monster, Identity.

To make this a little less abstract, I'd say that a Greek play came pretty close to a perfect, always precarious, balance between similarity and difference. There is similarity to life in the emotions of the principal characters, in the psychological responses they exhibit. But look at the differences: there is a Chorus that has no actual model in the universe at hand; there are subordinate characters—Messengers and sometimes Gods—that perform conventional rather than lifelike functions; there is verse, which no man has ever spoken in the daily round of his life; there is a rigid formulation of entrances, exits, and physical conduct on stage. (No murders may be shown; dead bodies must be wheeled on stage.) Life is mirrored here; but the degree of *surface* exactitude is terribly small.

That fifty-fifty balance is, of course, hypothetical, and if you want to call Shakespeare's work about sixty per cent similar to the surface of life and forty per cent dissimilar to the surface of life nobody is going to argue with you—except to point out that you are now becoming involved in an absurd effort to weigh intangibles.

Let's skip the mathematics, and consider the general movement of our theater. Few plays strive for the absolute identity of Belasco's boardinghouse or Stanislavski's beggar; total destruction of the imitative principle and the imitative faculty is rare. But the rough goal of the realistic theater is near-identity: the walls must be as solid as possible, the properties perfectly practicable, the deportment of the characters photographic, the speech of the characters close to stenographic. If we do not hit the mark, we aim at it; we are not trying for a balance between similarity and difference but for a maximum similarity and a minimum difference.

As we approach our goal—and it probably isn't overstating the case to say that we come within eighty to ninety per cent of total similarity—that delicate balance which gives an imitation its precise character recedes farther and farther from us. At the same time that we are taking pride in the increasing perfection of our imitation we are denying the very nature of imitation. The closer I come to identity the less am I engaged in the act of imitating.

I'm afraid that Mr. Hospers' position must be boldly reversed. A work of art does not become less and less imitative as it moves away from exactitude; it becomes less and less imitative as it moves toward exactitude.

The contemporary theater has not really been making better imitations, then, but worse ones. It has attended to one half of the imitative process, the half that has to do with similarity; it has sadly neglected the other and equally vital half, the half devoted to difference. If our realistic theater seems to have been chugging along at half energy, and if it has seemed to fly its performance flag at half mast, this is one of the reasons.

There is a point to so much semantic quibbling: the playwright who is reluctant to part with the notion of imitation, out of an honest fear of losing sight of reality and becoming mired in an unintelligible no man's land, need not be forced into the copycat's corner, into a confining literalism; he is free to reverse his field and go skylarking. Between the point at which he now stands and that midway point at which the imitative balance might be upset in the other direction there is a vast, rich territory open to imaginative adventure. The good imitator is actually invited to junk whole sections of the surface of life without running the risk of breaking faith with life.

The areas of similarity and difference are roughly definable. The similarity is to the emotional, psychological, and spiritual behavior of man; similarity is largely interior. The dissimilarity lies in the manner in which these things are revealed; it is largely exterior. As an imitator, I may alter the visible surface of life quite radically: I may employ unrealistic language to reveal a realistic emotion; I may make an arbitrary arrangement of the stage to expedite my journey into emotional depths that are anything but arbitrary; I may falsify the routine of a man's day in order to reach the profounder truths of his heart.

Dissimilarity is—or should be—most pronounced at the surface. We have been working the other way round: striving for intense similarity at the surface. And it may be that our preoccupation with similarity at the surface—where it is least needed, least interesting, least revealing—has kept us from achieving or even working toward any very high degree of similarity at the more difficult, more subjective, level. We have had a great many plays in which the surface deportment was near-perfect and in which the underlying motives seemed to have no truth at all in them.

On the whole, we are likely to achieve truth where we try hardest for it; we have been trying hardest in an area where it doesn't matter very much.

Since the current concept of imitation—whether we have consciously analyzed it or not—lies at the root of every move we now make in the theater, so any vigorous overhauling of our understanding of the term is bound to influence every move we make in the future. Enlivening the theater isn't really a matter of jolting each of its facets separately; shake up the underlying assumption and you will find half a dozen departments going into their dances spontaneously.

The moment we open one door toward difference we are sure to see other doors flying open ahead of us. We have, in a limited way, already seen this chain reaction at work.

Death of a Salesman and *A Streetcar Named Desire* both took certain liberties with normal play structure, electing to replace the sustained and realistic act rhythm with a short, lively, broken-field scene rhythm. As soon as this first rhythm was broken, there was a change in tempo as well: the plays moved more rapidly and covered more ground. With the change in rhythm and tempo came an unavoidable scenic change: we began to look at the inside and the outside of the backgrounds at the same time, to peer through once impenetrable walls, to cut away physical barriers. Lighting this fluid stage posed something of a problem; in solving the problem, lighting immediately became more poetic than it had been before.

Poetry is catching. Even language began to feel a possible freedom; a latch had been left half open. Neither Williams nor Miller turned poet overnight. But they began to poke at the poetic edges.

Williams wrote:

"He was a telephone man who fell in love with long distances; he gave up his job with the telephone company and skipped the light fantastic out of town. . . ."

Miller wrote:

"He's a man way out there in the blue, riding on a smile and a shoeshine. And when they start not smiling back—that's an earthquake. And then you get yourself a couple of spots on your hat, and you're finished. Nobody dast blame this man. A salesman is got to dream, boy. It comes with the territory."

This wasn't a speech he'd have written for an earlier, more "accurate" play.

I suspect that an adventurous dramatist can begin almost anywhere, can start by taking just such liberties as he feels competent to take. Stretching one muscle, he will sooner or later feel the itch to stretch them all—sooner or later they will involve one another.

Similarity has been pushed to its logical limits, and it may be time to go looking for differences.

There's just one difference I'd stay shy of. I'd cut through the red tape of realism with abandon, leaping from one concrete image of life to another concrete image of life. But I'd always want to be sure that the ultimate image, when I got there, was nothing less than concrete. A playwright may leap —but he's got to have somewhere to land.

15. *Cloud Cuckoo Land*

IN ENLARGING the scope of the theater, profundity is to be avoided at all costs. By profundity I mean what everyone seems to mean nowadays—abstraction. The contemporary world—in other forms of literature as much as in the theater —seems to have got it into its head that the only way an artist can become more profound is by becoming more abstract. The result is a group of plays in which God turns up as a stationmaster at a murky railroad junction, in which the principal characters are called Friend Ed, Joe Saul, and Mordeen, and in which unidentified desperadoes stagger into symbolic patios to be shot down by unidentified gunmen and carted off in garbage cans by white-jacketed collectors.

I think we must have some sense that our picky, small-bored realistic plays say very little about the universe. We conclude that the only way we can say something about the universe is by becoming Universal, with capital letters strewn all over the place. The curious thing is that no one has ever succeeded in writing a universal play by this method.

Like most of the other idiocies that occur to us as fresh inspirations, the method has been tried. It is, in fact, one of the first methods that is regularly tried whenever drama is getting ready for a rebirth. Aeschylus worked with it in his earliest days, before he had quite got hold of the nature of the theater and before Sophocles had helped him clear his head. A glance at the *Prometheus Bound* will turn up one character named Force, another named Power, and another named Oceanus. Mighty abstractions stalk one another, talk weightily at one another, in a play that has a certain majesty but is never majestically human.

Medieval drama took the same tack. The more ambitious playwrights of the period—those who were not content with coining little folk farces to be inserted into the Biblical narrative—drew themselves up to impressive height and wrote solemn homilies in which Death, Lust, Ambition, and Good Deeds contended for the soul of man. Man himself, however, did not put in a recognizable appearance until the stage was cleared of such august universals and given over to the specific spectacle of one foolish specimen cuckolding his neighbor, killing his wife, or picking his teeth.

Graham Greene, in his brief *British Dramatists,* has remarked that there is but a single step involved in getting from Ambition in a morality play to Macbeth in an Elizabethan play. It is, though, the step that makes all the difference.

The use of theatrical abstraction—nonexistent locales, symbolic characters, action that is to be understood not as an event taking place but as a hieroglyph requiring translation—does not represent a dramatic advance but a reversion to primitive stabs at importance. The mature dramatist invariably works in the concrete. The primitive dramatist often works in the abstract because abstraction is the easiest, crudest, roughest, most *approximate* way of saying something that is difficult to say.

It is, really, a lazy man's method. The dramatist stares—fondly enough—at the people he sees about him. He is aware that each is different from the other. He is also tantalized by the sense that each has something in common with the other.

These curious faces are alike and unlike at the same time. What makes one man different from another is easy enough to spot—not just by the shape of a nose or the drawl of a voice but by habits of thought and flareups of passion. What links these men together is much more difficult to see. We catch a glimmer of it now and then; but we can't name it.

Because human differences are readily detected, the playwright has no particular problem with uniqueness. He can simply keep book on the man he is interested in: jotting down his peculiar practice of picking at his trouser crease, his odd failures of memory, his idiosyncratic spurts of gaiety. When the dramatist has taken a sufficiently large inventory, he can add the items together and present us with an arresting "character."

The serious playwright may, however, be dissatisfied with this sort of "character." It will have its virtues: the figure is no mere cliché; it is painfully accurate. But it is, after all, a case study, a medical report. The sense of something larger —which is an actual sense keenly felt in life—is irretrievably lost. The idiosyncratic is too special; it seems stubbornly atypical, representative of nothing.

How to bring this throw-off back into the fold, give him some part in the common humanity we know he was born to? The dramatist's first temptation is not to look for this man's commonness *within* the unique personality that defines and identifies him, but outside it and apart from it. The logic goes something like this: the quality I miss so sorely is a quality that belongs not to this man alone but to a great many men, perhaps all men; my best bet, then, is to start with All Men, to take a kind of statistical average of so many men that the qualities they have in common may be justly determined; when I have located this bond, this commonness, by statistical means, I must project it in the manner in which I found it—by a character who is statistically representative, a composite, an abstraction.

Thus, if I wish to say something about the human instinct for friendliness, I dare not rest my case on the spectacle of one friendly man. So long as the man is merely unique, his friendliness may be an accident—the irrelevant result of his heredity, his basal metabolism. He may be friendly, all right, but he may not suggest that mankind as a whole is given—is almost driven —to kindliness. Since I am convinced that this last *is* true of the species as a whole, and wish to make use of the observation in my play, I promptly put Species on the stage. I do not draw a particular man who has the common instinct for friendship. I draw an outline of the instinct itself, devoid of all particulars. I do not call this instinct Philip Weinberg, since even a particular name might bog me down in unrepresentative specifics again; I call it Friend Ed.

In John Steinbeck's *Burning Bright*, Friend Ed talks like this:

> Now look, Joe Saul, you're nervous. . . . That's a new thing you're doing there. That's a nervy thing. . . . I've seen it coming on you, Joe Saul. It's no surprise to me except it's late. It's very late. I wonder why it is so late. Why, I remember when your Cathy died. You were strong when you lost your wife. You were not nervy then. And it's eight months since Cousin Will missed the net [the characters in the scene are, symbolically, acrobats]; you were not nervy then. Victor's a good partner, isn't he, you said he was. It's not the first time a Saul missed the net in all the generations. What's the matter with you, Joe Saul? You're putting an itch in the air around you like a cloud of gnats on a hot evening. . . . Do I have the right to ask a question? . . . Is there any trouble between you and Mordeen? . . . That's a fine girl, Joe Saul, a fine wife. . . . I'll take some of the itch from you if you'll let me. I held you weeping when your Cathy died. I lifted Cousin Will off the ring rim. I stood left-hand with you to Mordeen. I think I know your

sickness, but you'll have to say it first, Joe Saul. . . . Talk it out, Joe Saul. Let's find your poison.

I suppose we ought not to be surprised that a man who is not meant to be a man should be unable to talk like one. The playwright who is conceiving his characters generally is almost bound to write in generalities.

But what is essentially wrong with this is its ironic lack of universality. Since no one man ever talked like this, or behaved like this, it is difficult for us to believe that all men do. The struggle to be widely representative has ended in something that is utterly unrepresentative.

The difficulty is inherent in the method, which, like the case study it is opposed to, is a half method. The case study, relying solely on particulars, fails to catch that glimpse of the universal that haunts us in life. The abstracted universal, hoping to recapture the glimpse, wipes out the very particulars it came from.

Neither method produces first-rate drama because neither method faces up to the teasing, elusive simultaneity of nature. Of the two, the case-study technique, the accumulation of specifics, is far and away the better because it reproduces *some* of the conditions that confront us in life. The symbolic try reproduces none of them—not as we know them—and thereby leaves us appalled at its frigid inhumanity.

Life as we know it presents us with the universal *in* the particular. Brotherliness does not stroll the streets, to be run into as I turn a corner. Individual men stroll the streets—short, tall, mean-tempered or mild—and if any one of them should possess the quality of brotherliness I can come to know of it only by first coming to know the peculiar, particular man. I must meet him, formally. I must make tentative, awkward efforts at establishing communication. I must spar, waiting to find out if I like him enough to bother meeting him again. I must look at him carefully enough to remember him

—out of all the other thousands I meet—in the event that we do meet again. A second meeting over lunch will be only a little less gingerly. He is still essentially a stranger, a baffling complex of unpredictable attitudes, beliefs, sensitivities. I touch a sore spot, and shy away. I stumble on a sudden, happy point of agreement and develop it. I am often misled; what seemed agreement cannot be pursued too far and I am thrown back, stung and embarrassed.

He, of course, is all this time doing the same thing to me. We are both worming our ways through labyrinthine particularities—the things that make each of us individual and all but impenetrable—in the hope that, digging deep enough, we shall uncover similar qualities of mind. My acquaintance may, in the end, turn out to be Friendship itself. I never can, however, treat him as though that friendship were abstract, stable, or divorced from idiosyncrasy. I dare not trade on his friendliness or put it to too severe a test. I cannot keep him waiting in a bar unreasonably. I cannot push my praise for something he despises. I cannot say anything I like about his wife. I cannot suggest that he clean his fingernails. I cannot keep him up when he is tired. The price of our common liking is a common patience with much that is irritating, with much that is merely crotchety and fetishist and puzzlingly out of place.

After I have known him a long, long time, after I have practiced anticipating his moods, after I have learned to take barometer readings of his very special personality, I may venture to make generalizations about him. I may say now that he is essentially kind, or proud, or ambitious, or romantic. Even as I say it I have a certain sense of falsification—little contradictions leap to mind—and I hasten to qualify what I have said. ("Yes, he's proud, although not exactly in that way.") No one word is ever quite right, I am soon immersed in additional adjectives. But I can have a shot at it, anyway. I am entitled to try describing the general man because I know the particular man so intimately. Without this intimacy, of course, I have no credentials.

And as I describe the general man I have always at the back of my mind the precise cast of features, the explicit gestures, of the particular man. The validity of my generalization depends wholly upon the particular man's capacity to carry it. (Does the word *fit* him?) The moment I lose sight or sense of the face, voice, and physical weight of my subject, I begin—if I continue to generalize—to talk pompous nonsense. Any minute now I am going to be talking about the Common Man, that faceless fellow whom no one has ever met.

This, then, is our experience of life: from a mass of concrete details we arrive at a vague, not quite fenced-in, universal. We do not start, say, with a concept of Pride and then interview men to accommodate it. People who go looking for Friendship are people who never find it; we have all got to take our chances with Mildred, Fred, Frank, Barbara, and John.

I do not know John through the concept of Friendship. I know just a little about friendship through the actual existence of John.

If this is the routine that nature has imposed on us, and if drama is—as we are always saying it is—a matter of holding up the mirror to nature, the playwright's course is clear enough. He is an admirer of the concrete, a passionate addict of particulars. And he will hope, as he gains in intimacy, as he unfolds layer after layer of highly personal passion, to strike upon a root that looks familiar, to uncover at last a seed we have all noticed growing in our own gardens. When he has dug this deep, when he has worked his way down through all that exists and found something beneath it, he may lay claim to profundity. Profundity is not the result of seeing truth above and apart from the stubborn, finicky, flesh-bound body. It is the result of seeing through it.

Macbeth is plainly ambitious—so plainly that we haven't

the least doubt that Ambition is the theme of the play, that Ambition is the key to Macbeth's character, that Ambition in a morality play is only one step removed from the ambitious man here. But what a curious way to be ambitious! When Macbeth appears on the scene, he seems not to have given a moment's thought to his own advancement. When he is told that he is Thane of Cawdor, he does not leap at the possibility; he doubts it. When it is prophesied that he is to become king, he apparently dismisses it from his mind. When an opportunity presents itself to kill the king, he shrinks from it. When he has been all but forced into doing the deed, he is aghast at himself. When he finds himself on the throne, he is at once a model of insecurity. Never has an ambitious man been so pushed, shoved, coddled, bullied, terrorized, and artificially bolstered. There are many times in the play when you feel that this gentle knight would have been happy enough with a garden hoe and a game of chess in the evening (after prayers). Yet Macbeth *is* ambitious—in one, small, dark recess hidden far beneath the military integrity, the husbandly warmth, the moral scrupulousness, the nervous sensibility of the man there lies a kernel of ambition just big enough to overbalance him when the scales are properly tipped. There is, in Macbeth, just about as much ambition as there is in all the rest of us; barring outside pressures is there really more? On the face of things, Macbeth is one of the world's least likely candidates for Ambition's crown; and that is one of the reasons he is so interesting.

I doubt very much that anyone who had started out with the notion of dramatizing Ambition could have wound up creating this exasperating man. He does not possess the attributes—abstractly speaking—that we normally associate with the vice. He is not bold, he is not headstrong, he is not vain, he is not shrewd. Shakespeare does not seem to have adopted a generality and dressed it suitably. He seems to have thought of a person and found ambition in him.

Nor do I think that this is mere ingenuity on Shakespeare's part, that he succeeded in fooling us about his procedure. There are a few Shakespearean heroes whose universal traits may be quickly identified, whose counterparts might have been found in a morality play: there is Othello, of course, and there are—perhaps—Cressida, Angelo, Antony, and Shylock. (Wantonness, Hypocrisy, Lust, and Greed.) But there are so many others difficult to platitudinize about. Who has found the word for Lear? For Hamlet? For Romeo, for Cleopatra, for Brutus? There is universality in all of them, and we do not doubt it as we hear them speak. But it exists as an intuition, as a shadow in the eyes, as an echo imperfectly traced. It is there, but—as is so often the case in our own experience—it is not named.

We are seriously misled in our pursuit of the arts by the talk that goes on about symbolism. We find symbols everywhere, not just where the author has patently put them—not just in a Billy Budd or a Caliban—but in a Bottom, a Feste, a Huckleberry Finn. We discover that everything in a play or a novel stands for some aspect of the author's own thought and we love to distinguish and detach, as we might detach the wings from a fly, this generalized meaning.

The practice has its uses. They are, however, critical rather than creative uses. Let's say that I am a literary critic and wish to perform the literary critic's function of analysis. I may wish to analyze a certain work for various reasons. I may admire the work intensely and wish to dissect it in order to explain my own admiration to myself or to others. I may dislike the work and wish to dissect it in order to explain, and to justify, my dislike. I may break a work down into its isolated parts—or into some of them; I never succeed in getting them all—because I want to relate those parts to a social impulse that helped produce them, because I want to use them as the basis for a new aesthetic, or because I am by nature a critic and began taking watches apart at the age of two. (The critical mentality is an identifiable mentality, generally unrelated to the creative. I have twin sons to whom I show motion pictures: one of them wants only to take pleasure in the films, the other is uninterested in the films and wants only to examine the machine.)

The critic, bent upon examining a work not as an object of pleasure but as a machine that has produced a pleasurable effect, is forced to take a number of arbitrary actions. He must sever elements that are, in the work, inseparable and indivisible. (He must talk of Falstaff's worthlessness and his attractiveness in separate breaths, as though they were in fact distinguishable.) He must extricate Character from Situation, so that he can talk about Character and talk about Situation, though neither has ever actually existed apart from the other. Worst of all, he is forced to name every element he isolates, and this is where the real trouble begins.

He may be naming something that is, in the work and in the author's mind, nameless. T. S. Eliot suspects, for instance, that Shakespeare never did have any formal or objective concept of Hamlet's character, that he wrote out of a burning intuition he had never analyzed for himself. Or he may be giving a simple name to something that has no simple name. He may accept Greed as a symbol for Shylock. But Shylock is a pathetic figure, as much victimized as victimizing, the man who is so touching about his wife and so moving about his essential humanity ("Hath not a Jew eyes?"). What, then? Is Shylock a symbol of Victimized Humanity turned Vengeful? Is he an Impatient Job? Or is there some word, some phrase, that will successfully unite both the greed and the pathos—some word or phrase we have not found yet? We go on coining new names, trying them on for size.

It should be noticed, though, that in cases such as these it is the critic and not the playwright who has created the symbol. A vast amount of the discussion of symbolism we have heard down the ages is of this kind: we speak of the symbolism in a work and mean the symbolism that can be deduced from it.

There are other possibilities. In our struggle to name an elusive reality, we may come upon a word that has, at one time or another, occurred to the playwright but that has been abandoned or altered during the intricacies of composition. Scholars, for instance, have turned up some evidence that Shakespeare may have meant Romeo to symbolize Fury. There are many references to Fury in the play to support them —and Fury was a vice that the Elizabethans liked to talk about. But to accept Fury as the name for Romeo is to go against the grain of our experience of the play in the theater. Romeo does not seem a tragic figure possessed of a vicious flaw; he seems an idealized lover accidentally cheated of his happiness. The author may once have meant a certain symbol, and we may seize upon the symbol in the quiet of our libraries. But something has happened during the process of composition to alter the author's intention and to destroy the usefulness of our carefully assembled evidence. As any playwright will tell you, the process of putting true flesh and blood on an initial idea very often plays tricks with the idea. You can christen a baby but you can't always control its growth.

Then there are surely times when the critic's search for a symbolic word coincides quite satisfactorily with what the author has had in mind. No one is going to quarrel about the just word for Othello. (Well, some didacticists do; there are those who insist that Shakespeare was writing a tract on the perils of miscegenation, but I think we may safely pass on.) Even when we have all agreed, however, that the word Jealousy is an eminently suitable symbol to stand for the central quality in Othello, we still have not captured Othello. We weren't trying to capture him, of course; we were trying to kill him, in order to see what made him work. We are, as critics, always performing autopsies. We deliberately drain the blood from Othello in order to be able to deal with one of his dissected parts. The removal of blood, the clinical isolation of one or more lifeless members, has value for us: now that we have abstracted certain nameable qualities, we are able to use the abstractions in our critical discussions, in our technical laboratories. But we must always remember that we have made a sharp break with the character, and with the play, as they actually exist. We have left the created world and entered a hypothetical one. Even if our hypotheses are quite correct, we are breathing a different air. To suppose that a play can be written in this air, to usher these hypothetical qualities onto the stage under their abstracted and symbolic names, is to perform an autopsy in the theater.

The critic is a kind of philosopher, and he does use the philosopher's tools of hypothesis, abstraction, and symbol. The philosopher isolates a quality from its flesh-and-blood manifestation in order to be able to work with it in the study, without human interference and without that erratic tipping of the scales that occurs whenever the individual personality is taken into account. (A symbol is an arbitrary sign meant to stand for something absent.) The philosopher speaks of Catharsis, though we never *think* "catharsis" as we watch Lear die in the theater. The philosopher speaks of the Recognition Scene, though we never think "recognition scene" as we watch Hamlet become certain that Claudius has killed the King. The philosopher speaks of The Ideal Prince, though we do not think "ideal prince" as we watch Hal horse around with his low companions nor do we really think it even as we watch Hal bid Falstaff a curt good-by. All of these critical terms are accurate statements of values present in the plays. But they are statements after the fact. It is as though the plays had been drained of fact and left to hang sacklike in a drying air. The philosopher works—for good reason—with a fleshless universality. And he acquires—really, he was born with—an abstractive habit of mind.

This habit of mind is a habit ruthlessly opposed to the

creative artist's. One dissects; the other unifies. One examines part after part in antiseptic isolation; the other lets the parts walk together in their wholeness. The two habits of mind are such contraries that it is by now an old saw—to which we pay too little practical attention—that good critics never write good plays and that good playwrights never are good critics. Over the years a number of first-rate critical minds have turned their energies to creative work—Lessing and Dryden leap to mind as examples. But there is no mistaking the state of mind that was native, and fruitful, in each of these cases: we continue to read the criticism of Lessing and Dryden; we have long since stopped producing their plays. The difficulty of swapping one state of mind for another is given elaborate illustration in our own time by the career of Edmund Wilson. It has been possible to watch a genuinely distinguished critic write plays of disturbing naïveté: plays in which a sonorous gardener speaks with a Swedish brogue in one act, an Irish brogue in another, and then—at eleven o'clock and in a blinding spotlight—turns out to be Ahasuerus, the Wandering Jew. The theatrical innocence and theatrical ineptitude that mark these plays derive not from a mind that is essentially naïve but from a mind that is essentially critical.

Conversely, the true dramatist who gives himself over to abstract speculation or to the writing of plays out of an abstractive state of mind stumbles just as badly. *Camino Real* has been Tennessee Williams' most decisive failure. It is a play in which Kilroy, Don Quixote, Camille and a character known simply as A. Ratt struggle to gain Passports to a better world, attempt to board an airplane called *The Fugitivo*, and eventually march through an unlabeled archway to the cry of "The violets in the mountains have broken the rocks!"

The failure of the play need not puzzle us once we have read Mr. Williams' preface to it, his explanation of the theories that guided its composition. Mr. Williams says:

"I can't deny that I use a lot of those things called symbols but being a self-defensive creature, I say that symbols are nothing but the natural speech of drama. . . . I hate writing that is a parade of images for the sake of images; I hate it so much that I close a book in disgust when it keeps on saying one thing is like another; I even get disgusted with poems that make nothing but comparisons between one thing and another. But I repeat that symbols, when used respectfully, are the purest language of plays."

Mr. Williams has, in this instance, entered the world and adopted the tools of the philosopher-critic. He is analyzing his play at the same time he is writing it; or, rather, he is giving us the analysis without ever having written the play. A. Ratt is an analysis of a character, not a character. Furthermore, Mr. Williams is explicitly rejecting—as he must, if he is to be consistent—all those techniques of imagery that remind us of how things look, feel, smell, and actually are. A poet tells us that one thing is *like* some other thing in order to help us see it more exactly, to bring us closer to it. If a symbol is a handy sign meant to stand for something absent, an image is a handy picture of a thing meant to intensify its presence. The symbolist is always working away from reality, trying to grasp it in an arbitrary way; the imagist is always trying to worm his way back into it.

When a dramatist finds a symbol that pleases him, he has no doubt made his abstract meaning clearer to *himself;* but he has also destroyed all that might have been vivid or graphic for his audience. Mr. Williams inadvertently gives us a useful illustration:

"To take one case in point [in *Camino Real*]: the battered portmanteau of Jacques Casanova is hurled from the balcony of a luxury hotel when his remittance check fails to come through. While the portmanteau is still in the air, he shouts: 'Careful, I have—' and when it has crashed to the street he continues '—fragile—mementoes. . . .' I suppose that is a symbol, at least it is an object used to express as directly and vividly as possible certain things which could be said in pages of dull talk."

The symbol is clear enough, as Mr. Williams writes about it. It is even attractive enough—as a symbol. That is to say, I can examine and relish and approve the notion while I think about it, while I toy with it as an *idea*. The experience is intellectually profitable in a philosophical sense, in something of the same way that Plato's "cave" image is intellectually provocative.

But it has no power at all in the theater. Jacques Casanova has not been presented to me as a man but as a symbol of certain kinds of men. Therefore I have taken no interest in him as a man. I do not believe he has any mementoes, I do not believe that there is anything in the portmanteau. If I were told that there were real things in the portmanteau—I never am, of course—I should doubt it; or rather, I should begin to think of the other, abstract values these things were meant to stand for. Because there are no real things in the portmanteau, I have no apprehension about their crashing. When they crash, I am not moved. No matter what Casanova says, he cannot touch me—because he is not he, the mementoes are not mementoes, the crash is not a true crash. Nothing is broken except an idea; in the circumstances my heart cannot break.

By contrast, in the shoddiest play ever written an actress might convince me that she cares about a dress—a real dress, her own dress, the only dress she owns. The sound of its tearing—because I care for her and care for what she cares for—might distress me deeply. I might even—if I had a busy mind—deduce a certain symbolic value from the episode, later on. But what stirred me in the theater was my belief in the dress as a real dress, a concrete and possessible and desirable dress. I have believed in the desire, too, as a personal, particular desire.

Nor are we given any choice between plays of emotional identification and plays of abstract reasoning. The abstract play, intending to offer us an interesting thought to chew on, defeats its own specialized purpose. Because the people of the play do not engross us, the thought that might have sprung from their activities does not engross us, either. It is gratuitous, premature, cold: we are asked to take a speculative interest in someone we do not know, someone who has not even been carefully described to us. We cannot do it; we cannot summon the patience to deal with anything so remote, so hypothetical. In the theater, as in life itself, the brain must be reached through the senses.

And even when symbolic value may be quite justly deduced from a given play, the deduction does not describe the manner in which the play was composed, does not serve as a guide to future composition. An artist works in many ways. He may compose without any sort of conscious abstraction, interested only in a story or a situation or a character he has observed. He may compose with a shadowy abstraction at the back of his mind, half aware of the generalizations that might be made on the materials but principally interested in the concrete shape of the materials. He may—some writers surely have done this—begin with a crystal-clear abstraction and then make the prodigious effort involved in swinging clear around to the other side of the world and creating a genuine, dirt-rooted image that will safely grow toward the abstraction. This last is, I think, the most difficult method of all, heavily mined with booby-traps. The abstraction may continue to predominate, and the image will never come to life; the image may come to life and refuse to rise toward the abstraction. If, however, the artist is prepared, and talented enough, to undertake a complete transmutation of his initial idea—to start with a word and then make that word thrillingly present in the flesh, so present that the word is contained in the flesh and need no longer be spoken—then the method need not be ruled out.

What must be ruled out is the refusal to leave the study, the academy, the intellectual laboratory—the refusal to honor the flesh and to let the blood flow. The writer who is determined to offer his symbolic thinking just as he thinks it, to put his concepts on the stage in the form of precepts, becomes one of two things: he becomes vulgar or he becomes obscure. The bare bones of thought, when they are made utterly clear, have a habit of seeming simple-minded on the stage. The clear symbol is never complex enough to pass as a picture of life; the audience is offended at the unnatural simplicity that passes before it and dismisses the playwright—usually with laughter—as pretentious, platitudinous, and not quite bright. As George Meredith once said of Allegories, "To be of any value, [they] must be perfectly clear, and when perfectly clear, are as little attractive as Mrs. Malaprop's reptile."

The writer who anticipates this obvious—and hence vulgar—effect, and who does not want to be caught out as a rude and penny-plain philosopher, takes pains to conceal the too-easy outlines of his thought. He does not conceal it, though, by incorporating it in a valid and self-moving image. He conceals it by drawing a veil over it, by refusing to make his abstractions explicit. He is dealing only in names, but he will not name names. In this way he becomes obscure.

There is no escaping this two-pronged fate except through the living image of nature itself. The playwright of intellectual bent must of necessity exchange the technician's scalpel for the painter's brush.

I did not mean to be so literal about it, but here is Tennessee Williams' autopsy:

> *La Madrecita is seated; across her knees is the body of Kilroy. Up center, a low table on wheels bears a sheeted figure. Beside the table stands a Medical Instructor addressing Students and Nurses, all in white surgical outfits. . . .*
>
> INSTRUCTOR: This is the body of an unidentified vagrant.
> LA MADRECITA: This was thy son, America—and now mine.

INSTRUCTOR: He was found in an alley along the Camino Real.

LA MADRECITA: Think of him, now, as he was before his luck failed him. Remember his time of greatness, when he was not faded, not frightened.

INSTRUCTOR: More light, please!

LA MADRECITA: More light! . . .

[As the INSTRUCTOR dissects the body on the table, LA MADRECITA continues to keen over the body of KILROY. . . .]

LA MADRECITA: His heart was pure gold and as big as the head of a baby.

INSTRUCTOR: We will make an incision along the vertical lines.

LA MADRECITA: Rise, ghost! Go! Go bird! "Humankind cannot bear very much reality." (*At the touch of her flowers,* KILROY *stirs and pushes himself up slowly from her lap. On his feet again, he rubs his eyes and looks around him*). . . .

KILROY: Hey! Hey, somebody! Where am I? (*He notices the dissection room and approaches.*)

INSTRUCTOR (*Removing a glittering sphere from a dummy corpse*): Look at this heart. It's as big as the head of a baby.

KILROY: My heart!

INSTRUCTOR: Wash it off so we can look for the pathological lesions.

KILROY: Yes, siree, that's my heart! . . .

INSTRUCTOR: Look! This heart's solid gold!

KILROY (*Rushing forward*): That's mine, you bastards! (*He snatches the golden sphere from the* MEDICAL INSTRUCTOR. *The autopsy proceeds as if nothing had happened as the spot of light on the table fades out, but for* KILROY *a ghostly chase commences. . . .*)

GUTMAN: Stop, thief, stop, corpse! That gold heart is the property of the State! Catch him, catch the golden-heart robber! (KILROY *dashes offstage into an aisle of the theater.*

There is the wail of a siren: the air is filled with calls and whistles, roar of motors, screeching brakes, pistol-shots, thundering footsteps. The dimness of the auditorium is transected by searching rays of light—but there are no visible pursuers.)

KILROY (*As he runs panting up the aisle*): This is my heart! It don't belong to no State, not even the U.S.A. Which way is out? Where's the Greyhound depot? Nobody's going to put my heart in a bottle in a museum and charge admission to support the rotten police! Where are they? Which way are they going? Or coming? Hey, somebody, help me get out of here! Which way do I—which way—which way do I—*go! go! go! go! go!* (*He has now arrived in the balcony.*) Gee, *I'm lost! I don't know where I am!* I'm all turned around, I'm *confused!* I don't understand—what's—happened, it's like a—*dream,* it's—just like a—dream. . . .

It cannot be said that Mr. Williams writes badly even when he is busy cutting solid-gold hearts out of representative dummies. But his power to move us evaporates. This is a power that comes to him naturally enough when he is focusing on individual faces and on hearts that are not solid gold. Listen to the affected, well-meaning, overeager Alma Winemuller, in *Summer and Smoke,* speak to a man whose advances she has long ago rejected:

ALMA: Why don't you say something? Has the cat got your tongue?

JOHN: Miss Alma, what can I say?

ALMA: You've gone back to calling me "Miss Alma" again.

JOHN: We never really got past that point with each other.

ALMA: Oh, yes we did. We were so close that we almost breathed together!

JOHN (*With embarrassment*): I didn't know that.

ALMA: No? Well, I did, I knew it. (*Her hand touches his face tenderly.*) You shave more carefully now? You don't have those little razor cuts on your chin that you dusted with gardenia talcum. . . .

JOHN: I shave more carefully now.

ALMA: So that explains it! (*Her fingers remain on his face, moving gently up and down it like a blind person reading Braille. He is intensely embarrassed and gently removes her hand from him.*) Is it—impossible now?

JOHN: I don't think I know what you mean.

ALMA: You know what I mean, all right! So be honest with me. One time I said "no" to something. You may remember the time, and all that demented howling from the cock-fight? But now I have changed my mind, or the girl who said "no," she doesn't exist any more, she died last summer—suffocated in smoke from something on fire inside her. No, she doesn't live now, but she left me her ring—You see? This one you admired, the topaz ring set in pearls. . . . And she said to me when she slipped this ring on my finger—"Remember I died empty-handed, and so make sure that your hands have *something in them!*" (*She drops her gloves. She clasps his hand again in her hands.*) I said, "But what about pride?"—She said, "Forget about pride whenever it stands between you and what you must have!" (*He takes hold of her wrists.*) And then I said, "But what if he doesn't want me?" I don't know what she said then. I'm not sure whether she said anything or not—her lips stopped moving—yes, I think she stopped breathing! (*He gently removes her craving hands from his face.*) No? (*He shakes his head in dumb suffering.*) Then the answer is "no"! . . .

Or compare John Steinbeck in cosmic mood with John Steinbeck in earthy mood. This is a conversation, in *Burning Bright*, between a man who is afraid he cannot have a child and the friend in whom he confides:

JOE SAUL (*Moving tensely. . . .*): A man can't scrap his blood-line, can't snip the thread of his immortality. There's more than just my memory, more than my training and the remembered stories of glory and the forgotten shame of failure. There is a trust imposed to hand my line over to another, to place it like a thrush's egg in my child's hand. You've given your blood-line to the twins, Friend Ed. But I . . .

FRIEND ED: Maybe you should go to doctors. There might be remedy you haven't thought of.

JOE SAUL: What do they know? (*Sitting, his head going down into his hands.*) There is some kind of dark curse on me and I feel it.

FRIEND ED: On you alone, Joe Saul? Do you feel singled out, pinned up alone? It's time we sing this trouble out into the air and light, else it will grow like a cancer in your mind. Rip off the cover. Let it out. Maybe you're not alone in your secret cave.

JOE SAUL (*Looking up calmly*): I know. I guess I'm digging like a mole into my own darkness. Of course, Friend Ed, I know it's a thing that can happen to anyone, in any place or time. And maybe all these have the secret locked up in loneliness. . . .

There is loneliness and friendship in *Of Mice and Men*, too, but it reads like this:

GEORGE: There's beans enough for four men.

LENNIE (*Sitting on the other side of the fire, speaks patiently*): I like 'em with ketchup.

GEORGE (*Explodes*): Well, we ain't got any. Whatever we ain't got, that's what you want. God Almighty, if I was alone, I could live so easy. I could go get a job of work and no trouble. No mess . . . and when the end of the month come, I could take my fifty bucks and go into town and get whatever I want. Why, I could stay in a cat-house all night. I could eat any place I want. Order any damn thing.

LENNIE (*Plaintively, but softly*): I didn't want no ketchup.

GEORGE (*Continuing violently*): I could do that every damn month. Get a gallon of whiskey or set in a pool room and play cards or shoot pool. (LENNIE *gets up to his knees and looks over the fire, with frightened face.*) And what have I got? (*Disgustedly*) I got you. You can't keep a job and you lose me every job I get!

LENNIE (*In terror*): I don't mean nothing, George.

GEORGE: Just keep me shovin' all over the country, all the time. And that ain't the worst—you get in trouble. You do bad things and I got to get you out. It ain't bad people that raises hell. It's dumb ones. (*He shouts.*) You crazy son-of-a-bitch, you keep me in hot water all the time. (LENNIE *is trying to stop* GEORGE'S *flow of words with his hands. Sarcastically*) You just wanta feel that girl's dress. Just wanta pet it like it was a mouse. Well, how the hell'd she know you just wanta feel her dress? How'd she know you'd just hold onto it like it was a mouse?

LENNIE (*In panic*): I didn't mean to, George!

GEORGE: Sure you didn't mean to. You didn't mean for her to yell bloody hell, either. You didn't mean for us to hide in the irrigation ditch all day with guys out lookin' for us with guns. Alla time it's something you didn't mean. God damn it, I wish I could put you in a cage with a million mice and let them pet you. (GEORGE'S *anger leaves him suddenly. For the first time he seems to see the expression of terror on* LENNIE'S *face. He looks down ashamedly at the fire, and maneuvers some beans onto the blade of his pocket-knife and puts them into his mouth.*)

LENNIE (*After a pause*): George! (GEORGE *purposely does not answer him.*) George?

GEORGE: What do you want?

LENNIE: I was only foolin', George. I don't want no ketchup. I wouldn't eat no ketchup if it was right here beside me.

GEORGE (*With a sullenness of shame*): If they was some here you could have it. And if I had a thousand bucks I'd buy ya a bunch of flowers.

The difference between the two passages is very much a difference of words. One is crammed with "blood-line," "immortality," "darkness," "loneliness," "dark curse," "glory," and "the forgotten shame of failure." The other is crammed with "beans," "ketchup," "fifty bucks," "whiskey," "pool room," "cat-house," "that girl's dress," "a mouse," and a "bunch of flowers." The choice of words in each case stems from a habit of mind: the one is general, and the words remind us of nothing that is real; the other is specific, and the words crackle. The abstract habit of mind is so overwhelming that when an image intrudes—the "thrush's egg" or the "mole"—it seems absurdly out of place. Indeed when anything specific intrudes —say, Friend Ed's suggestion that Joe see a doctor—there is a clash of styles and an impulse to mirth. Here is the clash again:

MORDEEN: . . . I am aching to get on with birth. My baby is crowding for the light. My mind . . . my body are driving toward birth.

VICTOR: Sit down, Mordeen.

Abstractions do not have to sit down. And the world of the theater *is* a world of chairs and tables, of getting up and sitting down.

This is not to say that we are once more committed to the dreary catalogue of total realism. In taking account of the concrete universe, there is no need to take inventory. It is still possible to cut away a thousand irrelevant details and to cut through to that one detail, that one bristling image, that will summon up all the rest.

The break with exhaustive "realism" does not require a break with reality, a flight into the symbolic stratosphere.

There is no breathing in the stratosphere, and the play that is most certain to fail is the play that announces itself as follows:

> ACT ONE: Anywhere. The day the hydrogen bomb fell.
> ACT TWO: That evening.

16. *All That Is Spoke Is Marred*

IN ONE WAY, realism has made it easy for the playwright. It has relieved him of the obligation of writing his speeches.

In the dim and dusty past, from which no traveler seems to have returned, it was customary for the dramatist to develop an emotion through the medium of language. If a character felt passion of one kind or another, he was expected to communicate the passion in passionate words. If a principal figure was about to die, he breathed his last at some length, and with some literacy:

> Soft you; a word or two before you goe:
> I have done the State some service, and they know't:
> No more of that. I pray you in your Letters,
> When you shall these unluckie deeds relate,
> Speake of me, as I am. Nothing extenuate,
> Nor set downe ought in malice.
> Then must you speake,
> Of one that lov'd not wisely, but too well:
> Of one, not easily Jealious, but being wrought,
> Perplex'd in the extreame: Of one, whose hand
> (Like the base Indean) threw a Pearle away
> Richer than all his Tribe: Of one, whose subdu'd Eyes,
> Albeit un-used to the melting moode,
> Drops teares as fast as the Arabian Trees

Their Medicinable gumme. Set you downe this:
And say besides, that in Aleppo once,
Where a malignant, and a Turbond-Turke
Beate a Venetian, and traduc'd the State,
I took by th' throat the circumcized Dogge,
And smote him, thus.
 (*Led.* Oh bloody period.)
 (*Gra.* All that is spoke, is marr'd.)
I kist thee, ere I kill'd thee: No way but this,
Killing my selfe, to dye upon a kisse.
 (*Dyes*)

Othello must be feeling something as he stares at the dead Desdemona, as he at last grasps the treachery of Iago, as he reaches for a dagger to end his own life. The playwright assumed that this feeling—all of it—must be expressed.

It was the habit of earlier theaters to regard verse as the natural language of the arts, prose as the natural tool of the sciences. The virtue of prose was that it could make explicit, define exactly. Law, medicine, and philosophy needed such a tool. The virtue of verse was that it could, through imagery and rhythm, touch all the secret things that never can be made explicit. An art that meant to move its audiences, rather than train them in the fact-finding processes, needed poetry.

The abandonment of poetry came about through an excess of common sense. They were a reasonable bunch, those middle-class merchants and hardheaded bankers of the English eighteenth century. Kings didn't matter so much any more, and they wanted plays about clerks in the counting-houses. But clerks in the counting-houses didn't speak verse. (Neither did kings, for that matter; nobody seems to have noticed the fact.) It was time for the playwright to sober up, get down to business, pay attention to what was going on around him, and stick to the truth.

England got its first prose tragedy in 1731. George Barnwell, in Lillo's *The London Merchant*, had been a clerk in a counting-house but an untrustworthy one. With his mistress Millwood, he is being led to the gallows:

> OFFICER: Make way there; make way, and give the prisoners room.
>
> LUCY: They are here: observe them well. How humble and composed young Barnwell seems! but Millwood looks wild, ruffled with passion, confounded, and amazed.
>
> BARNWELL: See, Millwood, see, our journey's at an end. Life, like a tale that's told, is passed away. That short, but dark and unknown passage, death, is all the space between us and endless joys, or woes eternal. . . .
>
> MILLWOOD: Encompassed with horror, whither must I go? I would not live—nor die—That I could cease to be—or ne'er had been!
>
> BARNWELL: Since peace and comfort are denied her here, may she find mercy where she least expects it, and this be all her hell! From our example may all be taught to fly the first approach of vice: but if o'ertaken,
>
> By strong temptation, weakness, or surprise,
> Lament their guilt, and by repentance rise.
> Th' impenitent alone die unforgiven:
> To sin's like man, and to forgive like Heaven.
>
> LUCY: Heart-breaking sight!—Oh, wretched, wretched, Millwood!
>
> TRUEMAN: How is she disposed to meet her fate?
>
> BLUNT: Who can describe unutterable woe?

I have clipped a big middle stretch out of this passage, and it's only fair to tell you that George and Millwood do express themselves extensively, in the same sort of language that is quoted. The playwright has not yet given up his right to sound off. You'll notice, too, that verse is not something to be ditched in a hurry. The words may be more commonplace than those Marlowe used, but the old rhythms keep ringing in the ear, pushing against the prose like a cataract against a dike. The itch becomes, in fact, intolerable—and George Barnwell cannot let his spirit go without first singing out a quatrain. (And quite a bad quatrain it is: how shall it now be good?)

But there are more important things to keep an eye on: for the future, anyway. Lucy, for instance, has quite a bit to say; and what she says tends to describe, from the outside, a passion we may not be able to tease from the inside. Millwood's final speech is quite lifelike; the girl is gasping and stammering, turning this way and that, working herself up to a splendid incoherence. And Blunt's remark is crucial: who indeed could describe unutterable woe? Well, Aeschylus, Sophocles, Euripides, Racine, Marlowe, Kyd, Shakespeare, Webster, Ford, and a fair number of others could have—and did. The theater in general has always gone along on the assumption that unutterable woe was utterable. Uttering it seemed more or less the theater's business. But author George Lillo is a shade self-conscious. He senses that, for all his fidelity to the speech of men, something has been left unsaid. His little confession is the signature of realism.

For in life, after all, people don't get things said, especially when they are dying or otherwise preoccupied. They breathe heavily, make false starts, forget what they had in mind, run off at tangents, become distracted, and at last lapse into a merciful confusion.

By 1753, or roughly twenty years after *The London Merchant*, playwrights were getting a good grip on the new technique. Edward Moore knew how gamblers die:

> Lend me your Hand, Love—so—raise me—No—'twill not be—My life is finish'd—O! for a few short Moments! to tell you how my Heart bleeds for you—That even now, thus dying as I am, dubious and fearful of Hereafter, my Bosom

Pang is for your Miseries. Support her Heaven!—And now I go—O, Mercy! Mercy!

Among other things, the dash is coming into its own.

And the character would still *like* to have had a few moments to tell his sister how he feels, but somehow or other the moments are not vouchsafed him. We shall never know the things locked in his heart.

The nineteenth century? We like to think of the nineteenth century as quite a purple period. We remember Little Eva dying and we imagine a riot of heart-rending rhetoric. Do you know what Little Eva said as she lay dying? Here is the entire scene:

(EVA *discovered on a couch.—A table stands near the couch, with a lamp on it. The light shines upon* EVA'S *face, which is very pale.—Scene half dark.*—UNCLE TOM *is kneeling near the foot of the couch.* OPHELIA *stands at the head.*—ST. CLARE *at the back.—Scene opens to plaintive music.—Enter* MARIE, *hastily.*)

MARIE: St. Clare! Cousin! Oh! what is the matter now?

ST. CLARE (*Hoarsely*): Hush! She is dying!

MARIE (*Sinking on her knees, beside* TOM): Dying!

ST. CLARE: Oh! if she would only wake and speak once more. (*Bending over* EVA.) Eva, darling!

EVA: (*Uncloses her eyes, smiles, raises her head and tries to speak.*)

ST. CLARE: Do you know me, Eva?

EVA (*Throwing her arms feebly about his neck*): Dear papa! (*Her arms drop and she sinks back.*)

ST. CLARE: Oh, heaven! this is dreadful! Oh! Tom, my boy, it is killing me!

TOM: Look at her, mas'r. (*Points to* EVA.)

ST. CLARE: Eva! (*A pause*) She does not hear. Oh, Eva! tell us what you see. What is it?

EVA (*Feebly smiling*): Oh! love! joy! peace! (*Dies.*)

Eva turns out to have been a girl of few words, too weak, really, to ramble on. St. Clare does rather better:

> ST. CLARE: I was wrong, Tom, very wrong, to neglect it. I may be the cause of much suffering to you hereafter. Marie, my wife—she—oh!—
>
> OPHELIA: His mind is wandering.
>
> ST. CLARE (*Energetically*): No! it is coming *home* at last! (*Sinks back*) at last! at last! Eva, I come! (*Dies.*)

And Uncle Tom does better still:

> Don't call me poor fellow. I *have* been a poor fellow but that's all past and gone now. I'm right in the door, going into glory! Oh, Mas'r George! *Heaven has come!* I've got the victory! the Lord has given it to me! Glory be to His name! (*Dies.*)

But *Uncle Tom's Cabin* is something less than a lather of words. Playwrights of the nineteenth century made a number of remarkable labor-saving discoveries. One of them was the interrupted line:

> "You have heard me assert your guilt: Dare you as solemnly assert your innocence?"
>
> "I dare, but—"
>
> "Swear then."
>
> "To need such a test is—"
>
> "Swear, I say!—"
>
> "Count, if you refuse—"
>
> "Refuse?—Be patient! I obey."
>
> "Silence!" (*A dead pause.*)

(I haven't made this up. It is from Monk Lewis' *Adelmorn the Outlaw.*)

The pleasant thing about an interrupted line, of course, is that the playwright doesn't have to write out what the character might have said if he hadn't been interrupted. He doesn't even have to *know* what the character might have said.

Another discovery was the pause, variously known as the dead pause, the long pause, or the expressive pause. The point of the pause is obvious enough: it may somehow or other imply feeling that is not actually contained in the lines. Let a silence fall, and no word be spoken. The word that is not spoken is a word that does not have to be written; the dramatist is relieved of a tiresome duty; and the effect is extraordinarily lifelike.

Most felicitous of all, though, was the dramatist's discovery of the stage direction. You may have noticed the number of parenthetical signposts that pop up by the time of *Uncle Tom's Cabin.* If I have counted correctly, Little Eva's death throes embrace exactly one hundred words of stage direction to sixty-nine words of dialogue. I don't know what the corresponding proportions would be in, say, the later plays of William Gillette, but I suspect the spoken word would be found in even greater retreat.

Having learned the arts of verbal suppression, the nineteenth-century playwright arrived at a kind of literary shorthand:

> PAUL (*Aside*): And Diane!—Is she there?—I must see! (*Starts, stops.*) No, No!—They would know me; the hour is not up!
>
> CARRAC: You, Citizen Gouroc?—I don't believe it.
>
> GOUROC (*Holding out papers*): Here are our credentials.
>
> CARRAC: They may be forgeries.
>
> MOB: Aye—forgeries! forgeries!
>
> CARRAC (*To the* MOB): Silence! While we proceed in our examination. (*The* MOB *utters low murmurs.* CARRAC *turns to* NANETTE.) Who are you?
>
> NANETTE (*Advancing defiantly*): I am Citizeness Nanette Potin.
>
> POTIN (*Aside*): My wife!—(*Sneaks behind comrades.*)

CARRAC: Ha, wait! (*Seeing* DIANE, *he drags her forth.*) By the gods!—here's a feast for Jupiter himself—Speak out, delicious wench, and tell us who you are.

DIANE: I am Diane—

GOUROC (*Interrupting quickly*): She is Diane Gouroc. (*Pointing at the* DUKE): His daughter and my wife.

PAUL (*Exploding*): Liar! (*All start and turn toward* PAUL, *who speaks aside.*) God help me!—I forget; the hour is not ended.

CARRAC: Who is it calls this citizen a liar?

GOUJON: The prisoner.

CARRAC: Ah, ha! It seems he knows these citizens.—In the name of the law and the Republic, I summon instantly as a witness Henri de la Rochejacquelin.

DIANE: My cousin captured? (*All turn toward her, amazed.*)

GOUROC (*Starting*): My God!—We're lost!

CARRAC: So—the prisoner is the beauty's cousin. (*To* GOUROC): Traitor! You have lied!—This convicts you all.

MOB: To the guillotine!—To the guillotine!

BOURDOTTE: No! A marriage! A Republican marriage!

MOB: Aye! A marriage! A marriage! (BOURDOTTE *drags forth* NANETTE.)

NANETTE: What are you going to do?

BOURDOTTE: Tie you to this man and throw you in the river.—That's the way we marry Royalists! (*The* MOB *laugh mockingly.*)

NANETTE (*Shrieking*): Help!

POTIN (*Exploding*): Damnation!—Tongue or no tongue, I must save her. (*Bounds forward and frees his wife.*) Nanette!

NANETTE (*Joyfully embracing* POTIN): Dodolphe?

CARRAC: What does this mean? . . .

What this means is that the spoken word has lost all functions save one: it is still of some slight use in conveying scraps of essential information. It may identify characters; it may telegraph situations; it may tell us what time it is—and that's about all. The passage is from a highly regarded play of 1887, Steele Mackaye's *Paul Kauvar.*

In general, we don't think of ourselves as writing in the manner of George Lillo, Edward Moore, Monk Lewis, George L. Aiken (whose version of *Uncle Tom's Cabin* is quoted here), or Steele Mackaye. And, of course, we have made certain idiomatic advances since 1877. But have we altered the basic style?

Eugene O'Neill killing off a character in the Pulitzer Prize play for 1920:

> ROBERT (*in a voice suddenly ringing with the happiness of hope*): You mustn't feel sorry for me. Don't you see I'm happy at last—free—free!—freed from the farm—free to wander on and on—eternally! (*He raises himself on his elbow, his face radiant, and points to the horizon.*) Look! Isn't it beautiful beyond the hills? I can hear the old voices calling me to come—(*Exultantly*) And this time I'm going! It isn't the end. It's a free beginning—the start of my voyage! I've won to my trip—the right of release—beyond the horizon! Oh, you ought to be glad—glad—for my sake! (*He collapses weakly.*) Andy! (ANDREW *bends down to him.*) Remember Ruth—
>
> ANDREW: I'll take care of her, I swear to you, Rob!
>
> ROBERT: Ruth has suffered—remember, Andy—only through sacrifice—the secret beyond there—(*He suddenly raises himself with his last remaining strength and points to the horizon where the edge of the sun's disc is rising from the rim of the hills.*) The sun! (*He remains with his eyes fixed on it for a moment. A rattling noise throbs from his throat. He mumbles.*) Remember! (*And falls back and is still.* RUTH *gives a cry of horror and springs to her feet, shuddering, her hands over her eyes.* ANDREW *bends on one knee*

beside the body, placing a hand over ROBERT'S *heart, then he kisses his brother reverently on the forehead and stands up.*)

ANDREW (*Facing* RUTH, *the body between them—in a dead voice*): He's dead. (*With a sudden burst of fury.*) God damn you, you never told him!

RUTH (*piteously*): He was so happy without my lying to him.

ANDREW (*pointing to the body—trembling with the violence of his rage*): This is your doing, you damn woman, you coward, you murderess!

RUTH (*sobbing*): Don't Andy! I couldn't help it—and he knew how I'd suffered, too. He told you—to remember.

ANDREW (*stares at her for a moment, his rage ebbing away, an expression of deep pity gradually coming over his face. Then he glances down at his brother and speaks brokenly in a compassionate voice*): Forgive me, Ruth—for his sake—and I'll remember—(RUTH *lets her hands fall from her face and looks at him uncomprehendingly. He lifts his eyes to hers and forces out falteringly.*) I—you—we've both made a mess of things! We must try to help each other—and—in time—we'll come to know what's right—(*Desperately*) And perhaps we—(*But* RUTH, *if she is aware of his words, gives no sign. She remains silent, gazing at him dully with the sad humility of exhaustion, her mind already sinking back into that spent calm beyond the further troubling of any hope. The curtain falls.*)

For the record, the passage quoted contains two hundred and sixty-three words of stage direction to one hundred and ninety-six words of speech. There are twenty-eight dashes. Some of the dashes indicate realistic gasps within completed constructions. Others—approximately twelve, I'd say—indicate thoughts left unfinished. The diction itself does not represent a notable advance over that used by Uncle Tom.

By means of the stage direction, the dash, the pause, and

the interruption we continue—in the twentieth century—to mirror the inarticulate surface of life magnificently. People stammer in crises; we stammer. People flush and fall silent; so do we. Under pressure, people utter not powerful revelations of the state of their hearts, but the first halting words that come into their heads; we have learned the trick. But in respecting whatever is inarticulate in nature, we have finally—inevitably—become inarticulate ourselves.

We are unable now to express the simplest emotion. We can organize a few words that might, or might not, be used by someone feeling the emotion; but we cannot write the emotion itself.

Let's say that a character is being left behind by someone she loves. She is wretched, but she is weak; she can only wring her hands and wistfully inquire if her lover is going. I may, if I am a conscientious playwright, give some attention to this girl's feelings. I may try to write a line that has a certain weakness in its rhythm, a certain helpless sorrow in its words. This will, of course, be difficult; truly evocative writing is never a simple chore. I may chew at my pencil, or xxx out a great many false starts on my typewriter, struggling to create a phrase that says "Are you going?" but says it in such a way that regret and ineffectuality are present in the words.

I do not have to struggle for very long, though. Under the new dispensation the creative process has been expedited. I may, at any time, abandon the struggle as unnecessary and even unnatural, and simply write what has always been in my head:

"Are you going?"

Then, with a flourish, I whip out a parenthesis and add:

"(*Piteously*) Are you going?"

I have done my work and am off to lunch with a clear conscience.

Furthermore, I can use the line in my next play. In my next play some other character will be leaving; this time, however, he is off to England on a Fulbright grant, and his adoring companion is delighted for him. So I write:

"(*Thrilled*) Are you going?"

I have picked up a knack that will do me for years. Play after play tumbles from my typewriter:

"(*Angrily*) Are you going?"

"(*Sullenly*) Are you going?"

"(*Impatiently*) Are you going?"

"(*Slyly*) Are you going?"

At the end, of course, I will never have composed a piteous, thrilled, angry, sullen, impatient, or sly line. But why should I, when I need only tell the actor how to lend color and force and even meaning to what I have jotted down? And I am left with a delicious advantage. Should, by some mishap, my play fail or never seem to communicate quite the touching or rousing sensations I meant it to have, I can justly complain that the actor has not played it properly. "Are you going?" should have been read very movingly, I can say. I am in an excellent position all round.

The "realistic" playwright has shrewdly learned, over the long years since poetry passed away, how not to write a play and how *to* write friendly little letters to the actor. Pick up any play written in the twentieth century and you will be bombarded with emotions enclosed in parentheses. Take away the parentheses and you are likely to feel nothing at all; you will be lucky if you can grasp what the play is about.

Let's reread Andrew's curtain speech from *Beyond the Horizon* with the parentheses left out:

"Forgive me, Ruth—for his sake—and I'll remember—I—you—we've both made a mess of things! We must try to help each other—and—in time—we'll come to know what's right—And perhaps we—" (*Curtain*).

The tongues of the world are tied these days. "And perhaps we—" means a little bit more when (*desperately*) is placed in front of it. But I'm not sure that it means much more. O'Neill, unlike the majority of his contemporaries, really intended to become a dramatic poet, really hoped that his words would sing. Yet in the short passage quoted earlier he found it necessary to fall back on (*Exultantly*), (*Mumbles*), (*With a sudden burst of fury*), (*Piteously*), and, at the last, (*Desperately*). The essential content of the scene, its very coherence, is confined to the author's parenthetical remarks.

That is where our talent goes now: into the parentheses. We are no longer interested in the resources of language; we are fascinated by the wonderful devices by which language can be circumvented. In one way or another, we have made the evocative word superfluous.

Our habits are pretty well fixed.

We write:

"Should you—?"

(*Pause*)

"No."

and hope that some very kind actors will make the moment rich and warm.

Aware that feeling is called for, we shyly pass our impotence on to the character:

"How do I feel? I don't know, honestly. . . . Isn't that always the way? You feel something terribly, you want to shout it from the housetops, and then—then—there just aren't any words. I feel . . . well . . . I just feel, that's all."

(Geraldine Page will make this very touching for us.)

And always we write:

"(*Significantly*) It is five-fifteen."

These habits are going to be hard to break. The playwright is not going to be eager to part with such handy household helps. The right to leave a sentence unfinished is precious; the pause has a certain undefinable appeal; the mid-sentence dash makes for charming elisions; the parenthesis is great fun to type.

The playwright is apt to resist, too, the notion that any of his dodges is an actual defection from duty. They constitute, he will tell you, one or another form of subtlety. (*Piteously*) is not a substitute for some quality missing in the line; it is an additional shading, a grace note, a refinement not possible to the coarse syntax of dialogue.

I know of no subtler or more curious interplay of opposed emotions than that to be found in Octavius Caesar's reaction to the news of Anthony's death. Anthony has been his enemy; the news comes suddenly. Shakespeare does not say that Caesar pauses.

> The breaking of so great a thing, should make
> A greater cracke. The round World
> Should have shooke Lyons into civill streets,
> And Cittizens to their dennes. The death of Anthony
> Is not a single doom, in the name lay
> A moiety of the world. . . .
> Looke you sad Friends,
> The Gods rebuke me, but it is Tydings
> To wash the eyes of Kings. . . .
> Oh, Anthony,
> I have followed thee to this, but we do launch
> Diseases in our Bodies. I must perforce
> Have shewne to thee such a declining day,
> Or looke on thine; we could not stall together
> In the whole world. But yet let me lament
> With teares as Soveraigne as the blood of hearts,
> That thou my Brother, my Competitor,
> In top of all designe; my Mate in Empire,
> Friend and Companion in the front of Warre,
> The Arme of mine owne Body, and the Heart
> Where mine his thoughts did kindle; that our Starres
> Unreconcilable, should divide our equalness to this.

I suppose that you could dress this up with parenthetical prompt notes: (*Stunned*), (*Shaking his head*), (*Softly*), (*Re-*

gaining his composure), (*Sternly*), (*Fiercely*), (*Bitterly*), (*Philosophically*), (*Warmly*). You would be collecting excrescences, though. The speech does not ask for artificial hearing aids.

As a matter of fact, it defies them. There is no parenthesis you can add that does not degrade and limit the speech. The delicate juxtaposition of antithetical emotions is sustained throughout the speech; it *is* the speech. The contrasted thoughts move with swift and supple invisibility in and around and through the words, through all the words at once; it is impossible to say where one emotion ends and the other begins; the values are not parceled into the speech, still less are they wrapped and tied for immediate delivery. The words move as the emotion moves, they are born of it. (They cannot be vitamin-enriched later.) The language itself is alive, and any attempt to categorize its parts must kill it.

The parenthesis is admissible only when content is absent, as in our own theater. When content is present, the parenthesis merely insults it.

It is, of course, a convention to pretend that Octavius Caesar, at that unexpected moment in time, should have been able to organize his reactions so swiftly and to express them so superbly. But what an attractive convention to have inherited! The twentieth-century playwright has inherited a somewhat different one: the pretense that dashes and spaces and silences can stand for all that Octavius felt.

Shakespeare had no tradition of parenthetical shorthand. (*Dyes*) was about all that was permitted him. He was undoubtedly lucky in being forced to make the words do the work.

And I suspect that we might improve twentieth-century drama quite suddenly, and quite considerably, by the simple expedient of strapping every playwright to a chair and insisting that he complete at least one play that contained no (*Pause*), no ——, and no (*Crying a little*).

17. *Worst Foot Forward*

IT HAS BEEN CURIOUS, and not at all edifying, to watch the theater attempt to deal with its competition during the past thirty years or so. Along about 1920 the motion picture began to inherit the theater's disaffected masses, and, until quite recently, it has held the attention of those masses with Svengali-like power.

During the long reign of the film as undisputed box-office champion, the stage seemed able to respond in only two ways: (a) by straining every backstage nerve to become as much like the motion picture as possible; (b) by sitting down and crying about it.

The second response—a plaintive whimpering that the whole thing was simply unfair—needn't concern us. It didn't move the theater one way or another. It didn't move any hearts, either; self-pity never does.

But the first response, which had at least the merit of being an active one, was a king-sized mistake. Producers and playwrights looked at the screen and decided—not altogether wrongly—that its spellbinding qualities lay in its ability to leap, with the speed of lightning, from realistic locale to realistic locale. The screen could change its solid backgrounds in the bat of an eye; the stage, if it hoped to stay in business, had better be able to do likewise.

There followed a field day for the craft unions. Plays popped up in a dozen different sets: all of them solid, all of them painted with a canny respect for the film-trained eye. To keep them flowing, to let one follow another with breath-taking rapidity, wagon stages were rolled right and left, upstage and down, finally jackknifed for maximum speed; turntables were built and merrily spun; what couldn't be mounted on a wagon or double-mounted on a revolving disk was dropped from the wings and dovetailed below with split-second timing and daredevil skill. Nor was it necessary to drop a curtain while all this was being done; stagehands could manage it in the dark. Legend has it that one stagehand, crawling on his belly to clear stage before the lights went up, lost his way and lighted a match; but this sort of thing didn't happen very often. Generally one image disappeared as the lights dimmed down and, in something less than thirty seconds, another and equally substantial image rose into view. The audience, sensing the dangers involved from the size of the racket going on in the dark, gasped appreciatively.

It was a mock gasp, though. It really said "Isn't it wonderful what they can do, considering that they really can't do it?" For the effort was doomed.

It was doomed not simply because it was prohibitively expensive, or because most of the plays being written didn't really call for so much scenery. (One play, not too long ago, made use of one complete setting for the back seat of a taxicab and another complete setting for the front seat of a taxicab. The producer, asked why he wasn't taking the show out of town, snarled "Tour it? We can't even lift it!")

The effort was doomed because no matter how fast the stage jumped it still couldn't jump as fast as the film. The theater was competing in a league where it was automatically outclassed. Money could be spent; but the competitive image couldn't be met.

It is never wise to battle a competing medium in terms of what it can do best; it is much shrewder to offer, by way of competition, what you can do best.

There was one thing the screen never could do best: speak. This inability did not derive from any momentary lack of literary talent (the screen, at its richest, was in a position to buy up all the first-rate literary talent on the market). Nor did it derive from any lowbrow notion held by the makers of films that audiences could not grasp words of more than one syllable.

The silence—or comparative silence—of the screen was an inherent condition of the medium. The function of the moving-picture camera is to take moving pictures; the function of the moving-picture actor is to do something that will keep the picture moving; the function of the moving-picture director is to assemble his separate moving images in such a way that they will continue to move in relation to one another.

The wholly silent film was not, as film, inferior to the talkie. There are those who hold it to have been superior—an argument we won't go into. (We will go into it just far enough to point out that the silent screen seems to have been hospitable to the development of genius in a way that the talking screen is not; Chaplin, Keaton, Fairbanks, Garbo, Ford, Murnau, and Flaherty were all born under the sign of silence.) The ideal silent film was held to be a film with very few subtitles; Chaplin's sparse, blunt signposts were admired not for their expressiveness but for their brevity. Murnau made his reputation with a titleless film.

I once became curious about the decline of the motion picture during the late twenties. It seems there had been a brief period thereabouts when the distress signals were up. I got hold of a number of top-budget, name-star items of the period and ran them for myself. They were visually static and clotted with long, conversational subtitles. The essential content of the film was being conveyed on the titleboards; and an industry staggered.

The first flush of the talking film found words momentarily dominant. Speech was popular on the screen so long as it was novel on the screen. But the motion picture as such did not recapture its quality until microphones became flexible enough to follow the camera; to rerun an early talking film is to rerun an intolerable talking film.

Proportions were quickly restored: the visual image dominant, the verbal image a terse accessory. The good motion picture of today remains a cut-and-flash unreeling of meaningful pictures (the recurring railroad tracks, the clock, the deserted street of *High Noon*) helped along the way by verbal fragments but depending not at all upon these fragments for basic excitement.

As the stage imitated the screen, so the screen has, on one occasion or another, imitated the stage. The screen has, for instance, engaged in a running flirtation with Shakespeare. The sodden failures—*A Midsummer Night's Dream, Romeo and Juliet, The Taming of the Shrew*—are irrelevant here. But the semi-successes are very much to the point. Laurence Olivier's *Henry V* was a limited success, financially and aesthetically. By offering it to a specialized public under specialized conditions, the producers were gradually able to earn a profit. And the specialized public found much to admire in it. There were one or two moments that were interesting as Shakespearean speech, the St. Crispin's Day passage being the most effective of these. There were several soliloquies, so compromised by the camera that we were required to listen to them on a sound track the while we watched Olivier's immobile face from assorted angles—a practice that resulted in a maddening, two-headed bid for our attention. And there were, at the top of the film, magnificent mobile shots of an army roaring to battle. These last were the film's best scenes, as they were bound to be; they had nothing to do with Shakespeare and they had nothing to do with speech.

Shakespeare's greatest excitement was in his words; the film's is in the motion of its pictures. To put the two together is to declare war; one or the other will win out. The Shakespearean film will be a good film insofar as it succeeds in destroying, or at least circumventing, Shakespeare's method. Insofar as it respects that method it must cripple itself as film. The Houseman-Mankiewicz *Julius Caesar* offered the screen an excellent reading of the play, carefully photographed. One may be grateful to the producers for making such a reading available (the stage, at this time, could not have afforded the cast). But one cannot honestly assign the result a place alongside *The Informer* (a tattered poster being blown along a foggy street, a pocketful of coins falling to the floor, a hand losing its grip on a window ledge) or, for that matter, the lowliest two-reeler Chaplin made for Mutual (Chaplin examining a clock with a stethoscope, two dozen thugs dancing in and out of an alley).

The root difference between the two media lies in the manner in which they make their images. The screen makes its principal images by picturing them. The stage makes its principal images by speaking them. Each has an alternate method —the stage may have visual appeal, the screen a measure of literacy; but the alternate method is a subordinate method and the health of either medium will depend on its keeping its proportions in order.

The difference between the two ought not to be a crippling difference to either. Introspection, for instance, is possible to both. The screen is not, by its obligation to move, condemned to thoughtlessness. The camera may show, in a series of flashed images, what a character is thinking. The stage is not, by its physical limitations, condemned to stasis. It has words with which to make everything fluid.

The fluidity of the screen is visual, the fluidity of the stage verbal. Yet, when it came to do battle for the public dollar, the stage never seems to have considered fighting the battle on its own terms. It seems not even to have noticed that it held in its hand a weapon the screen dared not pause to use. It thought only—and very bitterly—of the intoxication of pictures; it forgot all about the intoxication of words.

Words can intoxicate an audience. To this day a kind of race memory keeps alive the moment when Marlowe first stunned a bunch of Elizabethan illiterates with a sledge-hammer music they had never heard before. They went to the theater one day expecting to hear the academic iambics of the *Gorboduc* tradition; they were confronted instead with a flashing cataract of words and came reeling from the playhouse gloriously drunk. The majestic thunders of *Tamburlaine* had burst about them, and, as J. R. Sutherland has remarked in his contribution to Phyllis Hartnoll's *Oxford Companion to the Theater*, they "could never again be content with the homelier rhythms of an earlier drama." An audience has but to hear the best to insist on it.

The English critic Kenneth Tynan, who is rather favorably disposed to our prose theater and inclined to be suspicious of any projected return to verse, points out that even Molière, nurtured on prose, turned to verse for his best work. Mr. Tynan is a bit rueful over Molière's decision, ascribing it to the tyrannous hand of tradition. But we cannot escape the fact that Molière, turning to verse, did then write his best plays. The fact is that every major serious play—and the lion's share of the comedies—that we cling to out of the past are verse plays. Three hundred years of prose have done well enough by the novel, beautifully by history and biography; they have left the theater grunting like an underprivileged child.

Verse is simply more pliable than prose, and for a form as swift and compact as the theater extreme pliability is wanted. The novel may, and does, take its time; the theater must have everything over and done with in two and one half hours. I may play along with Proust—or with Dickens or Tolstoi or Joyce—for hundreds of pages while, stealthily, a vast number of statements are added toward a composite image. (Very great novels are, characteristically, very long novels.)

The novelist writes: "Gradually my agitation subsided. Albertine was on her way home. I should hear her ring the bell in a moment. I felt that my life was no longer what it might have become, and that to have a woman in the house like this with whom quite naturally, when she returned home, I should have to go out, to the adornment of whose person the strength and activity of my nature were to be ever more and more diverted, made as it were a bough that has blossomed, but is weighed down by the abundant fruit into which all its reserves of strength have passed. In contrast to the anxiety that I had been feeling only an hour earlier, the calm that I now felt at the prospect of Albertine's return was more ample than that which I had felt in the morning before she left the house." (That's Proust—in translation, which hurts, but Proust.)

Try: "The shadows began now to descend larger from the high mountains; the feathered creation had betaken themselves to their dinners, and the lowest order to their suppers. In a word, the clock struck five just as Mr. Jones took his leave of Gloucester; an hour at which (as it was now midwinter) the dirty fingers of Night would have drawn her sable curtain over the universe, had not the moon forbid her, who now, with a face as broad and as red as those of some jolly mortals, who, like her, turn night into day, began to rise from her bed, where she had slumbered away the day, in order to sit up all night. Jones had not traveled far before he paid his compliments to that beautiful planet, and, turning to his companion, asked him if he had ever beheld so delicious an evening?" (Fielding)

Or: "The boy stirred, and smiled in his sleep, as though these marks of pity and compassion had awakened some pleasant dream of love and affection he had never known. Thus, a strain of gentle music, or the rippling of water in a silent place, or the odour of a flower, or the mention of a familiar word, will sometimes call up sudden dim remembrances of scenes that never were, in this life; which vanish like a breath; which some brief memory of a happier existence, long gone by, would seem to have awakened; which no voluntary exertion of the mind can ever recall." (Dickens)

Compare, for the rapidity with which the image is made:

"Night's candles are burnt out, and jocund day
Stands tiptoe on the misty mountain-tops."

We often think of verse as a rather roundabout way of saying something. It isn't. It is the fastest way of saying something provided that the thing to be said is difficult to say, provided that it is not a plain and literal statement of fact. Prose can say "He went to the door" more rapidly and succinctly than verse can. It cannot say "My way of life is fall'n into the sere, the yellow leaf" faster than verse can. (Rewrite the "yellow leaf" line in the manner of Proust and you will quickly see what I mean.)

The prose passages above are all—or at least two of them are—attractive even as excerpts. In the strictest sense, however, their effects are circuitously arrived at. Because prose is a tool devised for factual precision, it can arrive at imagistic evocation only by placing fact after fact after fact until some composite whole begins to gleam in the distance. The writer must, to crib a line from Zola, "pile fact upon fact until some degree of truth shall have been arrived at."

Thus the passages quoted are made up of dozens of separate statements of fact on the order of "Gradually my agitation subsided," "Now the highest order of mortals were sitting down to their dinners," "The boy stirred, and smiled in his sleep," "Albertine was on her way home," "The clock struck five just as Mr. Jones took his leave of Gloucester," "I should hear her ring the bell in a moment." Twenty or thirty of these put together will, in time, present a picture or begin to pierce a heart; but it is building with bricks.

There will be, in the process, a natural resistance to imagery. I begin to write "I felt that my life was no longer—" and instead of using a color word I add "what it might have become." I begin to write "the calm that I now felt at the prospect of Albertine's return was—" and instead of directly describing the sensation I add "more ample than that which I had felt in the morning before she left the house." I shy steadily from the illogical word combinations that are the magic of verse (night has no candles, really, and day is not itself jocund nor capable of standing on tiptoe). I wipe my feet, dry my pen, and keep reasonable control of my tongue.

There will be, in the same process, a sobriety in my choice of single words, and I shall be able to turn to the writing of committee reports when my creative fire has subsided. I shall write, in fact, that "my agitation subsided," giving neither the agitation nor the subsiding any value beyond the dictionary definition of the terms used. I shall write "to the *adornment* of whose *person* the *strength* and *activity* of my *nature* were to be ever more *diverted.*" Or "the shadows began now to *descend larger* from the *high* mountains." Or "as though these marks of *pity* and *compassion* had awakened some *pleasant* dream of a *love* and *affection* he had never known." I shall speak of "compassion" but give no immediate effect of compassion, speak of "adornment" but suggest no breath-taking bauble, say that mountains are "high" but give no sense of their height. Eventually, of course, I will summon up a vivid reality out of all this. But it will be a long-term process. I will let my sensations slip in, you might say, after the fact.

And, in the end, prose will have its images, too. Each of the passages quoted above contains at least one sample of the breed. Halfway through the paragraph from Proust there is a "bough that blossomed"; Fielding has his "dirty fingers of Night" and his red-faced moon; most of the Dickens excerpt is devoted to the "rippling of water" or "the odour of a flower."

But there are several things to be said about prose imagery. One of them is that its use must be sparing. The essential structure of prose is not imagistic but literal; to cram images into a prose passage with anything like the reckless liberality of verse is to produce that intolerable prose-poetry with which we are all familiar.

It will be noticed, also, that the neighboring prose casts a curious flatness over the occasionally introduced image. The image itself, if it is to feel at home, must not be too far removed from the commonplace. Aside from Fielding's "dirty fingers of Night"—you might almost know that Fielding had spent time in the more urgent and more graphic theater—we can do no better than the bare "bough that blossomed," the generalized "odour of a flower," the amorphous "sudden dim remembrances of scenes that never were." In none of these is there a genuine attempt to *create* an image; there is only a halfhearted attempt to borrow on the memory of one, to make almost footnoted reference to another kind of writing and another kind of reader experience. As images, they are not only extraordinarily simple; if they were to appear in a poem, they might seem simple-minded.

Indeed the best prose imagery is apt to have a deliberate air of flatness about it, an air of honestly belonging to a blunt and laconic context:

"The red sun was pasted in the sky like a wafer."

Stephen Crane's chapter ending slaps us in the face with such sting partly because it *is* an image following a context that has been carefully kept barren, partly because the words of the image belong to that same mundane, day-by-day diction that characterizes the novel as a whole. "Pasted" is a perfect word; its force here comes from the fact that it is a prosaic word.

Verse, by contrast, is lively language, language in a hurry, language that does not care what syntactical dust it kicks up so long as it is free to somersault right to the point. It is not necessary to plunge into the wonderfully reckless toss-and-tumble of Dylan Thomas to see its nature:

> It is Spring, moonless night in the small town, starless and bible-black, the cobblestreets silent and the hunched, courters'-and-rabbits' wood limping invisible down to the sloeblack, crowblack, fishingboat-bobbing sea.

It is only necessary to listen to:

Let the bloat king tempt you again to bed,
Pinch wanton on your cheek, call you his mouse,
And let him, for a pair of reechy kisses
Or paddling in your neck with his damned fingers. . . .

In these last four lines a lifetime of lust is made unbearably graphic. Now watch a character, so complete that no detail need be added, being carved out in six lines:

". . . And what's her history?"
"A blank, my Lord. She never told her love,
But let concealment, like a worm i' the bud,
Feed on her damask cheek; she pined in thought.
And with a green and yellow melancholy
She sat like patience on a monument,
Smiling at grief."

Or try to keep pace with the incredible hurry of:

Stand still, you ever-moving spheres of Heaven,
That time may cease, and midnight never come;
Fair Nature's eye, rise, rise again and make
Perpetual day; or let this hour be but
A year, a month, a week, a natural day,
That Faustus may repent and save his soul!
O *lente, lente, currite noctis equi!*
The stars move still, time runs, the clock will strike,
The Devil will come, and Faustus must be damned.
O, I'll leap up to my God! Who pulls me down?
See, see, where Christ's blood streams in the
firmament . . . !

Verse communicates its meaning more rapidly not because it is rhythmic—the rhythm is an empathic force producing emotion in us more rapidly—but because the word relationships are free of logical restraint. There is no such thing as a "green and yellow melancholy" and in prose I should be hard put to justify the shorthand; I should probably say of the girl that "she seemed more downhearted than she had before." (In the contemporary theater I would say "Helen hasn't been herself lately; is she depressed about something?")

Nor is "paddling in your neck" an altogether reasonable construction. Canoes are paddled. By analogy, fingers might be paddled in a pond, though "plashed" or "splashed" would be more appropriate words. To make the image in prose I should also have to make the logical connection, writing, perhaps, "as I lay beside her, my fingers moving idly against the nape of her neck, I remembered a day on the river, a day when I had paddled idly and rhythmically until it was time for lunch; it was like that now."

Verse is a wonderful excuse for skipping connections. (Notice the way the "paddling" passage plunges passionately ahead, hurling "bloat" and "wanton" and "reechy" and "paddling" pictures at the onlooker.) Verse is also a wonderful means of *making* connections—connections of an unpredictable, apparently irrational, shiningly intuitive sort.

Indeed the connections of verse imagery are not so much connections as collisions. Unlikely and unrealistic combinations of words come together with a crash, showering sparks in all directions. T. S. Eliot writes:

"The yellow smoke that rubs its muzzle on the window panes
Licked its tongue into the corners of the evening. . . ."

Or:

"The worlds revolve like ancient women
Gathering fuel in vacant lots."

Or:

"Miss Nancy Ellicott
Strode across the hills and broke them. . . ."

Or:

"His laughter tinkled among the teacups. . . ."

For the theater—and, most unexpectedly, for the theater of 1950—Christopher Fry writes:

> All right! You've done your worst. You force me to tell
>   you
> The disastrous truth. I love you. A misadventure
> So intolerable, hell could not do more.
> Nothing in the world could touch me
> And you have to come and be the damnable
> Exception. I was nicely tucked up for the night
> Of eternity, and, like a restless dream
> Of a fool's paradise, you, with a rainbow where
> Your face is and an *ignis fatuus*
> Worn like a rose in your girdle, come pursued
> By fire, and presto! the bedclothes are on the floor
> And I, the tomfool, love you.

The effective words in a verse line do not normally belong to one another. Miss Nancy Ellicott, a single woman, is not capable of "breaking" hills by simply walking over them. Smoke may have been granted tongues before, but from what vaporish dog has it acquired a muzzle? To suggest that the evening has corners is to outrage the visible universe.

Yet clarity—clarity swift and clarity absolute—comes from these lunatic mismatchings. A vision sharper and more precise than that possible to the precise tool, prose, has been granted us. Elaborate non-sense has brought us closer to concrete truth than strict sense could have. Have we ever known anyone more rapidly or more accurately than we now know Nancy Ellicott?

Verse gets at the truth by being untruthful, gives us our strongest sense of factual reality when it is most perversely destroying it. Verse is, in the Platonic eye of the logical realist, mischievous, irresponsible, indifferent to law, and contemptuous of order.

And to have it—in the theater or elsewhere—we must be

prepared to throw over law and order—that sober law and order that places one sturdy prose foot down after another sturdy prose foot. There are, I think, no really successful half measures. Prose and verse are two radically different methods of dealing with the universe. One adds the correct figures, and gets a sum. The other throws cabbages and kings onto the same scale, and gets a song.

The effort of the prose mind to arrive at verse without jettisoning its characteristic management of words and its characteristic sequences of thought leads to that dry and despairing "poetry" which marked Eugene O'Neill's *Lazarus Laughed:*

> Laugh! Laugh!
> Fear is no more!
> There is no death!
> There is only life!
> There is only laughter! . . .
> Laugh! Laugh!
> Fear is no more!
> Death is dead!

This is, as you will have noticed, still prose. The only change that has taken place is that O'Neill is now writing bad prose.

The effort to retain the shell of prose, while partially filling it with a kind of deviled poetry, does not so much enrich the final product as turn it indigestible. Here is George Tabori, in *The Emperor's New Clothes*, slipping a soupçon of verse imagery and a dash of verse rhythm into a prose format:

> Suddenly he got up and came towards me. Now he was after the last thing—no longer facts, or information: he wanted silence; the universal hush of conformity. DID YOUR SON TELL THE TRUTH? Did he? What did the child say, Bella? I tried to remember and saw his prophets' world of courage and goodness. I saw myself with his eyes—not a dog begging for a bone, but a man, Bella, a man enamored of the

moon. I heard his small voice: "Liar! Liar!"—Oh, but it roared in my ears like thunder, "STAND UP! DON'T BE AFRAID! LOOK AT HIM, LOOK!" and I looked, Bella, and saw this policeman through a child's eyes, too—I saw him naked, Bella, quite naked, divested of uniform, power and glory, just a plump little man who thought he was emperor. (*He rises.*) DID YOUR SON TELL THE TRUTH? (*In utter joy and triumph*): My son said I was good. I AM good. My son said I was brave. I AM brave; but what's this, who is this who wants to break me, remake me, unmake me, who the hell does he think he is, asking me again and again and again, "Did your son tell the truth? Did he, did he, did he?" (*Roaring*): YES! YES! (*Now his left fist, crushed and mangled, a bloody handkerchief around it, shoots out of his pocket, banging the table like a hammer.*) Yes, yes, yes—

Verse does not surrender its values piecemeal. The successful playwright is going to be candidly word-drunk, like Christopher Fry:

Girl, you haven't changed the world.
Glimmer as you will, the world's not changed.
I love you, but the world's not changed. Perhaps
I could draw you up over my eyes for a time
But the world sickens me still.

or he had best be candidly word-sober like Arthur Laurents:

"What would you do if I were unfaithful?"
"Kill you. No. Kill her and maybe you . . . Die, I guess."
"It wouldn't mean I didn't love you."
"It'd mean you didn't love me enough."
"Then I guess I don't love you enough."

Since these two ways of dealing with words are so spectacularly different, and since the shift from one to the other involves the destruction of one set of mental habits and the undoubtedly painful creation of another set, why urge the return to verse upon the already badgered playwright? No one is seriously urging the novelist to return to the verse epic, from whence he sprang. Why not leave the dramatist contentedly putting his sentences in order in the same commonsense way that the novelist does?

For one reason, because the novelist has been doing so much better at it. The past three hundred years have seen a great many major novels placed on the permanent bookshelf. The same three hundred years have seen very few plays—of the very few, most are comedies—so honored. The novelist has had the time and the space to make his effect in prose; the dramatist has not.

The novelist himself, turning to the stage, has invariably discovered his special effectiveness slipping away from him. Henry James labored long to capture the theater; but prose dialogue could not capture the James who had so many other prose weapons to work with.

Dialogue is a single, limited, terrifyingly compact tool. Take away from James the freedom to make a thousand objective statements about the thoughts, feelings, and behavior of a character—quite apart from such things as the character may actually say—and you have taken away an indispensable share of the sensitivity, and even of the understanding, James has to offer. Dickens, denied his circuitous effects and reduced to dialogue, became as baldly rhetorical as the nineteenth-century melodramatists we despise.

Confine any novelist to dialogue, and let that dialogue stand as prose, and you cannot escape this dimensional shrinkage. Graham Greene has recently attempted the theater, with relative success; yet the language of his play, *The Living Room,* is, alongside the language of his five or six best novels, noticeably defective in color and suppleness. When Mr. Greene turns to the theater he automatically takes on something of the flat and twangy accent of the prose theater.

Dialogue cannot assume the burden of three or four other tools unless, in some fairly radical way, it has itself become richer. If dialogue is to do double, triple, quadruple duty, it had best fatten itself, flex itself, find new and exhilarating sources of strength. The theater is, perforce, limited to this single literary tool; if it is to compete at all with other literary forms, it had best develop its one tool toward maximum power.

The theater labors under another, most peculiar, obligation: it must sustain an uninterrupted intensity. The novelist's intensity rides a gentler, more protracted rhythm, moving in long, slow swells and allowing for occasional calms. One rarely reads a major novel at a single sitting; nor is the novelist under any real pressure to give his language this sort of compulsive urgency. The dramatist, on the other hand, never dares relax the compulsive power of his words. Attention must be riveted at once, fixed so firmly that not a single auditor will ever go wool-gathering, and held at top pitch until the experience is concluded. The elongated rhythms and common-sense words of prose are not adequate to so electric a task; it has always taken the verbal fury of headlong verse to bring it off. Images must explode in my face (Shakespeare's explode so rapidly that we have trouble, syntactically speaking, tracking them all down). Words must flash into color, and keep changing color; rhythms must rush toward eleven o'clock. My ear must be continuously dazzled if I am not to turn it away before this pell-mell work is done.

Verse is constructed, by nature, to save the dramatist time and to bind the auditor fast. Its most characteristic power, however, is neither its surface hurry nor its stunning attack on the senses. The chief virtue of verse is its capacity for working in depth. Verse is able to descend into those recesses of personality and experience for which we have no adequate rational labels, to mine the soul of man for whatever is inexplicable about him. Verse goes, in quite a literal sense, where there is no prose.

Scholars have been trying to reduce Hamlet to prose for hundreds of years; no one has done it. Hamlet remains a mystery—that strangest of all creations, a clear mystery. We have no trouble with Hamlet when we are listening to Hamlet, only when we are listening to other people. Hamlet's secret thoughts touch our secret responses, and it is the imagery of verse that has flown between us. It is the business of prose to dispel secrets; it is the business of verse to keep them, thrillingly.

Verse, with its odd talent for giving to words far more than their literal meaning, has access to mysterious regions in which prose can only perspire and make clumsy approximations, to mysterious regions which the photograph cannot penetrate at all.

In its recent competition with the powerful screen, then, the stage had not only a weapon that might have matched the screen's fluidity. It had a weapon that might always have bested the screen's emotional power. There is no such thing as photography in depth; a picture cannot record more than meets the camera's eye. A succession of cannily related shots can suggest an impression of depth, can burrow by implication a few inches beneath the surface; but it cannot dig so deep as a brilliantly related succession of words can. Words are subtler than pictures, more flexible than pictures, capable of connoting a greater complexity than pictures. Inventively combined, they can cut closer to the heart's core; an imagined contest between the finest film ever made and the finest play ever written must inevitably end in victory for the play, by virtue of its verbal profundity.

But during its thirty-year struggle with the screen the stage never used its most distinctive tool at all. Just as it had given ground to the novel by speaking only as the novel spoke, without having the novel's other advantages, so it now gave ground to the screen by speaking only as the screen spoke, without having the screen's other advantages. The stage has been, so to speak, "out of character" the whole time.

I suspect that until it does learn to use its most distinctive tool it will continue to give ground to each new medium that comes along.

18. *Verse in Rehearsal*

IT ISN'T DIFFICULT to convince young playwrights that verse is the theater's natural vocabulary. I spent some years teaching playwriting and I had only to rattle off a little lecture about the glories of the poetic past to bring out in my students a rash of rhythm and imagery. The only trouble was that practically all of the plays were terrible.

And they were terrible not because they were structurally inept or psychologically immature, but because they were written in verse. You can do a talented young man a serious disservice in urging verse upon him; it might be kinder, all things considered, to cut his throat.

A drama critic, reviewing a recent volume of doggerel, found himself liking the poetry precisely because it was bad poetry. The author, this critic explained, was "perhaps the only poet (alive or dead) for whom I could honestly say a kind word; I was born with an inbuilt aversion to anything that is long hair."

This sounds, no doubt, like philistinism. But it isn't. It is the candidly expressed attitude of a man who has been exposed to the contemporary theater's occasional stabs at verse drama and found them stupefying.

They are, for the most part, stupefying. The stupefaction

begins long before the finished play finds its way to an unwary stage. It is a mental climate, a blanketing fog, a soft and padded and boneless unction that settles over the dramatist from the moment he decides that he is actually going to work in verse. Working in verse does mean walking into a new world; so far as the contemporary theater is concerned, it means walking into a somnambulist's world.

The world of verse, as we see it, has nothing to do with the coarse, tough, tinderbox scratch of ordinary life. It belongs instead to the limpid land of conscious, indeed self-conscious, Literature, to an alien country in which drowsy artifice has replaced down-to-earth actuality.

The causes for our attitude toward verse, and for the very real experience of such verse as we get, are many. There is the long-standing alienation of the poet—any sort of poet—from his more practical brethren. There is the excessively private and introverted universe into which the outcast poet has quite naturally retreated. There is the further separation of such poets as have survived from the day-to-day operation of the theater. There is the haughtiness of the poet, the deafness of the audience, the mutual recrimination that makes rapport impossible. There is the overpowering sense of strangeness that comes from all estrangement; and the best-intentioned labors toward a verse drama carry this sense of strangeness with them as awkward and crippling excess baggage.

Verse is not now written for the theater instinctively; when it is written at all, it is written deliberately. And deliberation is death.

Maxwell Anderson, let's say, deliberates on the desirability of verse and decides in favor of it. But Mr. Anderson, as a contemporary dramatist, has no natural habit of verse speech. He concludes that it will be necessary to borrow one. The Elizabethan habit is the best habit we have yet had in English; ergo, he borrows that one:

So now little Miriamne will go in
and take up quietly where she dropped them all
her small housewifely cares.—When I first saw you,
not a half-hour ago, I heard myself saying,
this is the face that launches ships for me—
and if I owned a dream—yes, half a dream—
we'd share it. But I have no dream. This earth
came tumbling down from chaos, fire and rock,
and bred up worms, blind worms that sting each other
here in the dark. . . .

The habit of another time has gone to sleep with the time. Nor can a drowsy form be jolted awake by an occasional jazz note in the content:

. . . My body turns
as if you were the sun, and warm. This men called love
in happier times, before the Freudians taught us
to blame it on glands. Only go in
before you breathe too much of my atmosphere
and catch death from me.

To hear the difference between the dead rhythms of the Elizabethan age, and the rhythms that are actually alive in our own age, one need only listen to the twentieth-century conversation of a Kenneth Fearing:

All right, I may have lied to you, and about you,
  and made a few pronouncements a bit too sweeping,
  perhaps, and possibly forgotten to tag the bases
  here or there,
And damned your extravagance, and maligned your tastes,
  and libeled your relatives, and slandered a few
  of your friends,
O.K.,
Nevertheless, come back.

Come home. I will agree to forget the statements that
you issued so copiously to the neighbors and
the press,
And you will forget that figment of your imagination,
the blonde from Detroit;
I will agree that your lady friend who lives above us
is not crazy, bats, nutty as they come, but on
the contrary rather bright,
And you will concede that poor old Steinberg is neither
a drunk, nor a swindler, but simply a guy, on
the eccentric side, trying to get along.
(Are you listening, you bitch, and have you got this
straight?)

Or, for something less obvious, hear the unmistakably authentic accent of W. H. Auden's simple:

"Stay with me, Ariel, while I pack."

Verse is of no value whatever unless, like every other part of the play, it mirrors the picture people have of themselves, echoes the rhythm with which they walk down a street or get up from dinner. Writing verse is almost like taking the blood-pressure of an age.

But a number of practicing poets who have, with great accuracy, taken the blood-pressure of their age have attempted the verse theater without winning the day for the cause. They have written good verse, but bad plays; or they have written curiously interesting plays which still failed to suggest that the theater was likely to give verse any permanent home.

Auden himself put several youthful years into the effort, and some of the fragmentary effects were hopeful. In *The Ascent of F 6* an angry son is accusing his mother of having always preferred his brother James. The mother answers, in specious but persuasive tones:

. . . Michael,
There is a secret I have kept so long
My tongue is rusty. What you have said
I knew and I have always known. Why do you start?
You are my Michael and I know my own:
A mother has no heaven but to look.
That was your secret; there is also mine:
From the good day when both of you were born,
And I first held you both in my two arms,
James, bigger, prettier, the doctor's pride,
Responding promptly to the nurse's cluck,
And you, the tiny, serious and reserved,
I knew your natures. You never knew your father:
But I can never see James toss his head
Or laugh, or take a lady's arm, but I
Must see your father in his popular pulpit.
Everyone thought your father wonderful
And so did I, until I married him
And knew him for a shell: James is like him.
He cannot live an hour without applause.
No one can say that I have stinted it.
But you, you were to be the truly strong
Who must be kept from all that could infect
Or weaken; it was for you I steeled my love
Deliberately and hid it. Do you think that it was easy
To shut you out? I who yearned to make
My heart the cosiest nook in all the world
And warm you there for ever, so to leave you
Stark to the indifferent blizzard and the lightning?
How many nights have I not bit my pillow
As the temptation fought to pick you out of bed
And cover you with kisses? But I won.
You were to be unlike your father and your brother,
You were to have the power to stand alone;
And to withhold from loving must be all my love.

After three or four plays, though, Mr. Auden's attack crumpled. T. S. Eliot has been less willing to quit. Mr. Eliot's earliest plays, *The Rock* and *Murder in the Cathedral,* were frankly lyrical, designed not for commercial performance but for specialized, semiliturgical use. Both contain extended stretches of magnificent verse. The music of *Murder in the Cathedral* proved so irresistible, in fact, that it eventually had what amounted to a commercial success, playing some seven hundred performances in a small London theater; it has since been successfully revived. It remains, however, a literary offshoot of the drama—or rather, a dramatic offshoot of another kind of literature—and offers no tempting pattern for the workaday playwright.

Stimulated by the popular response to what was actually poetry, but at the same time aware of the too specialized form in which *Murder* had been cast, Mr. Eliot now set about making his peace with the practical theater. *Murder in the Cathedral* had been, as much as anything, a choral work; the next play would deal with human figures in a contemporary environment. The play, *The Family Reunion,* did not succeed. The verse did not have that rude clarity needed to advance a story across the stage; the contrast between the difficult speech and the mundane setting proved troublesome; something was awry.

Mr. Eliot's subsequent work as a dramatist has been a steady, almost ruthless, process of pruning away a native lyricism in favor of a blunt conversational style. With *The Cocktail Party* success seemed in sight. But with *The Confidential Clerk* the worst has happened: the values of verse have been lost, the values of drama have not been seized.

The contemporary theater must be deeply grateful to Mr. Eliot for two reasons. He has kept the *idea* of serious verse drama alive, lent his weight to it. He has also shown such respect for drama, and for the production conditions that are peculiar to drama, that he has been willing to strip himself of his finest feathers to accommodate it. The loss of melody is terribly real; since melody is one of Mr. Eliot's greatest gifts, one can only gasp in admiration at the size of the sacrifice.

Gratitude, however, cannot conceal the fact that the sacrifice has been in vain. Mr. Eliot will, after all, be remembered for his lyric poetry, not for his plays. And the plays will not, in all likelihood, have spurred on the imitators who might give us a body of practical drama in verse.

Why not? Essentially, I think, because Mr. Eliot *is* a lyric poet, not a dramatic one. The two kinds of poet have much in common; yet each begins his work in a unique and untranslatable instinct. The fact that a play may have certain lyric qualities does not make it, at root, a lyric work; the fact that a lyric poem may, on occasion, have something like dramatic power does not transfigure it, formally or effectively, into a play. Coleridge, Shelley, Keats, Byron, Browning, Wordsworth, Southey, Landor, and Tennyson all wrote verse plays. The plays had so little survival value in the theater that the very announcement of their existence comes as a surprise today.

It should be possible to distinguish between the lyric and the dramatic instincts in a number of ways: we might call attention, say, to the natural brevity of the lyric impulse and contrast it with the sustained intensity that is required of the dramatic; we might point out that a lyric poem ceases to be a lyric and tends to become a ballad or an epic the moment it tackles a complex narrative, whereas the feeling for complex narrative is essential to the most rudimentary dramatic form. I think we might best and most fairly summarize, though, by saying that the lyric mood is a passive mood, the dramatic mood an active one.

The lyric poet is—or gives the impression of being—gently airborne, swept aloft on a current that is sudden, sensual, and single. He is a man exposed, open to such breezes as blow about him, acted upon by agents outside himself, content to record the subtle, affective state so produced; the experience will be short, elusive, submissive.

The dramatic poet, by contrast, is a man on a journey of exploration, committed to finding his way over difficult terrain; he will scuff the earth to see what he stands on, thrust his head forward in search of some sort of track, reach for a knife to slash at the tangle ahead of him. He is making a path, forging ahead under his own power, working toward a destination. Tranquillity may be his when the journey is ended; he is not tranquil now. He is not so much moved by the universe as moving ruggedly through it. He is the pursuer, not the pursued.

The dramatic poet will rarely think of himself as a poet. His first thought will not be for the evocative power of his words; it will be for the excitement of a scene, the tingling reality of a situation, the push and shove of characters shouldering their ways through a narrative. He will think of himself as a showman, take his most urgent fire from the thrill of getting a show on the stage. Language will be the last thing he turns to; it will be tremendously important in measuring his final effect, but he will come to it belatedly. If, when he comes to it, he decides to use verse, it will only be because verse may make all the other things clearer, more immediate, and more exciting. Instead of lavishing all his affection on his verbal imagery he will distribute it over a succession of unfolding images: an image of action, an image of character, finally an image of speech. The verbal image will, at last, reveal all the others; but it is a tool for a purpose, not an end in itself.

The lyric poet, differently equipped and differently stimulated, may humbly and honorably try to destroy much that is native to him in his effort to reverse his procedure and work as the playwright works. But the air of passivity is apt to linger; the concrete narrative is apt to seem what it is, an unfamiliar gesture; the structure of the piece is apt to leap from lyric crest to lyric crest rather than ride a steady road home.

The result is usually a cloudy business, a performance in which a veil has been dropped between the tangible reality of what is going on and the words that fall softly upon the audience ear. The spectator strains at the play as through gauze.

The contemporary critic who prefers doggerel—or, better still, prose—is, then, a man who has formed his aversion to verse on the basis of the out-of-tune borrowings of Maxwell Anderson or the out-of-order procedures of the lyric poet. He can make a good case for himself; the verse he hears, when he hears any, has not come crackling up from the floorboards on which the contemporary actor walks.

The audience is starved enough for some sort of magical speech to make nearly every one of Anderson's verse plays profitable, to seek out the difficult and unfamiliar choral practices of *Murder in the Cathedral*, to leap at the verbal liveliness of *The Lady's Not for Burning*. But neither the general audience nor our outspoken critic is going to accept verse as a steady, and quite plausible, diet until the trained theater man, passionate about the stage before he is passionate about anything else and committed only to the exuberance of a rousing show, reaches for verse as casually and as thoughtlessly as he reaches for a spotlight. When we can, with the playwright, take verse for granted as just one more device for increasing color and intensity, we shall find it no stranger than the lyrics we liked in the last musical comedy we saw.

IN GENERAL

I think two things have been clear to all of us for some time past. One is that our theater has not been an especially brilliant one; we have not felt that we were living among masterpieces. The other is that the physical theater has been dwindling away. Aesthetically, we have been at best second-rate; commercially, we have not been popular.

As a matter of habit, and perhaps out of snobbery, too, we dislike making any connection between these two things. We explain our aesthetic pallor by saying that our writers simply aren't skilled enough, and so on. We explain our commercial difficulties by saying that our audiences aren't bright enough, and so on.

The purpose of the preceding chapters has been to look a little more harshly at our aesthetic principles and a little less harshly at our audiences. For my own part, I am convinced that our theater has not risen to dazzling heights because it has substituted an editorial thesis for an orchestrated theme, because it has surrendered the vigor of forthright narrative, because it has diminished character to the size of a spot on a laboratory slide, because it has refused to budge and not bothered to speak. Theme, story, character, mobility, and language have all been severely constricted. (I am conscious that that is a staggering series of charges to be brought against any one kind of theater; but have we honestly done well by any one of these departments?)

I am further convinced that our commercial failure—our unpopularity—is directly due to our constricted aesthetic, to the very arbitrariness with which we have held to it, insisted on it. The audience has not deserted us because we were too good for it, but because we were not good enough.

I think the audience can be trusted to decide wisely, and that its current decision to stay away must be taken to heart.

Suppose this is true. What, if anything, can the young dramatist—or the young producer, or the young director, or the young play agent, or the young teacher—do about it?

We must admit immediately that there are serious difficulties standing in the way of the theater worker who might wish to dissociate himself from an exhausted and unappealing form and link himself to something more vigorous. It's obvious enough that no man knows the precise shape the next natural dramatic cycle may take; the novice is hard put to anticipate the character, and the world-view, of a social phase still struggling to be born.

The young dramatist is further inhibited by one of the facts of theatrical life: successful playwrights are not experimental playwrights. The men who have made the most of their careers are men who have unhesitatingly accepted the dominant patterns of their time, who have simply drawn blood from arteries opened by their predecessors. Shakespeare was not really an innovator. Molière rested squarely on two profitable formulas: those of the native French farce and the Italian commedia. The great playwright has usually been a lucky playwright: he has arrived on the scene just after the scene has been handsomely set. The innovator, on the other hand, rarely eats regularly. He stumbles along a path that is not yet perfectly defined; ripeness is a little while coming.

Even in our time—a time which finds the Ibsen-Chekhov passion virtually spent—a writer might well be forgiven if he chose to reread his John van Druten and to stand on this workable style. Mr. van Druten's work is literate; one could explore this placid vein and never feel himself a hack. It is also, averaged over the years, decently profitable; one could live comfortably, even though the theater continued to shrink. A man might do worse than bide his time, break his bread gently, and leave the problem of transition—and the pursuit of the disappearing audience—to the dedicated.

A writer who was waxing eloquent on my bourbon the other evening tackled the problem on fairly desperate terms. He didn't want to write a van Druten play; that was all right for van Druten, but he wanted to plunge into something with more energy, something with more sustaining power for the future. Neither did he want to write Camino Real: energy galloping toward chaos. It seemed to him that the only solution was to go into the form that has shown the greatest creative vitality in the past ten or fifteen years—musical comedy. I am an admirer of musical comedy and I agree that it is, at present, the only theatrical style exhibiting signs of spontaneous growth. But I doubt that, even in a time of morbid uncertainty and clear decline, we need give up the dramatic ghost altogether.

We might pause for a moment over musical comedy, though. It is interesting to note that, of all the forms of our time, musical comedy is the only one to make use of: free, unrealistic backgrounds; rapid leaps through time and space; bold color; heightened language (in its lyrics); rhythm (in its music); dynamic movement (not only in its dance, but everywhere); direct address to the audience. Musical comedy is the form that makes the most extensive use of theatrical convention in our time, and something of its theatrical vitality must stem from the fact. The form is eager to please its audiences, and to explore the theater as theater—two things that the serious drama has not thought of doing in quite a long while. We generally regard the popularity of musicals as a sign of public illiteracy; it may actually be a response to creative joy.

However, musical comedy is musical comedy, and we've been talking about the legitimate stage. Is there nothing that can be done—while we are caught between clearly defined cycles—to loosen its creative energies?

I doubt that the answer is to be found in deliberate experiment. "Experiment" is a horrible word. It conjures up visions of industrious playwrights building skeleton stages, plaster cycloramas, and plastic people. Conscious experiment is always like playing with blocks. It is a game, and all games have merely arbitrary rules. We aren't likely to revitalize the theater by imposing yet another cerebral construction upon it, and such a construction would, in any case, be premature. It would begin in a glorious manifesto, printed on embossed paper, and end with all the "new" scenery falling down.

But if we cannot hope to change the shape of our theater by main force, there is one thing we can change: our habits of thought. We can stop being so tensed up with virtue. We can relax our righteousness. We can stretch, and smile, and learn to feel comfortable.

I wonder how long it is since a playwright really felt comfortable in the theater—with himself, or with his audience. Ibsen wanted to make the audience bristle; and he must have bristled himself, anticipating all sorts of difficulties, as he strode through the lobby. George Tabori wants to irritate his audience; his own nerves must scratch a little as he sits next to his victims. There is a certain hostility now between the feared customer and the self-sacrificing playwright. Watch the playwright at intermission time, mingling with the smokers: worried as he listens, haughty as he hears what he doesn't want to hear. Read him in the newspapers after he has had a failure. Relations are edgy, not casual and affectionate.

We have grown used to this state of affairs, immunized ourselves, supposed that it was the necessary relationship between author and audience. In the same way we have supposed that however unattractive the theater might seem, its unattractiveness was to be endured in the interests of art. Recall van Druten watching a play he now admires: "I was amazed at the time it took over almost nothing. . . . I can remember thinking that I would not be able to bear it."

Mr. van Druten learned to bear it. He steeled himself. He formed a Spartan habit of tolerating the intolerable. He came to accept it as a mold for his own work. There may have been a day when Mr. van Druten liked his plays more interesting; he bravely banished such foolishness from his mind.

We've all done it. We have learned to accept what we do not like out of an honest conviction that what we do like is unworthy of us.

I wonder how long it is since a playwright wrote a play that was the kind of play he'd like to see. Do all of our young dramatists yearn to see on the stage, night after night, the Chekhovian plays of age and loneliness and frustration they sit down to write? Or are they simply making the kind of moody gesture that seems socially acceptable?

And I wonder how many producers actually produce the kind of play they themselves enjoy. I picked up the morning newspaper today to read that still another study of loneliness was on its way to town. (Six this season, and seven months to go.) I happen to know the producer. He is a very nice guy. He is also incapable of distinguishing between the literary styles of Anton Chekhov and Howard R. Garis. If he were to produce on Broadway the kind of entertainment he actually attends, he would be mounting night-club extravaganzas in the best Monte Proser manner. (I don't know that the theater would be notably enriched by this switch; as things stand, however, he isn't giving himself a good time and he isn't giving anyone else a good time, either.) Well-meaning producers are often found producing what they think will be respected by others, or what they think they can "get by the critics," or what they think will give them prestige. Quite a few of them haven't honestly answered the question "Would I like to see it?" in years.

In the time we must spend waiting before disaster overtakes us or a new imaginative impulse saves us we might put ourselves to the rather pleasant task of considering what we like.

Every one of us, for instance, likes stories. Some of us may pretend that the theater is no place in which to indulge this fondness, and some of us may feel a little sneaky about picking up a paperback between austere visits to the temple of stasis, but we cannot honestly conceal from ourselves the very human appetite for narrative we possess and we are always grateful when an otherwise respectable work of art manages to incorporate a little cliff-hanging. When we finally get around to seeing Oedipus, or when we run across a really well-staged fight in Romeo and Juliet, we are astonished at how suspenseful the theater can be.

Every one of us likes to watch things that go faster than we can go: horses, trains, plays. We like to be drawn ahead. made to lean forward for fear we shall miss something, carried out of our seats by an image that moves. In every other sphere of life we act on this principle: we stay up all night with a book that moves (we can't put it down because it is moving so fast); we refuse to leave a party that has hit high gear (we know we are enjoying ourselves because we're talking so fast); we cheerfully work overtime because ideas are now tumbling out and we are afraid of losing them (when the mind works rapidly, there is a heady sensation of creation and release). Conversely, we put aside a book that is standing still, we go home early from a snail's-pace party, we knock off work for the day when we find our minds working sluggishly. The theater that insists on a lazy rhythm because life is like that is reckoning without the life we know—or at least without the life we like. It is true that we are sometimes bored with life; but need the theater, to be honest, mirror only our boredom? We are delighted with a writer who makes us alert, who challenges us to keep up with him, who makes the breath come short and the blood race.

Every one of us has a great big appetite for experience. We will go to a fire any time we can find one; we can even be inveigled into seeing Cinerama, at least once. No matter how chaste our taste, we will still try to see the picture on the front of a tabloid across from us on a subway train. Let a roof cave in, or a car hurtle over a speedway embankment, or a hero be hacked to death in a play called Julius Caesar, and we will hardly be able to keep our eyes off the spectacle. We feel a little disgraced by this appetite. But why shouldn't the theater be disgraceful, now and then? It's always been called a disgraceful place, and I worry over its new respectability. When the theater was held to be at its most loathsome, it did some of its very best work. We like it splashy, and it's not quite honorable to pretend that we don't.

Every one of us is interested in interesting people. That is to say, we don't feel responsible for the rehabilitation of bores. In life, we avoid them. We feel no compunction about cutting them dead. If we have misgivings about our lack of charity, we contribute to a charity. When we notice a particularly dreary, unprepossessing, obviously frustrated fellow who lives in our apartment building, we do not invite him in to probe his malaise; his malaise is interesting only to him, anyway. We take great pains not to strike up an acquaintance. When we run across an arrogant oracle, terribly full of his own opinions and determined not to let anyone else get a word in edgewise, we are careful not to let him get us by the collar. When he invites us to dinner, we decline; when he calls us on the phone, we are polite but extraordinarily busy; when we are caught in a gathering with him, we drink heavily. We like people with lively minds and colorful ways and stimulating habits. We are grown-up now, and we like big people.

Every one of us is fascinated by language. This doesn't seem so obvious until we think about it. But listen to a man repeating a joke he has heard, and being careful that he gets it right. The joke may be only a pun, but a pun is language being playful, and the man is delighted with the mischief he has wrought. Watch a man reading Winchell and immediately repeating the jazzy word coinages to the friend sitting next to him. Listen to kids coining their own private lingoes, and notice the pride they take in the inventive twists they can give the mother tongue. Nor does this unconcealed delight in the manipulation of words end with casual Broadwayese or teen-age slang. Adlai Stevenson rocketed out of nowhere to national prominence in an incredibly short time largely because he made listening a pleasure. Mr. Stevenson's content was perfectly serious; but his management of it was linguistically exciting. Characteristically, a portion of our society complained that a man who could be so delightful couldn't be very responsible; the Puritan dies hard in us, and we keep insisting that whatever is important dare not be pleasurable. Just as characteristically, another portion of our society worried that Mr. Stevenson might be too literate for the masses, that his style was a style for "eggheads" only. (Intellectuals and anti-intellectuals actually hold to a common premise in our time: both camps believe that pleasure and profundity must be divided, that they are inimical, that they cannot coexist.) As it turned out, Mr. Stevenson earned some twenty-seven million votes in breath-taking time; and there aren't twenty-seven million eggheads. What happened? By taking pains to please twenty-seven million people—I count this a mass—Mr. Stevenson was able to carry the whole twenty-seven into some lofty regions indeed. They came happily, and not unintelligently. The mass is athirst for imaginative speech, as producer Paul Gregory found out when he gave it to them in a barnstorming tour of Shaw's Don Juan in Hell. Words are thrilling—when we take the trouble to make them thrilling.

Practically everything said in the last few paragraphs would boil down to simple philistinism if it weren't for the fact that the so-called philistine, the common customer with a vote at his disposal or a couple of bucks in his pocket, is possessed of an intuitive capacity for taking great delight in everything that is genuinely good. We haven't believed this for a long time; we haven't acted upon it. Yet history—theatrical history, anyway—suggests over and over again that the way to get Shakespeare is to honor the groundling.

But the groundling's capacity for delight in the best cannot be awakened by insult. If the customer is told, as he crosses the lobby, that his taste cannot be served because he has no taste, that his appetite cannot be appeased because his appetite is bestial, that his pleasure is of no moment because pleasure itself is vulgar, the ascent to King Lear can never begin.

There is a risk of vulgarity in turning our minds toward what pleases the common customer and what pleases ourselves. (We are brothers, after all.) We may quite possibly slip into banality as we try to stir up a good narrative, write a scene with the momentum of a shot, draw the kind of character who would be a bearable companion for roughly two and one half hours. (There is banality at the Chekhovian level, too; we see quite a bit of it in the course of a Broadway season.) But I think the risk must be run, for two reasons. One is that the theater must continue to shrivel if we do not do it. The other is that it seems to me, on the available evidence, to be a good risk. The theater was not created by a minority for a minority. It was created—in its Greek, Roman, and medieval beginnings—by a crowd for a crowd. It has, since these beginnings, been at its healthiest when it was closest to the crowd. There is a favorable chance, with the crowd, of arriving at serious art.

Lacking a new form, we can form new attitudes. Even within the general forms we know, and the theatrical practices with which we are familiar, we can teach ourselves to pay greater attention to what might attract an audience, to what might hold the audience rapt when it gets there, to what might send the audience away from the theater with a satisfied glow and a genuine desire to come back.

And I think we might test, for a while, the possibility that really laboring to please the audience might profit us not only financially but aesthetically. I think we must do this wholeheartedly, not with nervous reservations: that we must take off the hair shirts we have worn so long, and stop scratching our consciences with the fear of turning panderers. It would be good if we could bring ourselves to have quiet confidence in the common instincts toward pleasure and excitement—to believe that satisfying these instincts is one way of arriving at importance.

My guess is that by working with the universal audience we may get universal plays. By showing the audience some affection—rather than contempt, anger, or placid indifference—we may find the affection returned. And we may, to our horror, get rich.

ABOUT THE AUTHOR

WALTER KERR, drama critic of the New York Herald Tribune, was born in Evanston, Illinois. He attended De Paul University for two years and completed his studies at Northwestern, where he took his B.S. in 1937, his M.A. in 1938. For eleven years he was a faculty member in the Department of Speech and Drama at Catholic University of America, Washington, D.C. He was Drama Critic of Commonweal for two years, then became critic for the Herald Tribune in 1950. He has directed three plays on Broadway, including King of Hearts, a successful comedy of 1954 written by his wife, Jean Kerr (author of the great best-seller Please Don't Eat the Daisies). Mr. Kerr is associated with Omnibus and with several other television shows. He is also the father of five sons.